ABOUT ISLAND PRESS

Island Press is the only nonprofit organization in the United States whose principal purpose is the publication of books on environmental issues and natural resource management. We provide solutions-oriented information to professionals, public officials, business and community leaders, and concerned citizens who are shaping responses to environmental problems.

In 2003, Island Press celebrates its nineteenth anniversary as the leading provider of timely and practical books that take a multidisciplinary approach to critical environmental concerns. Our growing list of titles reflects our commitment to bringing the best of an expanding body of literature to the environmental community throughout North America and the world.

Support for Island Press is provided by The Nathan Cummings Foundation, Geraldine R. Dodge Foundation, Doris Duke Charitable Foundation, Educational Foundation of America, The Charles Engelhard Foundation, The Ford Foundation, The George Gund Foundation, The Vira I. Heinz Endowment, The William and Flora Hewlett Foundation, Henry Luce Foundation, The John D. and Catherine T. MacArthur Foundation, The Andrew W. Mellon Foundation, The Moriah Fund, The Curtis and Edith Munson Foundation, National Fish and Wildlife Foundation, The New-Land Foundation, Oak Foundation, The Overbrook Foundation, The David and Lucile Packard Foundation, The Pew Charitable Trusts, The Rockefeller Foundation, The Winslow Foundation, and other generous donors.

The opinions expressed in this book are those of the author(s) and do not necessarily reflect the views of these foundations.

RIVERS FOR LIFE

Managing Water for People and Nature

∽

Sandra Postel

Brian Richter

ISLAND PRESS

Washington · Covelo · London

ISLAND PRESS is a trademark of The Center for Resource Economics.

Library of Congress Cataloging-in-Publication Data

Postel, Sandra.
Rivers for life : managing water for people and nature / Sandra Postel
and Brian Richter.
    p. cm.
Includes bibliographical references (p.   ).
ISBN 1-55963-443-x (hard cover : alk. paper)
ISBN 1-55963-444-8 (pbk. : alk. paper)
1. Stream conservation. 2. Ecosystem management. I. Richter, Brian
D. II. Title.
QH75.P67 2003
333.91'6216—dc21

                       2003006051

British Cataloguing-in-Publication Data available.

Printed on recycled, acid-free paper ✪

Manufactured in the United States of America

09 08 07 06 05 04   10 9 8 7 6 5 4 3 2

To Amy, Henry, and Martha

WHO LOVE RIVERS AS MUCH AS WE DO
AND INSPIRE US BEYOND MEASURE

CONTENTS

ACKNOWLEDGMENTS

The seeds of this book sprouted in May 2000 at the annual conference of the North American Benthological Society, held in Keystone, Colorado, in the magnificent Rocky Mountains. We were both slated to give plenary talks in the opening session. Although we were familiar with each other's work, we had never before met, which made what transpired that morning all the more surprising: we gave such similar talks that it probably appeared to the audience like we'd conspired behind the scenes. Over lunch, it occurred to us that a good synergy might develop if we actually did collaborate on the water management challenges to which we were both devoted. Just over a year later, the idea for this book—and a synergistic partnership—was born.

We very gratefully acknowledge the financial support of The Nature Conservancy, which enabled us to dedicate the time and energy required to research and write *Rivers for Life*. Our hope is that the book will enhance the important work the Conservancy is doing to preserve the planet's freshwater biodiversity and ecosystems. The book's content and recommendations are fully ours, however, and do not imply endorsement by the Conservancy's staff, senior managers, or board of governors.

We have many people to thank. First and foremost is Nicole Rousmaniere, the book's illustrator. With creativity and remarkable efficiency, Nicole turned our pedestrian charts and graphs into attractive and compelling figures. We are extremely grateful for the time and talent Nicole so cheerfully put into the book. Karen Sanders provided research assistance that helped strengthen the book and also compiled the "Flow Restoration Database" for The Nature Conservancy, which proved immensely useful to us.

We thank Angela Arthington, Jackie King, and Kevin Rogers for sharing their deep insights on river management issues with us during travels and at conferences in Brisbane, Australia; Fort Collins, Colorado; and Cape Town, South Africa, as well as through numerous e-mail correspondences. They are true pioneers in this field. Their pathbreaking work on two separate continents has provided much inspiration for writing this book.

We benefited greatly from reviews of an earlier draft of the manuscript provided by many colleagues and professionals in the field. Michele Leslie and Amy Vickers offered particularly insightful suggestions, including the need to address the larger global context within which river conservation efforts are taking place, as well as to add a short final chapter and some key diagrams. Many people took time out of their busy schedules to comment on all or part of the manuscript, and in some cases to send us useful sources and information. We thank them all: Angela Arthington, Kristine Ciruna, David Galat, David Harrison, John Hawkins, Martha Hodgkins, Jackie King, Michele Leslie, Ruth Mathews, Patrick McCully, Ann Mills, Robert Muth, Sam Pearsall, LeRoy Poff, Catherine Pringle, Katherine Ransel, Holly Richter, Kevin Rogers, Nicole Silk, Chad Smith, Clair Stalnaker, Rebecca Tharme, Greg Thomas, Amy Vickers, and Robert Wigington.

At Island Press, Barbara Dean provided very helpful content and structure suggestions early enough that we could address them in the fundamental ways required. We thank Barbara and the entire Island Press team for their enthusiasm and hard work in bringing our book from manuscript to finished product.

Our families, friends, and work colleagues shouldered various burdens during the year long process of writing *Rivers for Life* and enabled us to persevere. For their love, support, humor, and understanding we especially thank Sue and Ralph Davis, Henry Green, Martha Hodgkins, Michele Leslie, Harold and Clara Postel, Walt and Ann Richter, Nicole Silk, and Amy Vickers.

Finally, we extend our gratitude and admiration to the many people and organizations working to protect earth's rivers. Too numerous to name, these dedicated conservationists form the vanguard of the flow restoration movement we hope this book will energize. Although we all may feel that we are paddling against the current, there is growing strength in our numbers, in our will, and in our collective dream of healthy and bountiful rivers—for life.

Sandra Postel and Brian Richter

June 2003

∽

CHAPTER ONE

Where Have All the Rivers Gone?

In his 1901 inaugural address, U.S. President Theodore Roosevelt set the tone for what would become a century of unprecedented and profound transformation of the earth's rivers. "[G]reat storage works are necessary," he said, "to equalize the flow of streams and to save the flood waters."[1] After passage of the National Reclamation Act the following year, the United States opened a new chapter in humanity's long history with water, one that viewed human control of rivers as fundamental to economic and social advancement. Government engineers built dams and reservoirs for irrigation, flood control, hydropower generation, and water supply. They dredged river channels for shipping and diked river banks to contain unruly floodwaters. River after river was transformed for human purposes as the U.S. economy's demand for water, electricity, and flood protection grew. Much of the world embarked on a similar path, often aided by U.S. engineers eager to share their experience and expertise.

Just shy of a century after Roosevelt's course-setting pronouncement, another U.S. political leader made a surprising and prescient statement of a different kind. During an interview for a 1997 documentary, Barry Goldwater, the 1964 Republican presidential candidate and former U.S. senator from Arizona, was asked how he would vote today if he could decide again on whether to support or oppose the construction of Glen Canyon Dam on the Colorado River. Completed in 1963, this super dam flooded a remarkable canyon and allowed for such complete control of the Colorado's flow that little of the river's water reaches the sea. "I'd vote against it," said Goldwater, who had advocated strongly for the dam sev-

eral decades earlier. "When you dam a river you always lose something."
For him, the price of progress had been too great.[2]

The words of Roosevelt and Goldwater serve as poignant markers to the
beginning and ending of the twentieth-century approach to rivers. Society's needs and values have changed. Equally important, scientists have
begun to uncover the severity of the ecological harm done by the large-
scale alteration of rivers to suit human purposes. Many rivers around the
world, large and small, are drying up before they reach their natural desti-
nations. In addition to the Colorado River, five of the largest rivers in
Asia—the Ganges, the Indus, the Yellow, and the Amu Dar'ya and Syr
Dar'ya—no longer reach the sea for large portions of the year.[3] Channelized rivers, such as the Rhine in Europe and a large stretch of the Missouri
in the U.S. Midwest, no longer meander but rather flow artificially straight
and deep to allow for the shipping and barging of goods. Levees have disconnected the mighty Mississippi River from 90 percent of its floodplain.[4]

Dams and diversions now alter the timing and volume of river flows
on a wide geographic scale. Worldwide, some 60 percent of the 227 largest
rivers have been fragmented by dams, diversions, or other infrastructure.[5]
Most of the rivers of Europe, Japan, the United States, and other industrialized regions are now controlled more by humanity's hand than by
nature's. Rather than flowing to the natural rhythms of the hydrologic
cycle, they are turned on and off like elaborate plumbing works.

Societies have reaped substantial economic rewards from these modifications to rivers—from the generation of hydroelectric power to the
expansion of irrigated agriculture to the growth of trade along shipping
routes. However, serious losses have mounted on the ecological side of the
ledger. In their natural state, healthy rivers perform myriad functions—
such as purifying water, moderating floods and droughts, and maintaining habitat for fisheries, birds, and wildlife. They connect the continental
interiors with the coasts, bringing sediment to deltas, delivering nutrients
to coastal fisheries, and maintaining salinity balances that sustain productive estuaries. From source to sea and from channel to floodplain,
river ecosystems gather, store, and move snowmelt and rainwater in synchrony with nature's cycles. The diversity and abundance of life in running waters reflect millions of years of evolution and adaptation to these
natural rhythms.

From a strictly human perspective, healthy rivers perform numerous
"ecosystem services"—the processes carried out by natural ecosystems
that benefit human societies and economies. Rivers, wetlands, and other

freshwater ecosystems constitute part of the natural infrastructure that keeps our economies humming. Like workers in a factory, wetland plants and animals are an organized and productive team—absorbing pollutants, decomposing waste, and churning out fresh, clean water. With great efficiency, periodic floods shape river channels and redistribute sediment, creating habitat essential to fish and other riverine life. Moreover, river systems do this work for free. Even if we knew how to replicate all the valuable functions that rivers perform, it would cost an enormous sum to replace them. The services performed by wetlands alone can be worth on the order of $20,000 per hectare per year.[6]

In little more than a century—a geologic twinkling of an eye—human societies have so altered rivers that they are no longer adequately performing many of their evolutionary roles or delivering many of the ecological services that human economies have come to depend upon. A significant portion of freshwater species worldwide—including at least 20 percent of freshwater fish species—are at risk of extinction or are already extinct. Because floodwaters are no longer getting cleansed by floodplain wetlands, more pollution is reaching inland and coastal seas, causing damage such as the low-oxygen "dead zone" in the Gulf of Mexico and the deterioration of Europe's Black Sea. In short, in many parts of the world, the harnessing of rivers for economic gain is now causing more harm than good. But because most of the harm goes unrecognized or unvalued, it gets left out of the cost-benefit equations that often determine how rivers get managed. As a result, far too little has been done to stop, much less reverse, the decline in river health.

To date, efforts to restore and protect rivers have focused primarily on two goals—improving water quality, and establishing minimum flow requirements so that rivers and streams do not run completely dry. These actions have improved river conditions in many locations. The Cuyahoga River in northern Ohio is no longer in danger of catching fire again, for instance, and many fish populations are benefiting from less-polluted waters. But the focus on minimum flows and water quality has done too little to restore the functions and processes that sustain the integrity of river systems overall.

During the last decade, scientists have amassed considerable evidence that a river's natural flow regime—its variable pattern of high and low flows throughout the year as well as across many years—exerts great influence on river health.[7] Each natural flow component performs valuable work for the system as a whole. Flood flows cue fish to spawn and trigger certain insects to begin a new phase of their life cycle, for example, while very low flows may be critical to the recruitment of riverside (or riparian) vegetation. Consequently, restoring rivers now under heavy human control requires much more than simply ensuring that water is in the channel: it requires re-creating to some degree the natural flow pattern that drives so many important ecological processes. Flow restoration may involve operating dams and reservoirs so as to mimic a river's pre-dam highs and lows. In rivers not yet heavily dammed or controlled, including many in developing countries, the challenge is to preserve enough of the natural flow pattern to maintain ecological functions even while the river is managed for other economic purposes.

In a nutshell, the challenge of twenty-first-century river management is to better balance human water demands with the water needs of rivers themselves. Meeting this challenge will require a fundamentally new approach to valuing and managing rivers. Fortunately, river scientists and policymakers in a number of countries—especially in Australia, South Africa, and the United States—have developed and tested some new ideas for achieving this more optimal balance. As described in Chapters 2 and 3, the most promising approaches incorporate new scientific knowledge, new management practices, and new policy tools. Bringing these promising initiatives to scale, however, will require new approaches to river governance—the process of establishing and administering the rules that dictate how rivers get managed and who benefits from them—which is explored in Chapter 5.

Although rivers around the world and the life they support are now in great peril, there is cause for optimism about the possibility of their return to health. As noted in Chapter 4, more than 230 rivers around the world are already undergoing some degree of flow restoration. Dams are being taken down, levees are being set back to reconnect rivers with their floodplains, conservation practices are enabling some water to return to nature, and reservoir releases are being modified to better replicate natural flow patterns. Viewed collectively, these actions constitute the vanguard of a movement to realign the health of our human water economy with that of nature's water economy. They also underscore the importance of preserving ecosystem-sustaining flows in rivers not yet harnessed by human infrastructure, so that the costly downsides of twentieth-century-style water management can be prevented in the first place.

Every once in a while the social and political stars align on an issue in a way that enables a quantum shift to occur in the way that issue is perceived and handled by human societies. For the health and conservation of rivers, that alignment is beginning to form. It consists of three key elements: (1) the growing recognition of the importance of biological diversity and the value of natural ecosystem services, (2) the scientific consensus that restoring some degree of a river's natural flow pattern is the best way to protect and restore river health and functioning, and (3) the emergence of new models of decision-making about river management that offer the promise of more inclusive, equitable, and ecologically sustainable outcomes.

This alignment opens new windows of opportunity, but the challenge ahead is large. It calls on scientists, conservationists, river managers, policymakers, and citizens to work together, across disciplines and professional boundaries. And it calls on society to adopt rules of water governance that recognize our interdependence with rivers—the blue arteries of the earth that course through and sustain the planet's life-support system.

WHY WE NEED HEALTHY RIVERS

Through the ages, rivers have played a central role in the evolution of human societies. Many great early civilizations sprung up alongside rivers—including the ancient Mesopotamians in the fertile plains of the Tigris and Euphrates rivers, the ancient Egyptians in the valley of the Nile, and the early Chinese societies in the valley of the Yellow, affectionately known in China as its "mother" river. As symbols of purity, renewal, timelessness, and healing, rivers have shaped human spirituality like few other features of the natural world. To this day, millions of Hindus in India immerse themselves in the waters of the Ganges in rituals of cleansing that are central to their spiritual life. Similarly, rivers have shaped the landscape in fundamental ways, carving remarkable canyons with their erosive power and creating huge deltas through their deposition of sediment. Evoking magic, mystery, and beauty, rivers have inspired painters, poets, musicians, and artists of all kinds throughout history, adding immeasurably to the human experience.

From a hydrologic perspective, rivers play a central role in the global cycling of water between the sea, air, and land. Along with underground aquifers, they gather precipitation and carry it as runoff to the sea, which then cycles moisture back to the land via the atmosphere. This cycle constantly renews the finite supply of water on the continents and thus sustains all life on land. From a human standpoint, rivers are principal sources of water for drinking, cooking, and bathing, for growing crops where rainfall is not sufficient, for generating electric power, and for manufacturing all manner of material items.

We need and value rivers for a host of reasons—some spiritual, some aesthetic, some practical. Yet only recently has scientific understanding of what constitutes a healthy river enabled us to grasp just how critical intact rivers are to the functioning of the natural world around us. Rivers are more than conduits for water. They are complex systems that do complicated work. They include not just the water flowing in their channels, but the food webs and nutrient cycles that operate within their beds and banks, the pools and wetlands that form on their floodplains, the sediment loads they carry, the rich deltas they form near their terminus, and even parts of the coastal or inland seas into which they empty. Along with their physical structures, river systems include countless plant and animal species that together keep them healthy and functioning.

Anyone who has traveled to the tail end of a heavily dammed and diverted river has seen what can happen when the health of river systems is destroyed. The people in the disaster zone of Central Asia's Aral Sea know these consequences perhaps better than anyone. They suffer each day with the legacy of Soviet central planners who calculated a half century ago that the water in the region's two major rivers, the Amu Dar'ya and Syr Dar'ya, would be more valuable if used to irrigate cotton in the desert than if left to flow into the Aral Sea, then the world's fourth largest lake. Today, the Aral Sea has shrunk to a third of its former volume, the fishing industry that provided jobs and livelihoods for local residents has been ruined, and the people themselves are afflicted with numerous diseases from the desiccated, salty, and toxic landscape that surrounds them.[8] No place on earth better shows the connections between the health of an ecosystem and that of the people, communities, and economies that depend upon it.

In recent years, a number of ecologists and economists have attempted to describe and value the functions that natural ecosystems perform in conventional economic terms in order to encourage the incorporation of these functions into societal decisions.[9] They have begun to talk of forests, watersheds, soils, and rivers as "natural capital," which, just like manufacturing or financial capital, provides a stream of benefits to society. These benefits are often referred to as ecosystem goods and services. The idea is not to suggest that nature's worth consists only of ecological services that directly benefit people monetarily. Rather, the valuation of ecosystem services is a tool that enables the health and conservation of natural ecosystems to be taken into account more directly in decision-making. To date, the economic benefits of ecosystem conservation have largely been ignored because most of nature's life-sustaining services are not valued in the marketplace or by any other conventional mechanism. We do not measure or track the worth of natural assets, nor of the benefit stream that derives from them. As a result, we are prone to squandering the wealth of nature without ever tallying the losses.

In the case of rivers, wetlands, and other freshwater ecosystems, these natural services include very tangible items, such as providing clean water to drink and fish to eat, as well as more complex functions such as moderating floods and droughts, maintaining food webs, and delivering nutrients to coastal estuaries (see Table 1-1). Some of these services are easier to value monetarily than others. For example, a minimum value for freshwater fish might be derived from the market value of commercial catches plus tourism and other receipts related to recreational fishing. It is far more difficult, however, to quantify the cultural and aesthetic values of river fish, as well as the value people place on just knowing that ancient salmon runs or native fish populations continue to exist.

Similarly, it is possible to value rivers and other freshwater systems for their water supply services by estimating the cost of replacing natural supplies with de-salted seawater. Substituting the entire volume of fresh water now consumed by the global economy—some 2,000 cubic kilometers a year—with desalinated water (assuming this could be done, which is questionable) would cost on the order of $3 trillion annually, not counting the expense of distributing the water to users, or the air pollution and climate change impacts of so many energy-intensive de-salting plants.[10] In other words, if rivers, lakes, and wetlands dried up, at least 7 percent of the entire global gross national product (GNP) would have to be devoted to creating water supplies that nature now provides for free. Many forms of recreation—boating, swimming, and fishing, for instance—would vanish, and these losses might be quantifiable as well. But humanity would also lose the aesthetic, cultural, and spiritual benefits that emanate from sparkling rivers, mountain streams, and the knowledge that a rich diversity of freshwater life exists—losses that cannot be expressed monetarily, but that may be even more important than those that can.

Despite the danger that ecosystem service valuation may elevate quantifiable values over nonquantifiable ones, the practice has helped

TABLE 1-1 Life-Support Services Provided by Rivers, Wetlands, and other Freshwater Ecosystems

Ecosystem Service	Benefits
Provision of water supplies	More than 99 percent of irrigation, industrial, and household water supplies worldwide come from natural freshwater systems
Provision of food	Fish, waterfowl, mussels, clams, and the like are important food sources for people and wildlife
Water purification/ waste treatment	Wetlands filter and break down pollutants, protecting water quality
Flood mitigation	Healthy watersheds and floodplains absorb rainwater and river flows, reducing flood damage
Drought mitigation	Healthy watersheds, floodplains, and wetlands absorb rainwater, slow runoff, and help recharge groundwater
Provision of habitat	Rivers, streams, floodplains, and wetlands provide homes and breeding sites for fish, birds, wildlife, and numerous other species
Soil fertility maintenance	Healthy river-floodplain systems constantly renew the fertility of surrounding soils
Nutrient delivery	Rivers carry nutrient-rich sediment to deltas and estuaries, helping maintain their productivity
Maintenance of coastal salinity zones	Freshwater flows maintain the salinity gradients of deltas and coastal marine environments, a key to their biological richness and productivity
Provision of beauty and life-fulfilling values	Natural rivers and waterscapes are sources of inspiration and deep cultural and spiritual values; their beauty enhances the quality of human life
Recreational opportunities	Swimming, fishing, hunting, boating, wildlife viewing, waterside hiking, and picnicking
Biodiversity conservation	Diverse assemblages of species perform the work of nature (including all the services in this table), upon which societies depend; conserving genetic diversity preserves options for the future

illuminate the tremendous worth of natural ecosystems that are often not given any economic weight at all. During the mid-nineties, University of Vermont researcher Robert Costanza and a team of ecologists and economists assessed the current economic value of seventeen ecosystem services for sixteen biomes.[11] For the earth as a whole, they estimated the value of these ecosystem services to range between $16 and 54 trillion per year (in 1994 dollars), with an average of $33 trillion per year—roughly equal to the mid-nineties global GNP. This finding suggests that, in monetary terms, ecosystem services contribute as much to human welfare as all goods and services valued in the marketplace do.

These global estimates can give only a very rough approximation of nature's economic worth. The value of the same ecosystem function (mitigating floods, for instance) will vary from one country and culture to the next, so estimating global values based on a small sample of local estimates is problematic. There is also the contradiction of placing a finite value on an irreplaceable life-support system. Suggesting that Nature's services are worth on the order of $33 trillion a year implies that if society came up with an extra sum in this amount and invested it in re-creating nature's functions, we could in fact do without Nature—when, of course, we could not. Society can and does use technology to substitute for some ecosystem goods and services—for example, raising fish in aquaculture pens when natural fish stocks get depleted, and desalting seawater when drinking water becomes scarce—but these substitutions are imperfect and can be made only to a point. More important, scientists and engineers have no idea how to re-create many of the more complex processes that natural ecosystems perform.

Notwithstanding the conceptual and methodological difficulties, the $33 trillion price tag captured people's attention, and did a great deal to spotlight ecosystem services as extraordinarily valuable. From a practical standpoint, the total value figure is less important than the unit values attributable to each ecosystem service that the research team analyzed. Again, analytical problems notwithstanding, these values help to highlight the tremendous worth of ecosystems that are often not given any tangible value at all.

Freshwater swamps and river floodplains, for example, were estimated by the Costanza team to yield annual benefits of nearly $20,000 per hectare ($8,000 per acre)—a value second only to that of estuaries among the sixteen biomes studied. Their roles in storing and retaining water, mitigating floods, and breaking down pollutants emerged as particularly valuable. Rivers and lakes, which the research team assessed together, were valued at $8,500 per hectare per year, with the greatest value attributed to their roles in regulating the hydrological cycle and providing water supplies. All told, wetlands, lakes, and rivers emerged from the analysis as extremely valuable natural assets, producing ecological services collectively valued at nearly $6.6 trillion per year.

The great benefit in generating even very approximate estimates of the worth of ecosystem services is that it makes it far more difficult for decision-makers to ignore those services when assessing the costs and benefits of particular projects. A river floodplain becomes more than just unused land ripe for "development." It becomes a capital asset worth several thousand dollars per hectare per year. The actual value will vary from place to place and probably cannot be known with complete accuracy, but nowhere can it justifiably be assumed to be zero, as has often been the assumption in the past. Moreover, because ecosystem services are irreplaceable life-support systems, their value climbs toward infinity as they become increasingly scarce.

Healthy river-floodplain ecosystems rank among the most undervalued of natural assets. A good portion of modern water engineering has been geared toward replacing the natural flood-control functions of these ecosystems with dikes and levees intended to keep rivers from overtopping their banks. Not only has this substitution often proven unsuccessful and overly expensive, it also destroys other critical life-support functions that healthy floodplains provide. Seasonal flooding connects a river with the surrounding landscape, promoting the exchange of nutrients and organisms among a rich mosaic of habitats, thereby enhancing species diversity and increasing biological productivity. Many floodplains are critical breeding and feeding areas for fish. Researchers have found that in tropical rivers with large floodplains fish can achieve 75 percent of their annual growth during the time they spend in the floodplain.[12] Overall, river-floodplain ecosystems comprise some of the most biologically rich places on earth—including, for instance, the Pantanal of South America, the Okavango Delta in southern Africa, and the Sudd Swamps of Sudan.[13]

In parts of the developing world, especially in Africa, many rural people key their lives and livelihoods to the flood pulse and the biological productivity of floodplains. This is an age-old practice that extends back at least five thousand years to the Nile valley of ancient Egypt. Historically, Egyptian farmers celebrated the Nile flood, which arrived each year with nearly calendrical precision. Originating with the monsoonal rains of the Ethiopian highlands, the Nile flood reached Aswan, in southern Egypt, in mid-August. It then surged northward through the Nile valley, reaching the delta and the Mediterranean Sea some four to six weeks later. At its peak, the flood would cover the floodplain to a depth of 1.5 meters. After the floodwaters receded, some time between early October and late November, farmers planted their wheat and other crops. The floodplain retained enough moisture to support the plants until harvest time in mid-April or early May. Then the cycle would begin all over again. Even into modern times, June 17 was celebrated as the Night of the Drop, "when the celestial tear fell and caused the Nile to rise."[14]

This ancient Egyptian practice of flood-recession agriculture took great advantage of the ecosystem services provided by the annual Nile flood. The peak river flows delivered about 10 million tons of nutrient-rich silt to the floodplain and an additional 90 million tons to the delta, annually replenishing the soil's fertility. It also flushed away enough of the salts that had accumulated in the soils to prevent serious soil salinization—historically and presently a vexing problem for farmers in most dry regions. Little wonder the ancient Egyptians worshipped and sang hymns to Hapi, the god of the Nile. The Nile flood, and the Egyptians' sustainable use of it, kept the Nile valley in continuous cultivation for five thousand years—longer than any other place on earth.[15]

In recent years, a number of researchers have made attempts to quantify the value of particular floodplain ecosystems and the activities they support in ways that allow these benefits to be compared with those of conventional river "development" projects. Following the Western river-development model, such projects in Africa and elsewhere typically involve eliminating the flood by constructing a dam and reservoir and then storing the floodwaters for hydropower production and irrigated agriculture. Many African river floodplains are being degraded or completely destroyed by such projects, much as the floodplains of many U.S. and European rivers were destroyed earlier in the twentieth century.

One such case is in northeastern Nigeria, where an extensive floodplain exists at the confluence of the Hadejia and Jama'are rivers in the Lake Chad watershed. This floodplain provides food and income sources for many rural Nigerians who use it to graze animals, grow crops, collect fuelwood, and to fish. The floodplain recharges regional aquifers, which are vital water supplies in times of drought. The Hadejia-Jama'are wetlands also provide dry-season grazing for semi-nomadic pastoralists and critical habitat for migratory waterfowl. With the floodplain increasingly threatened by existing and proposed dams and irrigation schemes upstream, researchers Edward Barbier and Julian Thompson evaluated the economic benefits of direct uses of the floodplain—specifically for agriculture, fuelwood, and fishing—and compared these with the economic benefits of the irrigation projects. They found that the net economic benefits provided by use of the natural floodplain exceeded those of the irrigation project by more than sixty-fold (analyzed over time periods of both thirty and fifty years). Since water is a limiting factor in the region, Barbier and Thompson also compared the options on a per-unit-water basis and found the benefits of the floodplain to range from approximately $9,600 to $14,500 per cubic meter compared with $26 to $40 per cubic meter for the irrigation project. Had Barbier and Thompson been able to estimate habitat supply, groundwater recharge, and other critical ecosystem benefits provided by the intact floodplain, the disparity in values would have been even greater.[16]

The value of healthy rivers and floodplains is increasingly gaining recognition in the United States as well. Between 1990 and 1997, flooding caused damages totaling nearly $34 billion, despite public expenditures on river engineering works over the previous six decades that exceeded this sum.[17] In particular, the Great Midwest Flood of 1993—which caused $12–16 billion in property damages—sparked new interest in rethinking river management with an eye toward restoring and protecting the natural flood mitigation, habitat, and other benefits of natural floodplains. Subsequent to the flood, researchers estimated that restoration of 5.3 million hectares of wetlands in the upper Mississippi River basin, at a cost of some $2–3 billion, would have been sufficient to substantially reduce the flooding.[18] According to the U.S. National Research Council, restoration of about half of the wetland area lost in the continental United States would affect less than 3 percent of the land used for agriculture, forestry, and urban settlement—suggesting great possibility for cost-effectively regaining more of the flood mitigation and other ecosystem services of riverine wetlands.[19]

Just as major floods draw attention to the importance of healthy floodplains, so the decline of coastal deltas and estuaries is focusing greater attention on river connections with the sea. The timing and volume of freshwater flows into the coastal environment are key factors influencing deltaic and estuarine productivity. The maintenance of salinity gradients and the delivery of nutrients, sediments, and organisms to the coastal environment are especially important ecosystem services that natural rivers perform. In recent years, the lack of river flow through the deltas of the Ganges, Indus, Amu Dar'ya, Syr Dar'ya, Sacramento–San Joaquin, and Colorado rivers—to name a few—has caused dramatic declines in the biological richness and productivity of these important ecosystems. In both the Ganges and Indus deltas, for example, the reduction in freshwater outflow has caused a salt front to move across the delta, which is threatening valuable mangrove ecosystems. In the United States, a number of studies have documented links between large reductions in freshwater flows and the decline of important fishery stocks—including, for example, a link between flows from the Everglades into Florida Bay and production of pink shrimp in adjacent areas of the Gulf of Mexico.[20]

How much more destruction of freshwater ecosystem services can occur before whole life-support systems cease to function? We do not know. Even if we followed conservationist Aldo Leopold's rule of "intelligent tinkering" and kept all the pieces of nature's infrastructure as we dismantled it, we would have no idea how to reassemble them again. As irreplaceable and essential to life, freshwater ecosystem services fall in that important category of assets to which it makes sense to apply the "precautionary principle"—that is, to err on the side of preserving more than we really need rather than to risk the high and irreversible costs of preserving too little.

THE DISRUPTION OF NATURAL FLOWS

Human actions alter rivers in numerous ways. Unchecked pollution diminishes water quality and depletes the oxygen that fish and other riverine life need. The introduction of nonnative species, whether accidentally or intentionally, changes predator-prey relationships and other interactions among native biological communities (see Table 1-2). One threat to river health looms over the others, however, a force of ecosystem decline that has quite literally reached geologic proportions—the alteration of natural river flows by dams, diversions, levees, and other infrastructure.

An estimated 800,000 dams of all sizes now block the flow of the world's rivers.[21] Approximately one-fourth of the global flux of sediment carried by flowing water now gets trapped in reservoirs rather than nourishing floodplains, deltas, and estuaries.[22] Swedish scientists Matts Dyne-

TABLE 1-2 Threats to Freshwater Ecosystem Services
from Human Activities

Human Activity	Impact on Ecosystems	Benefits/Services at Risk
Dam construction	Alters timing and quantity of river flows, water temperature, nutrient and sediment transport, delta replenishment; blocks fish migrations	Provision of habitat for native species, recreational and commercial fisheries, maintenance of deltas and their economies, productivity of estuarine fisheries
Dike and levee construction	Destroys hydrologic connection between river and floodplain habitat	Habitat, sport and commercial fisheries, natural floodplain fertility, natural flood control
Excessive river diversions	Depletes streamflows to damaging levels	Habitat, sport and commercial fisheries, recreation, pollution dilution, hydropower, transportation
Draining of wetlands	Eliminates key component of aquatic environment	Natural flood control, habitat for fish and waterfowl, recreation, natural water purification
Deforestation/ poor land use	Alters runoff patterns, inhibits natural recharge, fills water bodies with silt	Water supply quantity and quality, fish and wildlife habitat, transportation, flood control
Uncontrolled pollution	Diminishes water quality	Water supply, habitat, commercial fisheries, recreation

sius and Christer Nilsson report that 77 percent of the large river systems in the United States, Canada, Europe, and the former Soviet Union—essentially the northern third of the world—are moderately to strongly altered by dams, reservoirs, diversions, and irrigation projects. They warn that, because of the extent of river modifications, key habitats such as waterfalls, rapids, and floodplain wetlands could disappear entirely from some regions, extinguishing many plant and animal species that depend on running-water habitats.[23] Perhaps the most startling finding about the scale of human hydrological impacts is that the weight of impounded

TABLE 1-2 (*continued*)

Human Activity	Impact on Ecosystems	Benefits/Services at Risk
Overharvesting	Depletes species populations	Sport and commercial fisheries, waterfowl, other biotic populations
Introduction of exotic species	Eliminates native species, alters production and nutrient cycling	Sport and commercial fisheries, waterfowl, water quality, fish and wildlife habitat, transportation
Releases of metals and acid-forming pollutants to air and water	Alters chemistry of rivers and lakes	Habitat, fisheries, recreation, human health
Emissions of climate-altering air pollutants	Potential for dramatic changes in runoff patterns from increases in temperature and changes in rainfall	Water supply, hydropower, transportation, fish and wildlife habitat, pollution dilution, recreation, fisheries, flood control
Population and consumption growth	Increases pressures to dam and divert more water, to drain more wetlands, etc.; increases water pollution, acid rain, and potential for climate change	Places virtually all aquatic ecosystem services at risk

SOURCE: Postel and Carpenter, 1997.

waters at high latitudes in the northern hemisphere has slightly altered the tilt of the earth's axis and increased the speed of the earth's rotation.[24]

The vast majority of human impacts on natural river flows has occurred within the last century, and especially within the last fifty years. The growing demand for irrigation, water supply, and hydroelectric power as population and economic growth surged after the Second World War led to an unprecedented boom in dam and reservoir construction (see Figure 1-1). Worldwide, the number of large dams (those at least 15 meters high) stood at five thousand in 1950; three-quarters of these were

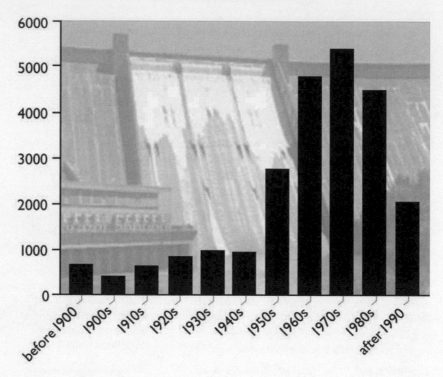

FIGURE 1-1. Worldwide Dam Construction by Decade. Note: dams in China are not included. (Source: World Commission on Dams 2000; background photo courtesy of U.S. Bureau of Reclamation.)

in North America, Europe, and other industrial regions. By 2000, the number of large dams had climbed to over forty-five thousand, and these were spread among more than 140 countries. On average, human society has built two large dams a day for the last half century.[25]

China, which is home to one-fifth of the world's people, has constructed nearly one-half of the world's large dams—some 22,000 in all. Ninety percent of them have been built since 1950. The United States, with just over 4 percent of the global population, ranks second with nearly 6,600 large dams, or 14 percent of the world total. India, with 17 percent of the world's population, has 9 percent of the world total, or about 4,300 large dams. According to the World Commission on Dams, approximately 40 percent of all the large dams now under construction worldwide are in India. Japan, with more than 2,600 large dams, and Spain, with nearly 1,200, round out the top five[26] (see Table 1-3).

Without question, dams and reservoirs provide substantial benefits to human societies and their economies. Through hydroelectric power generation, they currently provide 19 percent of the world's electricity supply. One in three nations depends on hydropower to meet at least half of its electricity demands. By capturing and storing flood flows for later use, dams and reservoirs have also contributed to the global supply of water for urban, industrial, and agricultural uses. Worldwide, water demands have roughly tripled since 1950, and dams and river diversions helped satisfy that demand (see Figure 1-2). About half of the world's large dams were built solely or primarily for irrigation, many of them in Asia as the Green Revolution spread. Today large dams are estimated to contribute directly to 12–16 percent of global food production.[27]

On the cost side of the ledger, however, dams and other infrastructure have proven to be primary destroyers of aquatic habitat and ecosystem services. Whether a dam is built and operated for flood control, hydropower, irrigation, water supply, or navigation, it alters the natural pattern of a river's flow throughout the year.

TABLE 1-3 Worldwide Distribution of Large Dams by Country

Country	Number of Large Dams	Percent of World Total
China	22,000	46.2
United States	6,575	13.8
India	4,291	9.0
Japan	2,675	5.6
Spain	1,196	2.5
Canada	793	1.7
South Korea	765	1.6
Turkey	625	1.3
Brazil	594	1.3
France	569	1.2
South Africa	539	1.1
Mexico	537	1.1
Italy	524	1.1
United Kingdom	517	1.1
Australia	486	1.0
Others	4,969	10.4
World Total	47,655	100.0

SOURCE: World Commission on Dams, 2000.

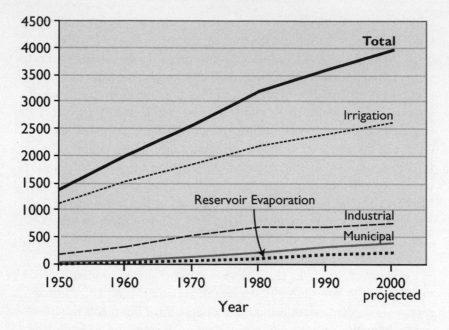

FIGURE 1-2. Estimated Global Water Withdrawals, 1950–2000. (Source: Shiklomanov 1996)

Every river has a unique flow signature that is determined by the climate, geology, topography, vegetation, and other natural features of its watershed. That signature can be depicted by a hydrograph—a line drawing of the river's flow over time (see Figure 1-3). In monsoonal climates, for example, river flows peak during the rainy season and then drop to very low levels during the dry season. Similarly, rivers fed primarily by mountain snowpacks will typically run highest during the spring melting season and then drop to low levels during the summer. Where there is no significant snowmelt nor a distinct rainy season, river flows will generally vary less between the seasons, but will rise and fall along with precipitation events in the watershed. Although a yearlong hydrograph can capture a river's typical flow pattern, it takes a flow record spanning several decades to capture extreme events—such as very high floods or very serious droughts—that may occur only once every half century but that are an important part of the river's natural flow regime.

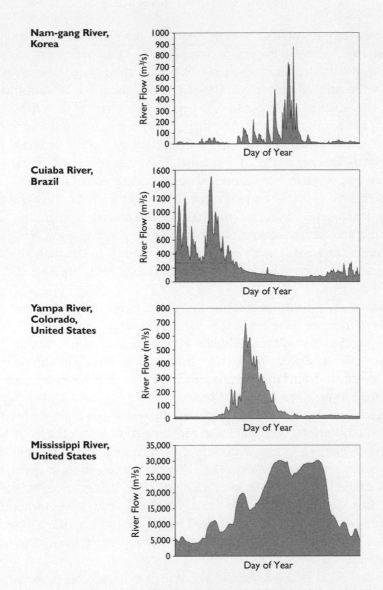

FIGURE 1-3. River Hydrographs from Around the World. Each of these four hydrographs portrays a river's flow variations over the course of a single year, which are influenced by different climates and watershed sizes. The Korean river is relatively small, and it rises quickly in response to seasonal rainstorms that occur midyear. The Brazilian river gathers rain-fed runoff from a larger watershed; its flow rises are more gradual and prolonged, and occur earlier in the year. The Yampa River in Colorado is fed by melting snows, producing a distinctive flood peak of long duration in late spring. The Mississippi River receives water from many large tributaries, and its flow increases slowly toward a midyear peak.

Each component of a river's hydrograph—the highs, the lows, and the levels in between—is important to the health of the river system and the life within it (see Figure 1-4). Large floods deposit gravel and cobbles in spawning areas, flush organic material (food for aquatic creatures) into the river channel, trigger insects to begin a new phase of their life cycle, and provide migration and spawning cues for fish—to name just a few of their critical functions. More regularly occurring high flows shape the physical character of the river channel, including pools and riffles, and aerate eggs that have been deposited in spawning gravels. Low river flows, also referred to as base flows, determine how much habitat space is available for aquatic organisms, maintain suitable water temperature and quality, and enable fish to move to feeding or spawning areas. Naturally occurring drought-level flows are also important—for example, for the recruitment of certain floodplain plants and to purge invasive species from the river.

Dams and other infrastructure that alter a river's natural flow pattern disrupt many of these ecosystem-sustaining processes (see Figure 1-5). Dams and levees built to control floods, for instance, will flatten out the peak flows and disconnect the river from its floodplain. The elimination of flood flows from large portions of rivers in the U.S. Midwest has contributed to the imperilment of prairie fishes that spawn during floods and rely on water currents to carry their buoyant eggs until they hatch.[28] Dams built primarily to store water for irrigation flatten the peaks and overly deplete base flows during the summer irrigation season. Before the construction of the Aswan High Dam on the Nile River in Egypt, the Nile's ratio of high flow to low flow averaged 12:1; after construction of the dam, that ratio dropped to 2:1.[29] Hydropower dams are notorious for causing huge and totally unnatural daily swings in a river's flow, as water suddenly is released from reservoirs to meet peak electricity demands.

Based upon a comprehensive global review of the ecological impacts of flow alteration, Australian scientists Stuart Bunn and Angela Arthington have suggested four major principles that explain why flow modifications have been so devastating to river species and ecosystems.[30] First, because river flows—and particularly floods—shape the physical habitats of rivers and their floodplains, changes in these flows strongly affect the distribution and abundance of plants and animals—and can completely eliminate species that are dependent upon habitats no longer available after the flow alteration. Second, aquatic species have evolved survival and reproductive strategies that are keyed to natural flow conditions. If the flow conditions needed for a species to successfully complete its life cycle no longer exist, the species will quickly decline or disappear. Third, many species require adequate water depth at critical times of the year to facilitate their movements upstream and downstream and from the channel laterally into floodplains. Flow alterations that inhibit these movements may prevent them from reaching feeding and breeding sites that are critical to their growth and reproduction. Finally, altered flow conditions often favor nonnative species that have been introduced into river systems, placing greater survival pressures on native species.

Consider the chain of effects that unfolded on the Colorado River after the completion of Glen Canyon Dam upstream of the Grand Canyon in 1963.[31] With the closing of the dam gates, the once-muddy, reddish waters soon began flowing crystal clear and emerald green, completely free of the sediments that gave the river its name ("colorado" means red in Spanish). Before the dam was built, water temperatures fluctuated naturally over the course of the year between the freezing point and 30 degrees Celsius (85 degrees Fahrenheit). But today, water is released from the dam's penstocks 60 meters beneath the surface of Lake Powell at a stable and cold 9 degrees Celsius. Sunlight, which previously had reflected off the surface of the opaque river, began deeply penetrating the clear water, setting off explosive growth in submerged aquatic plants and insects, which in turn fundamentally altered the river's natural food webs. Native fish, which had adapted to the river's muddy waters by locating their food through nonvisual means, were soon devoured and outcompeted by introduced nonnatives such as carp and trout, which could suddenly see their prey in the clear waters. Of the eight native fish present in the river prior to 1963, only three remain abundant today; the others are either locally extinct or barely hanging on.

Glen Canyon Dam also drastically curtailed the Colorado's natural floods, which had averaged 2,550 cubic meters per second (90,000 cubic feet per second) prior to 1963. Post-dam flows were determined not by snowmelt and other natural conditions, but rather by releases from the dam's hydropower turbines. These releases fluctuated wildly on a year-round daily basis, with daily high flows thirty times greater than daily lows. These dramatic swings in river level turned the fringes of the river into a death trap for larval fish and insects that had previously used the

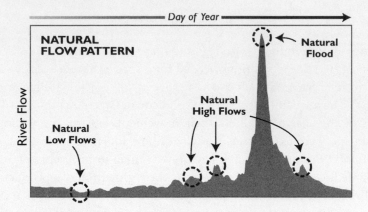

Natural Low Flow

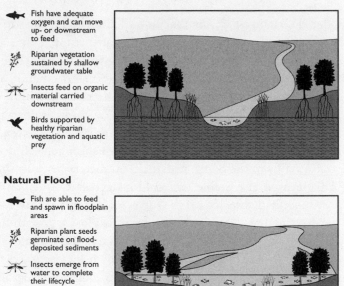

Fish have adequate oxygen and can move up- or downstream to feed

Riparian vegetation sustained by shallow groundwater table

Insects feed on organic material carried downstream

Birds supported by healthy riparian vegetation and aquatic prey

Natural Flood

Fish are able to feed and spawn in floodplain areas

Riparian plant seeds germinate on flood-deposited sediments

Insects emerge from water to complete their lifecycle

Wading birds and waterfowl feed on fish and plants in shallow flooded areas

FIGURE 1-4. Ecosystem Functions Supported by Natural River Flows. The natural flow regime supports many important ecosystem functions. During normal low flows, fish and other river creatures have enough space to feed and reproduce, and enough water depth to enable them to move upstream and downstream to find food or mates. Groundwater tables remain high enough to support floodplain vegetation. Higher flows flush wastes and restore water quality, shape the river channel, and transport food throughout the river system. Floods stimulate fish migrations and enable fish and other mobile creatures to move into warm, nutrient-rich floodplain areas to feed and spawn.

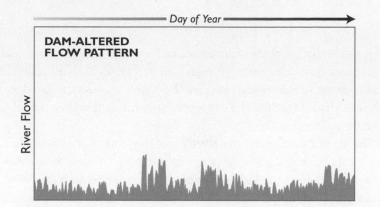

DAM-ALTERED FLOW PATTERN

Day of Year

River Flow

Inadequate Low Flow

 Fish are overcrowded in poor-quality water, cannot move to other feeding areas

 Riparian plants wilt when groundwater table drops too low

 Insects suffer when water levels rise and fall erratically

 Birds unable to feed, rest, or breed in tree canopy

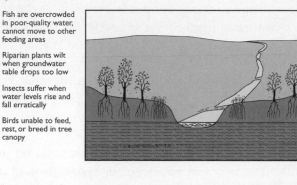

Absence of Flood

Fish unable to access floodplain for spawning and feeding

Riparian vegetation encroaches into river channel

Insect habitats smothered by silt and sand

Many birds cannot use riparian areas when plant species change

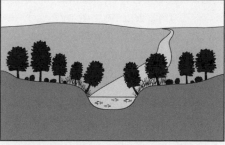

FIGURE 1-5. A Large Dam Alters River Flows and Disrupts Ecosystem Functions. This hydrograph is for the same river portrayed in Figure 1-4, but the river's flow pattern has been altered greatly by construction of a hydropower dam upstream. Operation of the dam causes the river's flow to fluctuate erratically. Unnaturally low flows lead to fish kills and deplete populations of species sensitive to higher water temperatures and lower oxygen conditions. Groundwater tables fall when not recharged by the river, desiccating floodplain vegetation. Without higher flows, vegetation encroaches into the channel, further reducing aquatic habitat space. In the absence of high flows, stressful conditions associated with low flows can last for long periods. Without floods, many fish species cannot access floodplains for spawning or feeding.

slow, shallow edges of the channel as a nursery and refuge from predators. Aquatic insects were either left high and dry or flushed away when they could not move fast enough to track the highly transient river edge. Tiny fish were drawn out into the deep, predator-infested main channel when river flows dropped rapidly.

The dam also plugged the river's massive conveyor system that had previously transported an average of 380,000 tons of sediment—five times the weight of the H.M.S. Titanic—downstream each day. With that sediment piling up in Lake Powell behind the dam, there was none to replace the sands and gravels that were flushed away by waters released from the reservoir. As a result, within a few years of the closing of the dam gates, the downstream riverbed was scoured more than nine meters. The dynamic and diverse channel habitat that had offered life-sustaining options for a wide variety of species was quickly converted into a homogenous, stable channel. More gradually, the river has eroded massive sand beaches, which are highly prized by river runners for camping and also provide critical habitat for riparian vegetation, insects, lizards, toads, small mammals, and birds.

Ecological changes of the sort that have occurred on the Colorado have unfolded in river system after river system around the world as flows have been altered to suit human purposes. Just as each river has a unique flow signature, each will have a different response to human disruptions of its flow regime, but in nearly every case the result will be a loss of ecological integrity and a decline in river health. In addition to harming the ecosystems themselves, these transformations also destroy many of the valuable goods and services that people and economies depend upon.

In the Mekong River basin of Southeast Asia, for instance, more than 50 million people depend upon fish for their nutrition and livelihoods. Ninety percent of these fish spawn in fields and forests that are naturally flooded under the river's flow regime. With numerous dams and diversions planned for the lower Mekong system, however, the subsistence livelihoods of people in the region are in jeopardy. Fisheries declined dramatically, for example, after completion in 1994 of the Pak Mun Dam on Thailand's Mun River (a large tributary to the Mekong), as well as the completion in 1998 of Nam Theun Hinboun, a hydropower project on the Theun River, another Mekong tributary, in Laos. Nam Theun Hinboun was built despite predictions that during the three-month dry season the river below the dam would be diminished to a series of pools, disrupting the habitat of 140 fish species.[32] In the Rio Grande, which forms 2,019 kilometers of the international border between the United States and Mexico, the loss of flood flows due to dam and reservoir operations has left the river unable to move the huge quantities of sediment brought into it by its tributaries. As a result, when tributary floodwaters enter the Rio Grande's choked channel, they spill out across the land and cause widespread economic damage.[33]

River systems in which dams, levees, or heavy channelization have destroyed the river-floodplain connection also have a greatly diminished capacity to purify water as it moves through a watershed, a very valuable ecosystem service. If rivers no longer spread out over their floodplains, their nutrient loads can no longer get taken up and cleansed by floodplain plant communities. Instead, rivers carry these heavy pollutant loads downstream. In the case of the U.S. Midwest, where corn and soybean farmers apply heavy doses of fertilizer to their lands, the loss of this important ecosystem service results in much greater pollution damage downstream. More than 90 percent of the freshwater inflow to the Gulf of Mexico originates in the Mississippi River basin, which drains about 40 percent of the land area of the continental United States.[34] The load of nitrogen at the mouth of the Mississippi is estimated to be double or triple the predevelopment quantity. These nutrients contribute to the algal blooms and the resulting "dead zone" of low oxygen that is killing fish and other aquatic life in the Gulf of Mexico.[35] The quantities of nitrogen carried by rivers to the coasts have increased greatly in many heavily polluted and altered watersheds of the world, including the Adriatic, Baltic, and Black seas in Europe as well as the Gulf of Mexico.[36]

Excessive water diversions and the cutting off of river flows from deltas and estuaries also pose major threats to aquatic life and valuable ecosystem services in many parts of the world. In river-estuarine systems, reductions in freshwater outflow often cause saltwater to penetrate inland, raising the salinity levels of brackish wetlands and estuarine waters. This has occurred in California's San Francisco Bay-Delta, for example, as river flows were diverted away from the delta in order to increase water supplies for Central Valley farmers and southern California residents. This diversion has caused the zone where saltwater and freshwater mix to move inland from the shallow embayments of San

Francisco Bay to the narrow, deeper channels of the delta, which is less hospitable to estuarine species.[37] The delta smelt has been driven to the edge of extinction by this loss of habitat, as well as by the large water pumps that have killed vast numbers of them. Similarly, the delta of the Ganges-Brahmaputra river system—the largest deltaic system in the world—is in a serious state of ecological decline. River diversions have reduced greatly the outflow of fresh water through the delta to the Bay of Bengal, causing a saline front to advance across the western portion of the delta, damaging valuable mangroves and fish habitat.[38] Some 5 million poor Bangladeshis depend upon fishing and other subsistence uses of the delta for their livelihoods.[39]

FRESHWATER LIFE AT RISK

As dams and other infrastructure have altered the habitats and flow conditions to which species have adapted over thousands of years, more and more life-forms have entered a perilous state of decline; many are at risk of extinction. Since healthy aquatic communities do much of nature's work, their disruption from the loss of key species is both a cause and consequence of the decline in river health. A look at the status of freshwater biodiversity can thus serve as evidence of the impacts of river flow modifications today, as well as a warning sign that ecosystem health will worsen unless critical trends are reversed.

Freshwater ecosystems account for less than 1 percent of all the habitat area on earth, compared with about 28 percent for terrestrial ecosystems and 71 percent for marine systems. Yet species richness relative to habitat extent is greater in freshwater ecosystems than either of the other two. Home to 2.4 percent of globally known species but comprising only 0.8 percent of earth's total habitat area, freshwater ecosystems have a higher species density than either terrestrial or marine systems.[40] This means that a significant share of the variety of freshwater life can be extinguished with the loss of relatively small portions of freshwater habitat. Many species may be lost even before they are found or named: indeed, for the last two decades scientists have been describing about three hundred new freshwater species each year.[41]

Unfortunately, a comprehensive global assessment of freshwater biodiversity is impossible because data are not available for most poor and middle-income countries nor even for many wealthy countries. Researchers estimate, however, that during recent decades at least 20 percent of the world's ten thousand freshwater fish species have become endangered, threatened with extinction, or have already gone extinct.[42] A significant, but unknown share of mussels, birds, amphibians, plants, and other species that depend on freshwater habitats are also believed to be at risk.

The high degree of imperilment of freshwater life is particularly evident in North America, a region for which biodiversity data are more complete. At least 123 species of North American freshwater fish, mollusks, crayfish, and amphibians have gone extinct since 1900. Biologists Anthony Ricciardi and Joseph Rasmussen estimate that in recent decades North American freshwater animal species have been extinguished at an average rate of half a percent per decade, and they project this rate to increase in the near future to 3.7 percent per decade.[43] This projected extinction rate is about five times greater than that projected for terrestrial species—suggesting that the variety of freshwater life in North America is proportionately more at risk than terrestrial life. Even more startling, the relative rate of loss of North American freshwater species is comparable to that of species in tropical rainforests, widely recognized as one of the most stressed ecosystem types on the planet. Although tropical forests contain many more species than North American fresh waters do, each of these ecosystems appears to be losing species diversity at a comparable rate.

The United States stands out as a global center of freshwater biodiversity. The nation ranks first in the world in the number of known species of freshwater mussels, snails, and salamanders, as well as three important freshwater insect groups—caddis flies, mayflies, and stoneflies. U.S. waters are home to a remarkable three hundred species of freshwater mussels—29 percent of those known worldwide—and nearly twice as many as are known to live in Europe, Africa, India, and China combined. With approximately eight hundred species of freshwater fish, the United States ranks seventh in freshwater fish diversity globally but has by far the most diverse assemblage of fishes of any temperate country. Indeed, one U.S. waterway—the Duck River in Tennessee—contains more species of fish than all of Europe. Darters, a type of perch, comprise the single most diverse genus of U.S. fishes, and most of its 125 species are endemic to the United States—that is, they are found nowhere else. Indeed, the United

States has a remarkably high degree of endemism of freshwater life generally: some two-thirds of the nation's freshwater fishes, for example, are found only in U.S. waters.

To date, the United States has been a poor steward of its rich and globally important patrimony of freshwater life. In the most comprehensive survey so far of the status of the nation's biological diversity, researchers with The Nature Conservancy and the Association for Biodiversity Information found that of fourteen major groups of plant and animal life in the United States, the five with the greatest share of species at risk are all animals that depend on freshwater systems for all or part of their life cycle[44] (see Table 1-4). An astonishing 69 percent of freshwater mussels are to some degree at risk of extinction, as are 51 percent of crayfishes, 37 percent of freshwater fishes, and 36 percent of amphibians—compared with 33 percent of flowering plants, 16 percent of mammals, and 14 percent of birds. Moreover, of the four categories of risk—presumed/possibly extinct, critically imperiled, imperiled, and vulnerable—freshwater-dependent organisms tend to have higher percentages in the higher-risk categories than other major species groups. For example, 38 percent of the nation's freshwater mussel species are either critically imperiled or possibly/presumed extinct, as are 18 percent of crayfishes and 14 percent of freshwater fishes. By comparison, 8 percent of all U.S. plant and animal species fall into these two highest at-risk categories—further evidence that freshwater life in the United States is proportionately at greater risk than terrestrial life.

The very high rate of mussel imperilment is especially disturbing both because mussels are good indicators of freshwater ecosystem health and because they play critical roles in preserving that health. Mussels, which are largely sedentary creatures, require a certain water flow, temperature, clarity, oxygen level, and substrate—traits important to other species as well, and that determine the overall health of freshwater systems. Ecologically, mussels act as natural water filters: they glean microscopic plankton from water flowing by them, helping to purify rivers and lakes and maintain water quality for human uses. Mussels also provide a source of food for a variety of birds and wildlife. Like the proverbial canary in the coal mine, the demise and high rate of endangerment of mussels signal trouble ahead for freshwater ecosystems and the life within them.[45]

Over millennia, mussels have evolved a myriad of fascinating and complex adaptations that, until recently, have enabled them to thrive suc-

TABLE 1-4 Risk Status of U.S. Animal Species Dependent
on Freshwater Ecosystems

Animal Group	Total Number of Species	Share That Is Extinct, Critically Imperiled, Imperiled, or Vulnerable (%)
Freshwater mussels	292	69
Crayfishes	322	51
Stoneflies	606	43
Freshwater fishes	799	37
Amphibians	231	36

SOURCE: Stein, Kutner, and Adams, 2000.

cessfully in their water environments. Since they do not move large distances, nearly all native mussels have come to depend on one or more species of fish to help spread their offspring and colonize new habitat. Scientists have only begun to uncover the diverse array of behaviors mussels have evolved to accomplish these tasks. For example, the orange-nacre mucket, a mussel found only in the rivers and streams of Alabama's Mobile River basin, has evolved an especially interesting way of tricking passing fish into taking its larvae to new locations. The female essentially uses her offspring to bait the fish, packaging her larvae at the end of jelly-like tubes that can extend a couple meters out into the water. To nearby fish, the larval packet looks like a tasty minnow. When the fish bites, the tube breaks open and releases the larvae into the stream. A few of the offspring succeed in attaching to the fish's gills, where they absorb nutrients and start to develop. After a week or two of moving about with their host fish, the young mussels drop off, float to the river bottom, and attach to new substrate, soon to begin performing their vital task of water purification.[46]

Unfortunately, along with numerous other mussels, the orange-nacre mucket's survival is now imperiled by the extensive damming and other alterations to its habitat brought about by human activities in the Mobile River watershed. A total of seventeen of the basin's mussel species are listed as threatened or endangered under the U.S. Endangered Species Act. The principal cause of their imperilment is the extensive development of the Mobile River and its tributaries for hydropower and navigation. The fifteen dams built for hydropower production and nineteen locks and dams built for navigation collectively impound some 44 percent of the Mobile River mainstem and even larger portions of some major tributaries, such as the Coosa River. As a result, free-flowing river habitat has been greatly diminished. Along with native mussels, numerous fish species are imperiled in the basin as well, including Alabama shad, Alabama sturgeon, and at least ten smaller fishes.[47]

A large share of the freshwater species at risk in the continental United States are found in the Southeast, a function of both the great richness of species in this region and the extensive alteration of its rivers. The north-to-south orientation of the vast Mississippi drainage allowed many species to migrate southward and thereby survive the advance of Pleistocene glaciers thousands of years ago. The resulting species diversity is greatest not in the Mississippi itself, but rather in its tributaries—particularly those that flow through parts of the Appalachian and Ozark mountains. Indeed, eighteen of the top twenty watersheds in the continental United States with the greatest number of species at risk are located in just four southeastern river basins—the Tennessee, Ohio, Cumberland, and Mobile. Topping this group is the upper Clinch River on the Tennessee-Virginia border, which is home to forty-eight imperiled or vulnerable fish and mussel species.[48]

Salmon, probably the most charismatic of U.S. fish species, have received more attention by far than other groups. Although most anadromous salmon are not that rare at the species level, their plight is certainly a dire one. Many individual fish stocks—which constitute genetically distinct populations within a species—are both rare and threatened. At least 214 salmon and steelhead stocks among seven different species are at risk of extinction. Especially in the Pacific Northwest, a combination of hydroelectric dam construction, overfishing, and unsound land-use practices have decimated salmon populations.[49]

Likewise, in both Europe and the northeastern United States, wild Atlantic salmon populations have plummeted. Historically, more than two thousand rivers on both sides of the Atlantic Ocean harbored this species. Now, a recent study by the conservation organization World Wildlife Fund (WWF) has found that wild Atlantic salmon have been wiped out in more than three hundred river systems. The fish has disappeared completely from Germany, Switzerland, Belgium, the Netherlands, the Czech Republic, and Slovakia. It is on the verge of being wiped out in Portugal, Poland, Estonia, the United States, and parts of Canada. Some 90 percent of wild Atlantic salmon populations judged to be healthy are in just four countries—Scotland, Ireland, Iceland, and Norway. The WWF study identified the major threats to wild Atlantic salmon populations as overfishing, dam construction, other river engineering projects, pollution, and commercial salmon farming, which spreads disease and erodes the gene pool of wild populations.[50]

Although no comprehensive surveys of the status of freshwater life exist for most of the developing world, numerous studies collectively suggest that the situation is not good. Undoubtedly it is worsening rapidly as dam construction, river diversions, and other engineering projects continue to alter rivers on a large scale. The Amazon River basin in South America, the Zaire River basin in central Africa, and the Mekong River system in southeast Asia top the list of river systems with the greatest total number of known fish species. The Amazon basin alone harbors more than two thousand species of freshwater fish—about one in five of those known worldwide—and scientists estimate that 90 percent of them are found nowhere else.[51] With more than seventy dams planned for Brazil's Amazonian region alone, a good portion of these species will undoubtedly experience similar problems of migration blockage, habitat destruction, and other alterations that have so jeopardized temperate freshwater species.[52]

Africa's rich freshwater species diversity derives from its diverse array of habitats. The continent harbors more semi-arid and desert area than any other, including Australia. More than 90 percent of Africa's total river length is made up of streams less than 9 kilometers long; many of these flow only seasonally, creating a diverse set of habitat conditions. Freshwater fish species in Africa are estimated to number around 2,800, similar to the estimated ranges (although estimates vary) for South America and tropical Asia (see Table 1-5).

While the dramatic decline of freshwater fishes in Lake Victoria has dominated freshwater biodiversity concerns in Africa, life in river systems is increasingly at risk as well. Dam construction, especially for irrigation and hydropower production, is proceeding rapidly. More than 560 large dams have been commissioned in African countries since 1980.[53] The construction of Egypt's High Dam at Aswan during the 1960s has greatly altered the habitat and diversity of life in the northern extent of the Nile

River. Out of forty-seven commercial fish species in the Nile prior to the dam's construction, only seventeen were still harvested a decade after the dam's completion.[54]

In the Zambezi River basin of southern Africa, the decline of the beloved wattled crane is signaling ecological trouble stemming from the disruption of natural river flows (Figure 1-6). The breeding of wattled cranes is tied closely to the river's natural flood regime: the recession of floodwaters following the seasonal flood peak appears to be the cue for crane pairs to nest. They build their nests in shallow open water on the floodplain, which protects their young from predators; because they wait until the flood period is over, their nests are not in danger of being washed away. Each pair raises a single chick on the pulse of plant and insect life produced by the flood. As dams and diversions have altered flows within the Zambezi River basin—which is home to more than 80 percent of the wattled crane population—the cranes have come under increasing pressure. Wattled cranes have nearly disappeared from the vast floodplains of the Zambezi Delta, which no longer receive the annual pulse of floodwaters so important to their survival.[55]

Asia has an incredibly diverse freshwater fauna, but much of it has not yet been adequately described or catalogued as to status or degree of risk. Indonesia alone has at least 1,200 freshwater fish species, and perhaps as many as 1,700. China's rivers support some 717 freshwater fishes, and Thailand's more than 500. Asian rivers are also home to three of the world's five true river dolphins—those that never enter the sea.[56] One is found in south Asia's Ganges and Brahmaputra rivers, another only in Pakistan's Indus River, and the third is restricted to China's Yangtze River.

TABLE 1-5   Freshwater Fish Diversity in Major
Regions of the World

Region	Estimated Number of Species
Africa	2,780
South America	2,400–4,000
Tropical Asia	2,500
North America	1,033
Europe	319
Central America	242
Australia	188

SOURCE: Stiassny, 1996.

FIGURE 1-6. The wattled crane builds its nests in shallowly flooded areas of the Zambezi River's floodplain, following the peak of the annual flood. (Photo by Richard Beilfuss.)

All three river dolphins are endangered. Tropical Asia also harbors the world's richest assemblage of freshwater turtles, as well as eight of the world's twenty-three crocodilian species. All eight are endangered. Less charismatic species are abundant as well: India alone may support four thousand species of caddis fly, an aquatic insect well known to people who fly-fish.[57]

Many Asian mammals classified as terrestrial species depend heavily on riverine habitats for part or all of the year. Aquatic ecologist David Dudgeon of Hong Kong University points out, for example, that the proboscis monkey, crab-eating macaques, Malayan tapirs, and the highly endangered orangutan all use riparian wetland and swamp forests as key habitats. Malayan tapirs, for instance, reside in dense swamp forest by day but then feed in marshy grasslands or floodplains by night. Though more wide ranging, Asian elephants and Javan rhinoceros rely on riverine wetlands for water and food during the dry season. Asian water deer graze on the grassy floodplains inundated by the seasonal monsoon. For example, Père David's deer, which has been exterminated in the wild, was confined to wetlands along China's Yangtze River. Marshland deer need open floodplains because their large antlers make movement through forests or other vegetative canopies difficult.[58]

As in tropical South America and portions of Africa, the outlook for Asian freshwater life is not promising. The ecology of many Asian rivers is driven by the monsoons, which create distinct wet and dry seasons and corresponding high and low river flow patterns at fairly predictable times of the year. The organisms that inhabit these systems have adapted to this flow pattern over time, and their life cycles are keyed to it. For example, fishes in the Mekong River migrate upstream to breed as river levels rise during the wet season, and migrate back downstream as levels drop during the dry season. Dams built to prevent flooding during the monsoon and to store water for the dry season smooth out the pattern of river flow and shorten the period of floodplain inundation, eliminating important habitat and environmental cues that fish and other species depend upon. Common engineering fixes that have been tried elsewhere, such as fish ladders to aid post-dam migration, are unlikely to be effective because most species in the Mekong do not jump.[59] The Mekong River Commission has identified a dozen sites for dams on the Mekong mainstem in Laos, Thailand, and Cambodia, although these are currently on hold (see Chapter 5). Meanwhile, China has seven large dams planned or under construction on the upper Mekong, and some of these already are impacting the river.

Life in China's largest river—the Yangtze—is also at great risk. Chinese leaders are proceeding with construction of Three Gorges Dam, which if completed will be the largest dam in the world. Already, the Gezhouba Dam on the Yangtze has blocked spawning migrations of the anadromous Chinese sturgeon, fragmented populations of the endemic Dabry's sturgeon, which is now nearly extinct downstream of the dam, and decimated the population of anadromous Chinese paddlefish, which can no longer access its upstream spawning sites. Because this paddlefish occurs nowhere else, it will almost certainly go extinct.[60]

Ecologist David Dudgeon sums up the situation: "Habitat destruction or degradation in and along Asian rivers is epidemic, with predictable consequences for resident and migratory species. . . . Tropical Asia is overpopulated, and many people are poor, landless, and crowded in burgeoning cities. All hope to improve their lives. The result will be per capita increases in resource use that will be accompanied by greater water consumption and further pollution, flow regulation, and habitat degradation. At the beginning of the third millennium, the prognosis for Asian rivers is grim."[61]

Although hidden from view and undeniably not charismatic, the algae, fungi, worms, and other freshwater species that live in the sediment of river channels, lake bottoms, wetlands, and floodplains play critical roles in the biological, chemical, and physical processes that drive ecosystem functions. They are the gears and levers that turn nature's aquatic machinery, quietly performing much of the work we call ecosystem services. They help maintain water quality, decompose organic material, take up and transfer contaminants, and produce food for animals higher in the food web. In comparison to fish and bivalves, much less is known about sediment-dwellers but they are unquestionably diverse and abundant. Globally, more than one hundred thousand species of invertebrates are estimated to live in freshwater sediments, along with ten thousand species of algae, and more than twenty thousand species of protozoa and bacteria.[62]

Information on the diversity and functioning of sediment-dwelling organisms in freshwater systems is poor. The most numerous organisms are microscopic and often live deep within the sediment column, making them difficult to sample and study. Scientists sometimes infer which species groups are present in a given location by the types of processes occurring there rather than by conventional sampling, detection, and cataloguing methods. Up to 1,500 different invertebrate species may live in a particular wetland, along with an equal or greater number of microscopic organisms. Lesser but still large numbers of sediment-dwellers also inhabit lake and river bottoms and groundwaters.[63] The activities of these organisms affect much that goes on in the water column above, and vice versa. For example, during the pulse of high productivity that occurs with flooding, sediment-dwelling animals may hatch, move into the water column, feed, and disperse.[64] Dams and other infrastructure that eliminate floods disrupt these important ecological processes since sediment-dwellers tend to be very sensitive to changes in water levels, flow magnitudes, flood frequencies, and other hydrologic alterations.

As rivers come under increasing regulation and freshwater habitats become increasingly altered, the composition and abundance of this critical assemblage of species will likely change as well—often in ways we cannot yet explain or predict, and with consequences that may be costly and irreversible. Indeed, the potential for nasty ecological surprises increases as the variety and number of freshwater organisms diminish.

A CONCEPTUAL VIEW FOR BALANCING
HUMAN AND ECOSYSTEM WATER NEEDS

Society is now confronted with a monumental design challenge. A large body of scientific evidence tells us that we have installed billions of dollars of engineering infrastructure that is killing the aquatic world. Freshwater species extinctions are rising. The ecosystem functions that sustain all life, including the provision of services that benefit human economies, are declining. Meanwhile human population and consumption levels continue to climb—driving humanity's demands for water, food, energy, and material items ever higher.

Projecting these trends into the future certainly does not create a desirable scenario. Yet the mind-set that has shaped water management practices up to the present time is deeply entrenched. For millennia, political leaders have used the successful control and manipulation of rivers to win favor with their citizens and to prove their power and legitimacy. Queen Sammu-Ramat, who ruled Assyria during the late ninth century B.C. in what is now northern Iraq, is reputed to have had inscribed on her tomb: "I constrained the mighty river to flow according to my will and led its water to fertilize lands that had before been barren and without inhabitants." Early in the twentieth century, this historically familiar political hubris was joined by advances in the science of hydraulics and water engineering to elevate human control over river flows by orders of magnitude. In 1908, after a military campaign on the Nile River, Winston Churchill prophesied that "One day, every last drop of water which drains into the whole valley of the Nile . . . shall be equally and amicably divided among the river people, and the Nile itself . . . shall perish gloriously and never reach the sea."[65] With the construction of Hoover Dam (originally known as Boulder Dam) on the lower Colorado River in the 1930s, engineers demonstrated the technical feasibility of taming a large river. At 220 meters high and able to store 1.7 years worth of the Colorado's average flow, Hoover broke all dam engineering records up to that time and unleashed an engineering frenzy that would dominate water development for the rest of the twentieth century.

Only within the last couple of decades, with advances in the science of river ecology, have we become aware of the high ecological price of these technological choices. Many governments and agencies have responded by altering the rules of water development somewhat—for instance, by requiring that the "environmental impact" of dams and other large water projects be studied before they are built. But these Band-Aid type measures are wholly inadequate to the scale of the problem at hand. Meeting the challenge of satisfying human needs while at the same time protecting the health of the aquatic environment will require a much more fundamental shift in how society uses, manages, and values fresh water—one that recognizes from the outset the importance of healthy ecosystems and humanity's dependence on them. Anything less than such a conceptual shift will not suffice. As the great physicist Albert Einstein observed, you cannot solve a problem within the mind-set that created it.

The conceptual view of water development that has dominated up to the present time considers freshwater ecosystems to be resources that should be exploited for growth of the human economy—to deliver more water to agriculture, cities, and industries, for example, and to enable the shipping of goods and the generation of electrical power. Because protecting the health of ecosystems themselves and the natural services they provide is not an explicit goal in this mind-set, nature's water needs go unrecognized and unspecified. For a period of time, this approach appears to work: economies reap the rewards of additional irrigation, hydropower, and other human water uses while the residual water is still sufficient to sustain natural ecosystem functions to a reasonable degree. Over time, however, as human pressures on water systems increase, the share of water devoted to ecosystem functions declines to damaging levels (Figure 1-7). In much of the world, nature's residual slice of the water pie is now insufficient to keep ecosystems functioning and to sustain freshwater life.

We suggest a shift to a new mind-set, one that makes the preservation of ecosystem health an explicit goal of water development and management. This mind-set recognizes that the human water economy is a subset of nature's water economy, and that human societies depend upon and receive valuable benefits from healthy ecosystems. To preserve these benefits, society therefore needs to make what we might call an *ecosystem support allocation* (or *eco-support allocation*, for short)—a designation of the quantity, quality, and timing of flows needed to safeguard the health and functioning of river systems themselves. This eco-support allocation implies a limit on the degree to which society can wisely alter natural river flows, a limit that we call the "sustainability boundary." Rather than freshwater ecosystems getting whatever water happens to be left over after human demands are met—an ever-shrinking residual piece of the pie—they receive what they need to remain healthy. As depicted in Figure 1-8, modification of river flows for economic purposes expands over time, but only up to the sustainability boundary, which is defined by the flows allocated for ecosystem support.

Contrary to initial appearances, this limit on river alterations is not a barrier to economic advancement but rather a necessary ingredient for sustainable development. Once human water extractions and flow modifications have reached the limit in any river basin or watershed, new water demands are met not by further manipulating rivers, but by raising water productivity—getting more benefit out of the water already appropriated for human purposes—and by sharing water more equitably. In this way, establishing an eco-support allocation unleashes the potential for conservation, recycling, and efficiency to help society garner maximum value from rivers, including instream and extractive benefits. Although this shift in river management will reduce jobs in dam-building and water project construction, it will create jobs in such diverse fields as native landscaping, green-building architecture, drip irrigation engineering, agroecological farming, and urban conservation planning. It also puts a premium on equitable allocations of water in shared river basins, both within and between countries.

Translating this ecological mind-set for river management into tangible policies and management practices will not be easy. The scientific basis for determining how much water a river needs, the topic of Chapter 2, is progressing steadily and is already sufficiently advanced to prescribe ecological flows for rivers. The policy tools for implementing these ecological flows vary with different legal and cultural settings, but as described in Chapter 3, there are enough instruments in the toolbox in most places to get going.

Just as rivers have been altered incrementally over the last two centuries—dam by dam, levee by levee—so they can be restored incrementally. In the United States, there is growing interest in removing dams that

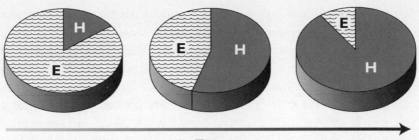

Time

FIGURE 1-7. Twentieth-Century Approach to Water Allocation. The conventional approach to allocating water is to permit human uses (H) for agriculture, cities, and industries to keep expanding, leaving for natural ecosystems (E) whatever slice of the "water pie" happens to remain. Over time, this residual slice becomes too small to support ecosystem functions adequately, causing the disappearance of species and the loss of valuable ecosystem services.

Time

- - - - Sustainability boundary

FIGURE 1-8. Proposed Twenty-First-Century Approach to Water Allocation. In this new approach to allocating water, scientists and policymakers define the quantity and timing of flows needed to support freshwater ecosystem health, and then establish a "sustainability boundary" that protects these flows from human use and modification. Human uses of water (H) can increase over time, but only up to the sustainability boundary. At that point, new water demands must be met through conservation, improvements in water productivity, and reallocation of water among users. By limiting human impacts on natural river flows and allocating enough water for ecosystem support (E), society derives optimal benefits from river systems in a sustainable manner.

no longer provide sufficient benefits to justify their environmental costs or safety risks. Twenty dams were removed nationwide during the 1970s, 91 during the 1980s, and 177 during the 1990s.[66] The vast majority of these are small dams, but even some large ones are under close examination, including four on the lower Snake River in the Columbia River basin. Former Secretary of the Interior Bruce Babbitt recently noted that "Five years ago, people asked of dam removal, Why? Or whether. Society now asks: Which ones, when, and how?"[67] Once considered extreme, the idea of removing dams is becoming increasingly mainstream. Just as important, however, is the emerging notion that dams still standing can be operated in ways that reinstate some of the river's natural form and function, and that dams not yet built can be designed and operated from the start with ecological goals in mind.

Although species that have already been driven to extinction are gone forever, many of the ecological impacts that dams and other alterations have had on rivers are reversible. When given a chance, many rivers can heal. Two million alewife returned just a year after the removal of Edwards Dam on Maine's Kennebec River, and American shad, striped bass, Atlantic salmon, and sturgeon were all sighted upstream of the former dam's location. After the mid-nineties floods in the U.S. Midwest, the natural communities of the Missouri River floodplain bounced back, demonstrating great capacity for recovery once the river's connection to its floodplain was re-established. Local groups in Thailand report that 152 species of fish have returned to the Mun River following the government's decision in 2001 to open the gates of the Pak Mun Dam.[68] And in northern Mexico, unusually high flows in the Colorado River during much of the nineties overwhelmed available reservoir storage and enlarged the area of wetlands in the Colorado delta.

Even as the work of restoring rivers gets under way in earnest, protecting the health, biodiversity, and ecosystem services of rivers not yet extensively developed remains an enormous challenge. Especially in poor and middle-income countries, demands for food, energy, and water supplies create great pressures to dam, divert, and otherwise modify rivers, just as industrial countries did during the twentieth century. The global challenge of sustaining the benefits and services people derive from rivers while at the same time meeting legitimate human needs requires efforts to both protect rivers from undue harm and to restore those that have already been damaged. The wealth of scientific knowledge gained over the last decade is creating the conditions for a very different relationship between people and rivers—a relationship of mutual health and coexistence that offers great benefits to this and future generations.

〜

CHAPTER TWO

How Much Water Does a River Need?

A river serpent, with the body of a snake and the head of a fish, lives in the sacred tribal belief systems of southern Africa. Native peoples communicate with their ancestors through this serpent god, Nyaminyami, when he is present in their rivers.[1] He is their link to ancient wisdom and to the creation. But Nyaminyami is elusive. He is found only in rocky shoals or boulder-choked reaches—only in those places where the river froths and cascades in a torrent of whitewater.

Africans look for Nyaminyami in different places along a river as water levels rise or fall. When the river is low, Nyaminyami can be found where the river tumbles over shallow cobbles. When the river is high, these same cobbles are too deeply submerged to form whitewater so the river serpent moves to areas where large boulders create swirling currents. Nyaminyami constantly moves up river and down, seeking out its whitewater habitat as river levels change from day to day, and season to season.

Elders of the Tonga people in southern Africa believe that Nyaminyami became very distressed during the construction of Kariba Dam on the Zambezi River in Zimbabwe during the late 1950s. As the dam was being built, heavy floods destroyed bridges, eroded riverbanks, and repeatedly delayed progress on the dam's construction. Tribal elders attributed these setbacks to Nyaminyami's wrath. How, they wondered, will the river serpent be able to move freely in search of its whitewater habitat with a large dam blocking the river? Will whitewater still exist when the dam is controlling the river's flow? Following the dam's completion in 1959, their fears came true: much of the serpent god's hallowed whitewater disappeared as operation of the dam dramatically altered the Zambezi's flow.

Kariba Dam has affected much more than the sacred realm of the river serpent, Nyaminyami. Some fifty-seven thousand Tonga people were forced to relocate from their ancestral homeland to make way for the Kariba reservoir.[2] Once-productive floodplain areas no longer receive nourishing floodwaters. Like Nyaminyami, many of the river's plants and animals depend upon particular habitat conditions that have been disrupted by the dam's alteration of natural river flows.

The damming of rivers like the Zambezi has been replicated time and again over the past century of major dam construction worldwide. The details of these transformations differ from river to river. But in each case, trade-offs—some anticipated and some not—have been made to enlist the service of rivers in economic growth and development.

As society becomes more alert to the damaging ecological and cultural effects of harnessing a river's flow, the question begging an answer is, how much water does a river need? Can a river serve the demands for hydroelectric power and irrigation water as well as the spiritual needs of local peoples and the ecological needs of the river itself? In the case of Kariba Dam, could the dam operators appease Nyaminyami and improve the river's ecological health by releasing water from the dam at different times and in different amounts? Could sacred whitewater be created periodically, at certain reaches, so that the Tongans can continue to communicate with their ancestors through Nyaminyami? Could improved water releases re-create the variety of habitats that support the Zambezi River's diversity of life? These are the types of questions that now challenge river scientists, sociologists, economists, and water managers around the world as they try to meet various human demands for water while maintaining healthy river ecosystems.

The plants and animals living in a river ecosystem depend upon habitat conditions that are determined largely by the river's flow. That flow can vary considerably over the course of a year and from year to year, forming an ever-changing, dynamic mosaic of river habitat. Over centuries or millennia, river species have adapted to the changing habitats created by naturally fluctuating water levels. When salmon are ready to leave the ocean and begin their upriver spawning migration, for example, they wait for the river to rise in flood, thus ensuring that they will have enough water to ascend rocky shoals or small waterfalls to reach their spawning grounds. After the flood season passes, lowered water levels and slower currents give recently hatched salmon fry a chance to grow strong enough to maneuver in the river without being washed downstream. When large floods do return, the fish are swept down river to begin the ocean phase of their life cycle.

In the Amazon River's floodplain, many tree species release their seeds at the onset of the flood season. The floodwaters carry the seeds across the river's massive floodplain, thereby maximizing the trees' chances for successful reproduction across an extensive area. The flood is a bountiful time for the river's fish, which gorge themselves on the downpour of fruit and seeds. During its annual flood, the Amazon rises as much as 13 meters, enabling manatees—an unusually large grazer in the Amazon basin—to feed in the submerged forest canopy. Without this opportunity to acquire huge amounts of body fat during the floods, they would not be able to survive the meager fare of the dry season.[3]

Each river-dependent animal or plant has different habitat needs or preferences, which typically vary during their life cycles, as well as different tolerances for unfavorable conditions. A river's native species have been "tested" by nature's variability over thousands of years. If individuals are able to grow and reproduce adequately when conditions are favorable, and their population does not lose too many members during hard times, the species is able to persist. When humans alter the natural variations in river flow, they change the probabilities of survival for each species. Big dams in the Columbia River basin of the northwestern United States have eliminated the natural floods that cued salmon to migrate upstream and then subsequently flushed their offspring back downstream to the ocean. Engineers now truck or barge adult salmon upstream past the dams, but too many young salmon perish because they cannot move quickly enough downstream, or because they lose their way in the slack waters formed by the dams.

The flow of water in a river is not the only factor influencing the plants and animals in river ecosystems. The chemistry and temperature of river waters greatly influence river life. Sunlight penetrating the water drives the growth of aquatic plants. Leaves and other detritus falling or washing into a river supply food to insects at the base of river food chains. The amount and size of sediments—sand, gravel, and cobbles—moving through a river affect the physical structure of river channels and floodplains. The fate of many river species depends on the species they feed upon, get eaten by, or compete with. However, each of these other factors, in turn, is affected by river flow to varying degrees, making the flow regime a powerful influence on river health.

In just the last decade, scientists have learned a great deal about the critical linkages between natural flow variations and the health of river species and ecosystems. This knowledge will be crucial in guiding society toward better ways of managing water that optimize the long-term provision of ecosystem services while meeting other human water demands. But realizing such improvement will require that water planners and managers do a much better job of incorporating scientific knowledge into their decisions and activities. As we describe in this chapter, the rapidly expanding field of river restoration will only achieve its potential if scientists and engineers work closely together. Some early successes are proving that when their brainpower is fused and directed toward a common purpose, they can find ways to better meet society's water needs while bringing rivers back to life.

THE EVOLUTION OF A NEW RIVER MANAGEMENT PARADIGM

When Donald Tennant stepped into his new job as a fisheries biologist with the U.S. Fish and Wildlife Service in 1956, he soon found himself out of step with many of his fellow Americans: He did not share their unbridled enthusiasm for building dams.

Recovering from the treasury-draining Second World War and emboldened by its outcome, Americans in the 1950s began focusing their attentions on building a strong nation, and investment in public works infrastructure was seen as an essential step. Federal and state highway systems expanded by leaps and bounds. Rural electrification projects brought power to the hinterlands. And nearly two hundred large dams were built each year in the 1950s and 1960s as the United States embarked on a dam-building binge unlike any the world had ever seen. These dams would enable Americans to grow crops in the desert, free western cities from their arid shackles, and protect their homes and livelihoods from the ravages of floods.

But Tennant knew that by depriving rivers of their life-giving waters, these same dams would devastate aquatic life. In 1975, he wrote in the journal *Fisheries*, "Philosophically, it is a crime against nature to rob a stream of that last portion of water so vital to the life forms of the aquatic environment that developed there over eons of time."[4]

Tennant became one of the first scientists to attempt to gauge how much water a river needs. From 1958 to 1975, he systematically collected biological and hydrological data from rivers across the United States, comparing the rivers' biological attributes with their hydrologic condition. On the basis of those observations, he proposed some guidelines for flow protection that became known as the "Tennant Method."[5] To sustain "optimum" biological conditions, Tennant suggested that 60–100 percent of a river's average flow would need to be protected. But to provide "excellent habitat," only 30–50 percent of the flow might be needed. Because it is rather simple and easy to apply, the Tennant Method became one of the most commonly used approaches for defining ecological flow needs in the United States, and it was eventually applied in at least twenty-four other countries.[6]

The Tennant Method came under mounting scrutiny, however, as water managers and dam operators began to equate water left in rivers with water unavailable for other uses, such as irrigating farms, supporting cities, and generating power. Increasingly it became the source of contention in court and regulatory proceedings resulting from new federal legislation, such as the National Environmental Policy Act of 1969, the Endangered Species Act of 1973, and changing policies for the licensing of private hydropower dams. Water managers and dam owners began questioning the scientific assumptions of Tennant's method, inquiring on countless occasions whether fish might do just as well with less water. What would happen with an incremental lowering of the flow requirements, for instance by releasing only 20 percent of a river's natural flow, or only 10 percent? Engineers and economists could readily enumerate the economic worth of each additional meter of water level in a reservoir for hydropower generation, or each additional cubic meter available for irrigation. Why couldn't biologists make similar judgments for fish?

The mounting pressure to justify the biotic worth of flowing water had a profound effect on the evolution of river science in the United States during the 1970s and 1980s. It engendered a new branch of aquatic biology focused on assessing the environmental impact of water development. Hundreds of fish biologists and water resource engineers working primarily for wildlife agencies or environmental consulting firms were swept up into the frenzy of developing new tools and methods to determine how much water should be left in rivers. These tools were needed to inform water negotiations and regulatory proceedings. Eventually these applied scientists became isolated from aquatic research ecologists in universities and other institutions, who continued studying and modeling the basic functions of river systems and the biology of their plants and animals. These two camps—applied scientists and research scientists—were not to reunite until the late 1990s.

The applied camp focused heavily on defining "minimum instream flow" requirements—the minimum amount of water to be left in a river—and its effects on fish. The emphasis on protecting minimum flows for fish sprang from at least three points of origin. First, most minimum flow assessments were based on fish simply because fish had received far greater study than had other river creatures, and the public could appreciate fish needs better than they could those of a mussel or snail. Second, because dam operators had not previously been required to release any flow, preventing rivers from going completely dry was a very real issue with obvious biological benefits. But most significant, these early ecological flow assessments focused on minimum requirements because biologists in the 1970s and 1980s generally believed that low flows in rivers were the primary constraint on the health of aquatic communities: the more water provided during low flow periods, the better the health of a river and its fish.[7] Many biologists suggested that providing more water during dry periods than Nature would have supplied could actually enhance rivers.[8]

Many of the ecological flow standards developed in the 1970s and 1980s reflected the focus on minimum flows and fish.[9] In the northeastern United States, an "aquatic base flow standard" issued by the U.S. Fish and Wildlife Service was based on minimum flows equal to the August median (August typically being the lowest flow month in the region). The "R2-Cross" method, used mostly in the western United States, identified the minimum level of water needed to let fish pass through shallow riffles. Other popular approaches such as the "Wetted Perimeter Method" were based on the idea that because most river channels have a characteristic "U" shape, it was most important to keep the rounded bottom of the "U" covered with water. Additional water simply deepened the aquatic area but did not substantially increase its width.

In the 1970s, a team of scientists, water policy specialists, and computer modelers working for the U.S. Fish and Wildlife Service developed an approach called the "Instream Flow Incremental Methodology" (IFIM).[10] While the IFIM included a suite of analytical methods and computer programs, one tool in this package became particularly popular with fish biologists and subsequently came to dominate the field of ecological flow analysis worldwide. This computerized "physical habitat simulation model," or PHABSIM (pronounced p-HAB-sim), was designed to quantify the habitat available for a species of interest, usually fish, at different levels of flow. Habitat preferences for different species could be described in the model using a number of variables, but most applications of PHABSIM have used only two to describe fish habitat: water depth and water velocity. Although the model can be used to estimate the habitat available for many different species, most applications of PHABSIM have examined only a few types of fish due to the considerable time and expense involved in collecting field data on each species' habitat preferences. Based on the model's predictions, fish biologists identify a level of flow at which the greatest amount of habitat is available for the target fish species.

This type of assessment—in which different levels of "return" (i.e., the amount of fish habitat available) can be associated with different levels of "investment"(i.e., the amount of flow provided)—is highly compatible with the way that water managers evaluate hydropower generation and other water management objectives. Not surprisingly, PHABSIM quickly became the most commonly used tool in the world for assessing ecological flow needs. PHABSIM modeling has been used to negotiate the minimum levels of flow to be released at hundreds of dams.

In the 1970s and 1980s, aquatic research ecologists working in universities and other institutions made some important discoveries and developed new ecological theories that diverged significantly from the way the ecological flow requirements were being defined by applied biologists. Their research led to a clash between the two aquatic science camps that began to foment in scientific journals in the 1990s.

Contrary to the flat-line minimum flow requirements being recommended by applied biologists, research ecologists argued that rivers require a much fuller spectrum of flow conditions to sustain their health and native species.[11] They disputed the accuracy or utility of models like PHABSIM that would predict benefits to fish on the basis of only a couple of factors like water depth and velocity, and that commonly led to the selection of a single minimum flow level for ecological protection.[12] The research scientists criticized the applied biologists' single-species and fish-centric focus as too narrow an approach to conserve healthy river ecosystems. Yes, they argued, it is vital to maintain adequate low-flow conditions to sustain fish and other aquatic organisms, but other flow conditions matter a great deal as well (see Box 2-1). Higher flows following rainstorms or snowmelt continually reshape physical habitats such as pools and riffles in the channel, provide increased mobility and food

BOX 2-1 Ecological Functions Performed by Different River Flow Levels

Flow Level	Ecological Roles
Low (base) flows	Normal level: · Provide adequate habitat space for aquatic organisms · Maintain suitable water temperatures, dissolved oxygen, and water chemistry · Maintain water table levels in floodplain, soil moisture for plants · Provide drinking water for terrestrial animals · Keep fish and amphibian eggs suspended · Enable fish to move to feeding and spawning areas · Support hyporheic organisms (living in saturated sediments) Drought level: · Enable recruitment of certain floodplain plants · Purge invasive, introduced species from aquatic and riparian communities · Concentrate prey into limited areas to benefit predators
Higher flows	· Shape physical character of river channel including pools, riffles · Determine size of streambed substrates (sand, gravel, cobble) · Prevent riparian vegetation from encroaching into channel · Restore normal water quality conditions after prolonged low flows, flushing away waste products and pollutants · Aerate eggs in spawning gravels, prevent siltation · Maintain suitable salinity conditions in estuaries
Large floods	· Provide migration and spawning cues for fish · Trigger new phase in life cycle (e.g., insects) · Enable fish to spawn on floodplain, provide nursery area for juvenile fish · Provide new feeding opportunities for fish, waterfowl · Recharge floodplain water table · Maintain diversity in floodplain forest types through prolonged inundation (i.e., different plant species have different tolerances) · Control distribution and abundance of plants on floodplain · Deposit nutrients on floodplain · Maintain balance of species in aquatic and riparian communities · Create sites for recruitment of colonizing plants · Shape physical habitats of floodplain · Deposit gravel and cobbles in spawning areas · Flush organic materials (food) and woody debris (habitat structures) into channel · Purge invasive, introduced species from aquatic and riparian communities · Disburse seeds and fruits of riparian plants · Drive lateral movement of river channel, forming new habitats (secondary channels, oxbow lakes) · Provide plant seedlings with prolonged access to soil moisture

sources for fish, and recharge shallow groundwater tables. Floods create floodplain habitat, maintain diverse riparian plant communities, and give fish access to spawning areas on the floodplain. Even extremely low water levels are essential, as they trigger reproduction in plants such as bald cypress and help to control highly competitive species that would eliminate others if they were not occasionally purged by stressful conditions. Freshwater flows from coastal rivers are also critical in maintaining the health and productivity of estuaries and other coastal marine habitats. Each of these factors must be considered when assessing how much water should be left in a river.[13] Research findings from hundreds of rivers around the world clearly demonstrate that when one or more aspects of hydrologic variability are removed or suppressed in a river ecosystem, many river species suffer.

Such criticism of habitat models and other popular instream flow methods shook the applied biology camp and others involved in regulating dams and water developments, bringing their modus operandi of prescribing flow requirements into serious question. This criticism also threatened to paralyze regulatory processes and even river restoration efforts. After all, how could one possibly consider the complex needs of hundreds or thousands of species in a river ecosystem, along with all the multiple interactions among flows, water quality, physical habitat, and species competition?

Recognizing the need to bridge the gap between research science and management, a number of river ecologists began in the early 1990s to sketch a new approach to river protection and restoration. Angela Arthington of Griffith University in Australia and seven colleagues from Australia and South Africa wrote in 1992 that new approaches should be based on the natural flow regime "as a guide to the environmental conditions that have maintained the river in its characteristic form."[14] That same year, Richard Sparks, a river ecologist at the Illinois Natural History Survey who has studied large river-floodplain systems around the world, wrote "rather than optimizing water regimes for one or a few species, a better approach is to try to approximate the natural flow regime that maintained the entire panoply of species."[15]

Implicit in Sparks' comment is the fact that species respond differently to hydrologic events such as floods and droughts. The same flood might benefit fish that reproduce during floods, but reduce the populations of crustaceans or aquatic insects that get flushed downstream. In years without large floods, insects and crustaceans are able to rebuild their populations. A natural flow regime provides a mix of good and bad years for each species over the course of many years or decades. Because good years occur sufficiently frequently, and bad years do not occur so often that they undo the benefits of the good years, all native species are sustained.

Keith Walker, a freshwater ecologist in Australia, wrote in 1995 that although many factors such as water quality, food supply, and interactions among species must be considered in any river management effort, the natural flow regime is of paramount importance because it exerts such considerable influence over these other factors. As Walker put it, flow is "the maestro that orchestrates pattern and process in rivers."[16] By the 1990s, Walker and many other ecologists had come to recognize flow as a "master variable" in river ecosystems.[17] While acknowledging the importance of other environmental factors, they asserted that efforts to maintain or restore river health must always consider the powerful influence of the flow regime.

Soon river ecologists around the world were calling for protecting or restoring natural flow regimes to the extent possible. Summarizing the emerging consensus in the research community around a "natural flow paradigm," LeRoy Poff and seven of his U.S. colleagues in 1997 suggested that the natural flow regime offers a time-tested recipe for river restoration and protection.[18] The needs of all river species are met, over the course of seasons, years, decades, and centuries, by the natural variations in a river's flow. Poff and his coauthors concluded, "the integrity of flowing water systems depends largely on their natural dynamic character," and "coordinated actions are therefore necessary to protect and restore a river's natural flow variability."

Although the scientific consensus to mimic natural flow conditions was instructive, applied biologists did not yet have adequate guidance for applying the natural flow paradigm. If natural flow conditions could not be preserved entirely on a managed river, how would applied biologists know how much water was needed to support the river ecosystem?

FLOW PRESCRIPTIONS AIMED AT ECOLOGICAL HEALTH

In South Africa and Australia, oceans away from the U.S. debates about river flow needs, ecologists were coming to their own conclusions about how to prescribe ecological flows for rivers. Concerned with the deteriorating state of their rivers and with intensifying water development pressures, many river scientists in the two countries had become active by the mid-1980s in defining the flow needs of river ecosystems.[19]

Ironically, by coming late to the ecological flows arena, the South African and Australian river scientists had an important advantage over their U.S. counterparts. Whereas the U.S. scientists were caught in a struggle to change old habits in the way that flow recommendations were made, the South Africans and Australians brought fresh and objective perspectives to the challenge of prescribing ecological flows. Informed by the writings of their international colleagues and decades of study in their respective countries, their work was guided from the beginning by an understanding that natural flows play critically important roles in river ecosystems.

Searching for methods and tools that could aid in determining ecosystem water needs, both South African and Australian scientists conducted comprehensive reviews of ecological flow methods and tools being applied in other parts of the world.[20] They found little to satisfy them. None of the existing approaches adequately considered the ecological influences of floods, extreme low flows, and other important hydrologic events on the health of whole ecosystems.[21] Few of the existing methods gave due consideration to the interactions of river flow with water quality, sediment movement, groundwater levels, or the need to provide fish and other aquatic animals with occasional access to floodplain areas. By the early 1990s, the South Africans and Australians had come to the conclusion that they would need to invent their own process for determining ecological flow needs. In 1991, an international conference on water allocation for the environment provided a propitious opportunity for scientific collaboration and cross-fertilization of ideas across continents. At that conference, eight South Africans and Australians outlined what they called a "holistic approach" to river flow protection that would address the whole river ecosystem and use the natural flow regime as a guide.[22]

The Holistic Approach and numerous variations on it began to evolve rapidly in Australia during the 1990s, while the South Africans began modifying it to fit their own needs.[23] At a national conference in July 1993, Jackie King and Rebecca Tharme of the University of Cape Town convened a workshop with seventeen South African scientists to discuss ways to apply a holistic approach in their country.[24] At the beginning of their deliberations, King and Tharme asked the scientists to draw a natural hydrograph, representing the typical natural fluctuations in water levels over the course of a year, for any river they knew well (see Figure 2-1). To

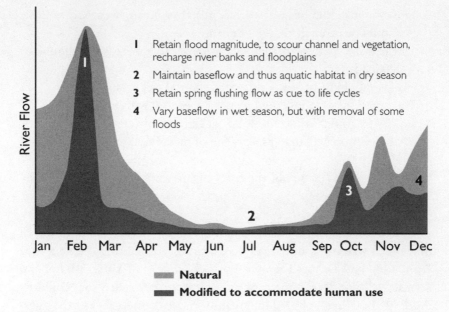

FIGURE 2-1. Natural and Modified Hydrographs in South Africa. At a 1993 workshop in South Africa, scientists drew natural hydrographs for selected rivers they knew well. They then drew modified hydrographs containing only half as much water to show how they would accommodate human uses while keeping the river as healthy as possible. Based on commonalities in their recommendations, they summarized some general principles for protecting flows adequate to maintain river health. (Adapted from Tharme and King 1998.)

simulate how best to provide water for human needs while keeping the river healthy, they then asked the scientists to draw a hydrograph that contained half as much water as in the natural condition but shaped in a way to protect river health to the extent possible. The scientists drew hydrographs for rivers in seven different regions of the country.

When they discussed the rationale for their modified hydrographs, the South African scientists found a great deal of consistency and agreement among their individual perspectives. Building from these common understandings, they then articulated eight general principles for managing river flows[25]:

> A modified flow regime should mimic the natural one, so that the natural timing of different kinds of flows is preserved.
> A river's natural perenniality or nonperenniality should be retained.

Most water should be harvested from a river during wet months; little
    should be taken during the dry months.

The seasonal pattern of higher baseflows in wet seasons should be
    retained.

Floods should be present during the natural wet season.

The duration of floods could be shortened, but within limits.

It is better to retain certain floods at full magnitude and to eliminate
    others entirely than to preserve all or most floods at diminished lev-
    els.

The first flood (or one of the first) of the wet season should be fully
    retained.

In essence, the South Africans had begun answering the question of
how much water a healthy river ecosystem needs. During the next four
years, King and Delana Louw of the Department of Water Affairs and
Forestry led the development of an approach they called the "Building
Block Methodology" (BBM) that would enable them to answer the question in a carefully structured, scientifically credible way.[26]

To apply the BBM to a particular river, a team of interdisciplinary scientists is assembled. A hydrologist characterizes the natural flow condition of
the river, defining the typical range of low-flow conditions and higher flows
that would be expected in each month as well as the size, duration, and
number of floods expected each year. A computer modeler develops graphs
showing how much of the river and floodplain would be inundated at different flow levels. Other scientists assemble available biological data about
the river's fish, mammals, aquatic insects, amphibians, aquatic and riparian
plants, and physical habitat and water quality information that will help
them understand how each species or natural community depends upon or
is affected by different flow events.

This information is summarized in graphs, tables, pictures, and notes
of various forms, and then brought to a workshop in which the scientists
work toward a consensus about the flow needs of the river. They decide
how much water is needed during low flow periods, how many high flows
or floods of each size are needed, how long the floods need to last, and
when they need to occur. These aqueous building blocks are then added
together to form the overall prescription for river management,
presented as a set of flow targets for water managers (Figure 2-2). The
resultant prescription is then used to protect a reserve of water in developing river basins, or to condition the operations of dams.

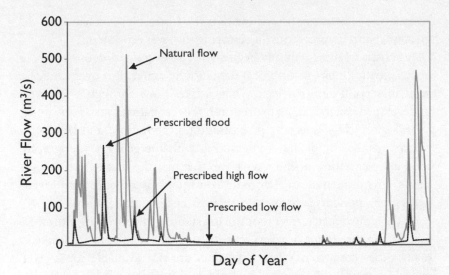

FIGURE 2-2. Flow Prescription for the Thukela River in South Africa. Ecological flows prescribed for the Thukela River using the Building Block Methodology (BBM) include the provision of adequate low-flow conditions during the dry season, occasional high-flow spikes during the wet season, and floods needed occasionally to sustain river health.

Variations on the basic scientific process used in the BBM or Holistic Approach are now emerging around the world.[27] Generally referred to as "holistic methodologies" due to their consideration of the entire river ecosystem rather than only selected species, each application is tailored to the unique set of ecological, water development, and socioeconomic conditions in a river basin. Because of differences in data, technical capacity, funding, and time available to complete ecological flow assessments in different places, no single model or tool is appropriate for all situations. Instead, a customized suite of tools is selected to fit each particular locale.[28] Initial determinations of flow needs are generated in some settings in just a few months at a cost of tens of thousands of dollars; others are requiring years and hundreds of thousands of dollars to complete. The common thread running through these holistic methodologies is their intent to define the river flows needed to protect or restore desired biological, physical habitat, and water quality features of the ecosystem while allowing for human uses of water.

A central element of holistic methodologies is the use of the natural flow regime as a guide or reference. By mimicking the natural patterns or variations of flow, scientists know that their prescriptions will have the greatest chance of protecting or restoring the river ecosystem.

A holistic analysis typically begins with an examination of the river's natural hydrograph—a graphical depiction of water flow over time at a particular point along a river. When a river flows through a relatively undeveloped watershed, its hydrograph reflects natural variations in the hydrologic cycle—especially precipitation, evaporation, and transpiration (water use by plants)—interacting with the geology, topography, soils, and vegetation of the river basin. Because the mix of each watershed's environmental and climatic conditions is unique, each river's hydrograph presents a distinct signature for ecologists to study.

In the United States, river monitoring stations measure daily flow fluctuations on thousands of rivers and streams, but such data are scarce in many other countries. When flow data are not available for a river, hydrologists use computerized hydrologic simulation models to synthesize estimates of natural flow conditions. River scientists use flow data to construct hydrographs, helping them to recognize repeating patterns in the river's flow.

A number of distinctive patterns can be detected in the natural hydrograph for northern California's Trinity River, for example (see Figure 2-3). From October through January, moisture-laden storm clouds travel eastward across the Pacific Ocean. When they crash into the Trinity Alps, they unleash heavy downpours, causing the Trinity River to rise suddenly. The river drops back down rather quickly after a rainstorm passes. Smaller rainstorms generate "high flows" marked as small rises in the Trinity's hydrograph; larger storms create floods. As air temperatures over the mountains drop in January and February, precipitation in the mountain range begins to fall as snow, which accumulates through early spring. Then, as temperatures warm from March to June, the snowpack begins to melt, triggering a slow but steady rise in river levels, which gradually recede over the summer. In the interludes between these rainfall- and snowmelt-generated river pulses, the river remains at a relatively low flow level.

By constructing hydrographs that span many years, river scientists are able to discern the repeating patterns in a river's flow. The basic flow patterns visible in the single-year hydrograph portrayed in Figure 2-3 can also be seen in the decade-long hydrograph of Figure 2-4. The magnitudes of floods, high flows, and low flows may vary from year to year, but the basic hydrograph patterns repeat in virtually every year.

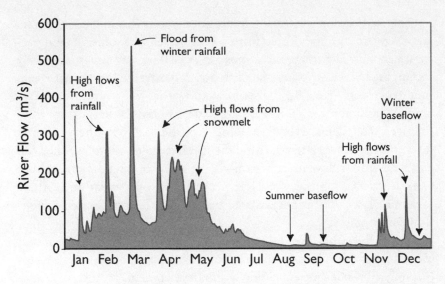

FIGURE 2-3. Annual Hydrograph from the Trinity River in Northern California.

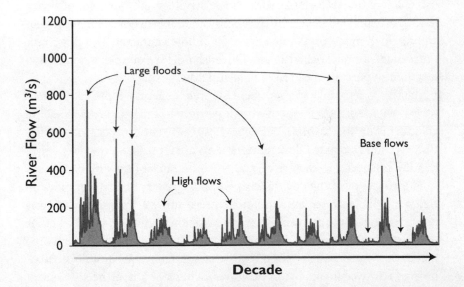

FIGURE 2-4. Decadal Hydrograph from the Trinity River.

The nature and variety of hydrographs vary from one region to another, and to some degree from river to river, but some general patterns can be identified for almost every river: low flows; regularly occurring higher flows; and large floods and extreme low flows that do not occur every year. Ecologists now know that these repeating intra-annual and inter-annual hydrologic patterns play very important roles in river ecosystems. When studying a particular river, they can link these natural flow patterns with their specific ecological roles. They can then develop a flow prescription—a set of recommendations on the size, frequency, timing, duration, and year-to-year variation in these essential flow patterns necessary to maintain or restore desired ecological conditions.

Given the rapid evolution of ecological knowledge in the recent decade, it is difficult to predict the future trajectory of the science supporting river management. Some recent developments in Australia, however, may be telling.

After participating in a number of exercises to develop flow recommendations for various Australian rivers, Angela Arthington became increasingly uncomfortable with the relatively small portions of water that were being prescribed for river ecosystems, particularly for rivers that still retained much or all of their original flow character. The flows recommended for the Logan River in Queensland, for example, amounted to less than 50 percent of the river's natural flow.[29]

Arthington speculated that scientists were generally quite cautious in their flow prescriptions, specifying flows only to the extent that they are able to justify them with solid ecological information. Because the life histories and associated flow requirements are typically known for only a handful of species in each river, and the influences of flow on ecosystem functions can never be known with complete certainty, Arthington worried that the flow recommendations were underestimating what was needed to fully sustain healthy river ecosystems. She wondered whether scientists would come to a different conclusion—a different flow recommendation—if they were asked to answer a different question. Instead of trying to answer the question of how much water a river needs, what if they were instead asked how much alteration of natural flow regimes was too much?

Arthington and her colleagues began developing a new assessment approach called the "Benchmarking Methodology" to enable them to identify the level of flow alteration at which important ecological changes would begin to be detected.[30] The method entails taking extensive measurements of the physical habitat, riparian and aquatic vegetation, aquatic insects, fish, and estuarine or marine conditions at many different sites across large river basins. The scientists rate the condition of each environmental variable along a gradient from "natural" or "near natural" to "very major modification from natural." Then, after compiling these ratings for the suite of environmental variables measured at the site, the scientists determine the level of hydrologic alteration at which ecological impacts are minor or undetectable and the level at which they become substantial.

Initial results from applications of the Benchmarking Methodology suggest that an ecological flow prescription built piece by piece to support particular ecological benefits might very well differ from a recommendation designed to prevent any significant ecological impacts. Arthington and her colleagues found that in the Burnett River basin in Queensland, 79 to 84 percent of the river's annual flow volume and 72 to 91 percent of natural flood magnitudes would need to be protected to ensure full ecological health.[31] These results suggest that a high degree of flow protection is needed to prevent any ecological damage.

These insights underscore the importance of carefully selecting scientific tools and approaches for prescribing flows to fit each particular situation. When a river is in relatively pristine condition but is being considered for further water development, the appropriate question is, how much alteration of natural flows is too much? The Benchmarking Methodology or similar approaches that evaluate the potential ecological degradation associated with increasing levels of flow alteration will be most useful in these situations. When a river has been degraded and its ecological health needs to be restored, the appropriate question is, how much restoration of flow is enough? In these cases, methods like the South Africans' Building Block Methodology and species-based tools like PHABSIM can help scientists determine how much restoration might be achieved by incrementally re-creating some features of the natural flow regime.

SETTING ECOLOGICAL GOALS

In order for scientists and river managers to put these new restoration tools to good use, an overarching question needs to be addressed by society at large: How healthy do we want any particular river to be? Is some degradation of river health acceptable? If so, what can be sacrificed? If the river in question is already degraded, how much ecological restoration is desired? Once again, experiences in South Africa provide some ideas about how scientists and civil society can work together in answering these questions.

As water managers in South Africa began applying ecological flow recommendations in the 1990s, they found that in some cases the recommendations were going to be very difficult, if not impossible, to satisfy because of rapidly growing demands for irrigation, domestic water supplies, and other human water needs. This caused them to go back to the scientists to ask them for revised flow recommendations, along with predictions of the likely ecological consequences of these alternative flow regimes. As Jackie King put it, "We would describe a flow regime, they would nibble away at it, we would describe a lower flow regime and a lower river condition, they would nibble some more, and so on."[32] Because each iteration of the exercise was time-consuming and expensive, such requests for revised flow prescriptions were placing considerable strain on both the scientific community and water planning efforts. King and her colleagues recognized the need to move from a prescriptive approach (the BBM) toward a more interactive scenario-based approach. King began working with Cate Brown, an ecological consultant with Cape Town-based Southern Waters, to convert the BBM into a method that would explicitly identify the different degrees of ecological health that would be expected as existing flow conditions in a river were either increasingly altered or restored. They gave their new approach the acronym DRIFT because it predicts the "Downstream Response to Imposed Flow Transformation."[33]

The heart of the DRIFT method is a classification scheme that describes several different levels of ecological health (or sustainability boundaries)—Class A to D (see Table 2-1). Protecting the highest level of ecological health, Class A, requires that the natural flow regime be maintained largely intact. Lower classes reflect greater deterioration of river health as flows increasingly are modified by dams and diversions (see Figure 2-5). Using the DRIFT method, scientists predict the class of river health that would be expected under various water management scenarios. For instance, they might predict how a river's condition would slip from Class A to B, or from B to C, as one or more of the natural floods are removed each year, or as low flows are reduced.

TABLE 2-1 Ecological Management Classes Used in South Africa

Class	Flow Regime	Ecological Condition
A (natural)	Close to natural condition	Negligible modification of instream and riparian habitats and biota.
B (good)	Largely natural with few modifications	Ecosystem essentially in good state. Biota largely intact.
C (fair)	Moderately modified	A few sensitive species may be lost; populations of some species likely to decline; tolerant or opportunistic species may become more abundant.
D (poor)	Largely modified	Habitat diversity and availability have declined; mostly only tolerant species present and they are often diseased; population dynamics have been disrupted (e.g., biota can no longer breed; alien species have invaded the ecosystem).

Some scientists dispute whether the ecological degradation associated with flow alteration can be predicted accurately, or whether the degradation of a river can be described using discrete categories. However, the DRIFT method is an important advancement because it makes explicit the implications of society's decisions about river use and management.[34] Because it also incorporates an analysis of the economic value of subsistence uses associated with a river, the method helps bring both ecological health and ecosystem services to the decision-making table.

In South Africa, river ecologists, water managers, and social scientists are working with local communities and government leaders to determine desired levels of ecosystem protection in each river basin. In each case, the desire to protect the river's health is weighed against present and future human needs for water, or the feasibility of restoring the river to a

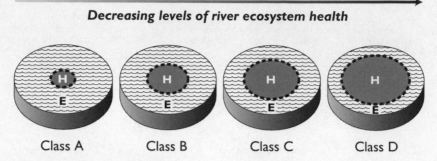

Increasing degree of flow alteration

Decreasing levels of river ecosystem health

Class A   Class B   Class C   Class D

━━━ Sustainability boundary

FIGURE 2-5. Setting Sustainability Boundaries to Attain Different Categories of River Health. As natural river flows are increasingly altered, the health of a river ecosystem will decline. Society must decide how much degradation is acceptable, represented here as a choice among different classes of river health.

higher level. It is important to note that in choosing to manage a river for any targeted ecological state—whether it is an A, B, C, or D—water managers and users are setting limits on the degree to which they will allow the river to be degraded. A decision to allow a river to deteriorate from Class A to B means holding the line at a targeted level of alteration corresponding to level B. In Figure 2-5, the line bounding each of the circles of human use demarcates the limits of acceptable alteration—the sustainability boundary—for each of the four ecological classes. Once society has chosen a level of protection for a river, scientists can develop an ecological flow prescription to support that desired condition.

The concept of setting ecological goals for rivers is not new. Human societies have been protecting their local streams, lakes, and watering holes for thousands of years using self-imposed limits or taboos on the use or pollution of water. In recent decades, many countries began implementing sophisticated systems for managing water quality based upon different river categories that reflect ecological goals. For instance, the United States applies categories of "designated uses"—such as cold freshwater habitat, agricultural supply, or water contact recreation—to set numerical water quality standards for each stream, river, and lake in the country. As the impacts of hydrologic alteration become better understood by society at large, it seems likely that the United States and other countries will eventually follow South Africa's lead in setting goals pertaining to flow protection.

The tools and methods developed by scientists during recent decades are enabling them to play a more integral role in water management. However, scientific understanding of the complex workings of river ecosystems remains far from complete, meaning that scientists cannot predict the ecological consequences of further water development or flow restoration with perfect accuracy. This uncertainty is all too often used as an excuse for inaction, even when existing water management practices are failing to protect the health of rivers. Water managers are reluctant to limit human water uses or to implement restorative actions when scientists are not perfectly certain about the flow conditions needed to attain ecological goals. Such management paralysis is unacceptable in a world in which more than two-thirds of rivers are substantially degraded and the rest increasingly are threatened by growing human needs for water and energy. Fortunately, water managers and scientists are embracing a new risk management philosophy—one that enables them to take action in the face of uncertainty and fosters learning from the results of those actions.

LEARNING BY DOING

A decision to restore river flows commonly arises when local communities experience the loss of highly valued ecosystem services, such as commercial or subsistence fisheries, or when a species nears extinction. Flow restoration necessarily requires a change in the water or land management practices influencing the flow of water. It might involve changing the amount of water being used, the way that water is being diverted from the river, or the way that water is being stored and then released from dams. It might also require changing various land management activities, such as timber harvesting or agricultural practices.

Figure 2-6 illustrates a situation in which the existing degree of flow alteration is greater than the desired condition—marked as the sustainability boundary. However, this limit is seldom known with a high degree of certainty. These two conditions—a need to restore flows to attain the desired degree of river health, and a lack of certainty about how much restoration will be enough—pose a quandary that is common to virtually every river restoration effort.

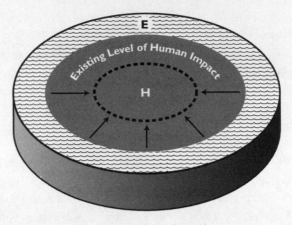

---- Sustainability boundary

FIGURE 2-6. Rebalancing Flow Allocations to Human and Ecosystem Needs. When natural river flows are altered excessively, flow restoration efforts must be undertaken to reduce human impacts to the desired level, represented by the sustainability boundary, and to restore key natural flow patterns that support river health.

A practical way of dealing with this situation has emerged through a process called "adaptive management."[35] As its name implies, adaptive management embodies a spirit of flexibility and adaptation sometimes referred to as "learning by doing." Based on their knowledge of river ecology, scientists work with water managers to develop flow restoration experiments geared toward improving river health. They monitor the effects of those experiments and then, based on their assessment of results, revise their flow prescriptions to move the river closer to the desired degree of ecological health. Through this iterative process, society approaches a more optimal balance between water allocations for human needs versus the river's needs.[36]

Adaptive flow restoration programs are now under way in many river basins, including the Colorado River in the Grand Canyon,[37] the Trinity River in California,[38] the Kissimmee River in Florida,[39] the Florida Everglades,[40] the upper Mississippi River system,[41] and the Murray River in Australia.[42] While each of these restoration programs are in different stages of development and each are practicing adaptive management in somewhat different ways, the basic process being employed in each case is similar (see Figure 2-7).

As emphasized earlier, it is critically important to define ecological goals at the outset of an adaptive restoration program, because these goals communicate the intended outcome of the restoration effort.[43] The goal might be to ensure that a particular species is sustained in the river, or to improve the river's overall health—for instance, moving it from a Class C to B. Once ecological goals have been determined, they drive the entire adaptive management process. Scientists develop an ecological model of the river ecosystem that depicts the impacts that are thought to be associated with the flow alteration. Next, using the tools and methods described earlier, they develop a flow prescription believed to be adequate to attain the goals. They then work with managers to develop strategies for modifying existing water management practices to achieve the desired flow prescription. Finally, they monitor the system as flow experiments are being implemented and assess whether ecological goals are being met:

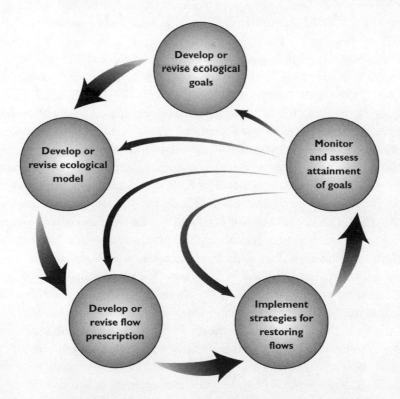

FIGURE 2-7. The Adaptive Management Process for Flow Restoration. Adaptive management is a continual, evolving process of developing ecological goals and testing and refining strategies for attaining those goals.

are the fish recruiting enough members into their population to sustain it, or is the river assuming its intended level of health? As scientists and managers assess their success in attaining goals, they may decide that changes are needed in one or more parts of the adaptive management cycle. They may then decide to modify the ecological goals, amend the ecological model, revise the ecological flow prescription, or they may decide that different strategies are needed to attain the goals.

An adaptive management program being proposed by a dam owner and a conservation organization for the Roanoke River in North Carolina provides an example of how this process can work. Two private hydropower dams have been impacting fisheries and an extensive floodplain forest along the lower Roanoke River since they began operations in 1955 and 1963. The original operating license for the dams, issued by the Federal Energy Regulatory Commission (FERC) in 1951, has expired, requiring the dam owner to obtain a new license. The relicensing process provided an opportunity for scientists and conservation interests to negotiate new operating agreements with the dam owner, Dominion Generation, subject to review and approval by FERC.

With considerable land holdings in the Roanoke River's floodplain, The Nature Conservancy, a private conservation organization, has a lot at stake in the outcome of these relicensing negotiations. Sam Pearsall, a Conservancy ecologist, knew that the dams were causing unnatural flooding in the floodplain forest downstream of the dams. During each summer growing season, young seedlings would sprout on the forest floor. But each year, prolonged high flow releases from the upstream dams would submerge and kill the young trees. Pearsall had formulated some hypotheses about how much flooding the seedlings could take, but he was sufficiently uncertain about his hypotheses to make him hesitant about locking in any new dam management requirements for 30–50 years—the typical term of a FERC license. He also knew that Dominion Generation would be reluctant to commit to license conditions that would require them to change their operations—and reduce their hydropower revenues—when they could not be assured that the new requirements would enable the forest to regenerate properly. To address environmental concerns about the relicensing, Pearsall asked Dominion Generation to implement an adaptive management program.

Under the terms of an agreement reached by the Conservancy and Dominion—recently approved by FERC—the dam-induced flow alterations will be reduced over time until the forest begins to reproduce at a sustainable rate. Specifically, Dominion will lessen the unnatural flooding caused by its dams by 50 percent in the first five years, and will continue to reduce its remaining flow impacts by half in each subsequent five-year period. The Conservancy and other conservation interests will monitor the response of the forest. Once the desired ecological conditions are attained, Dominion will need to make no further adjustments.

The adaptive approach proposed for the Roanoke River has many attractive features. Conservationists are assured that desired ecological conditions will be attained, even though it will take some time before the forest regains its health. The utility company is assured that the changes imposed upon its operations will not overshoot what is required to attain the ecological goals, because each restoration step is a short one. Furthermore, the restoration steps are taken at a pace that enables the company to develop ways to offset the loss of electrical power generation capacity and revenues from the Roanoke.

REBUILDING A RIVER'S NATURAL FLOW PATTERNS

The flow restoration efforts now under way around the world employ strategies ranging from modifying dam operations to reducing human uses of water through conservation measures. Most are targeted at re-creating key components of a river's natural flow regime. The examples provided here illustrate a variety of ecological problems caused by flow alteration, and some innovative ways that flows are being restored.

RESTORING LOW FLOWS

Low flow is the dominant flow condition in most rivers. As such, the low flow level imposes a fundamental constraint on a river's aquatic communities: it determines the amount of habitat available for most of the year. This has a strong influence on the diversity and number of fish and other creatures that can live in the river. Unnaturally depleted, as well as unnaturally augmented, low flows can both wreak havoc with a river's health.

In the Flint River of Georgia, low-flow periods provide a quiescent time of slow water that enables fish and other aquatic animals to conserve their energy reserves. During low flows, aquatic creatures are concentrated into limited habitat space, providing an easy feast for predatory fish, raccoons, and great blue herons. Occasional periods of extremely low flow are needed to enable certain trees like the bald cypress and water tupelo to reproduce. These trees spend most of their lives with their roots and lower trunks in water, but their seeds germinate only during extreme droughts when floodplain soils dry out sufficiently.

The Flint River is typical of streams that are strongly affected by rainfall events. When it rains in southwestern Georgia, it pours. Torrential downpours during the winter and spring frequently cause the Flint River to go from a low flow of 40 cubic meters per second to more than 700 cubic meters per second in a matter of hours. The Flint's annual hydrographs reflect the river's erratic and frequent variations, with sharp flood spikes interrupting low flow periods over the course of the year. Following the passage of each rainstorm, the river drops back down to its low flow level.

During the past few decades, however, average low flows have declined by 25–30 percent in the Flint. Although the area has experienced severe droughts in recent years, increases of more than 240 percent in groundwater pumping for agricultural irrigation have further depleted low flows. Many shallow wells near the Flint River have been intercepting groundwater that would have contributed to the river's low flow.

Low-flow depletion is causing serious ecological problems in the Flint. During the winter, many of the Flint's fish species congregate in places along the river where groundwater inflows to the river are concentrated, because these groundwater discharges are warmer than ambient river temperatures.[44] As groundwater contributions to the river decline, these thermal refugia will no longer be available to the fish. Because water table levels in floodplains are hydraulically connected to water levels in the adjacent river, lowered river levels cause water tables to drop, killing plants whose root systems cannot reach the lowered water table.

Some positive steps have been taken by the state of Georgia to ameliorate groundwater pumping impacts to low flows in the Flint River during drought periods. The Flint River Drought Protection Act of 2000 authorizes payments from the state to farmers who curtail irrigation in specified areas during droughts.[45] The challenge in implementing this new act is to identify the farms that are having the greatest ecological impact, and then to convince enough of those farmers to accept payments in lieu of irrigating their crops so that low flows can be restored.

The impact of groundwater pumping on river flows is a poorly understood but pervasive global issue.[46] Nearly one-fourth of the global human population and half of the United States population rely upon groundwater for drinking.[47] Approximately 85 percent of the water consumed in the United States goes to irrigated agriculture, and more than a third of that comes from groundwater.[48] The ecological consequences of groundwater withdrawals on rivers is dramatically illustrated in Kansas, where virtually all once-perennial rivers in the western third of the state now occasionally go dry due to groundwater overdraft.[49] In Arizona, groundwater pumping has dried up or degraded 90 percent of the state's desert streams.[50] Withdrawals of water for irrigation along the Great Ruaha River of Tanzania have caused severe depletion of low flows, triggering massive fish die-offs and severe overcrowding for hippopotami and crocodiles in river pools.[51]

Low-flow restoration has been pursued for a variety of ecological purposes, using many different strategies.[52] Minimum flow releases below a municipal water supply dam were increased on the Icacos River in Puerto Rico to restore populations of mountain mullet and river shrimp. The Nature Conservancy purchased an 870-hectare farm on the San Pedro River in Arizona with the intent of reducing irrigation by 90 percent. Computer model projections suggest that this reduced groundwater pumping will restore perennial flow to more than 30 kilometers of river that now flow only during large storms. In England, authorities have regulated municipal groundwater pumping in order to restore baseflows in the River Babingley in East Anglia and the River Itchen in Hampshire. A small irrigation dam was breached on Bear Creek in Oregon to benefit Pacific salmon during summer low flows. Also in Oregon, a donation of water rights to the Oregon Water Trust, a private environmental organization, improved conditions for steelhead and chinook salmon in Courtney Creek. The same group has secured additional low flow on numerous other streams by purchasing long-term leases of water rights. In Australia, flows have been improved below irrigation reservoirs to restore wetlands and aquatic health on the Murray and Murrumbidgee rivers, both in New South Wales. Low flows were restored below hydropower dams on the Coosa River in Alabama to benefit the Tulotoma snail, an endangered species, and on the River Kymijoki in Finland to improve fish passage.

Although it is too early to evaluate the ecological success of many of these low-flow restoration efforts, the results from the Tallapoosa River in Alabama suggest that ecological dividends can be dramatic. Low flows were restored below Thurlow Dam in 1991 from an average of 2.5 cubic meters per second to 34 cubic meters per second. Six years later, the diversity of fish species had increased from twenty-five to forty-six and overall fish abundance increased by 70 percent.[53]

RESTORING HIGHER FLOWS

Higher flows provide important and necessary disruptions in low flow, inserting a staccato in the river's rhythm. This is particularly true during droughts, when low flows have dropped to stressful levels. Even a small flush of fresh water can provide much-needed relief from high water temperatures or low oxygen conditions that typify warm-season low flows, and deliver a nourishing subsidy of organic material or other food into a river reach to support the aquatic food web.

Restoring high flows is a critical aspect of restoring a river's original character because they fundamentally shape the river's basic geometry— its width, depth, and the physical complexity of aquatic habitats—and therefore dictate the river's general utility for an array of native species. Restoring high flows will also likely generate many other tangible benefits in addition to those associated with ecosystem restoration, including increased hydropower generation, improved navigability, and better dilution of wastewater discharges from cities and factories.

High flows from snowmelt used to come down California's Trinity River each spring like clockwork. For many of the river's denizens such as chinook salmon and black cottonwood trees the arrival of the spring high flows was a wake-up call, triggering them to begin a new phase of their life cycle. Cottonwoods disperse their fluffy white seeds in late May and early June to coincide with the natural recession of the snowmelt pulse, enabling their seeds to land on fresh, moist floodplain soils. For young salmon, the flush of cool, clear water is the ticket for a free ride to the ocean.

The snowmelt runoff on the Trinity would begin with a rumble then build to a roar. At first, sand particles and organic matter lying in the riverbed would start to move. Then, as floodwaters rose higher and accelerated, gravels and cobbles would begin to roll and bounce downstream. High flows like those on the Trinity are extremely important in shaping the physical character of a river channel. High flows act like a fluid bulldozer, pushing sediment around and dumping it in areas of slack water. This dynamic erosion and sedimentation carves the shape of the channel and sifts the sediments in the riverbed, forming key habitat features such as riffles, pools, gravel bars, and islands.

A river's plants and animals are greatly affected by this sculpting of the river's physical template. The character of a river's bed—its mixture of sand, gravel, cobbles, and boulders—makes a great deal of difference to aquatic insects and fish. By flushing away smaller particles like silt and sand, the high flows act like hydraulic dental floss, keeping the gaps between cobbles clear and open for tiny salmon fry to occupy.

Each of these ecological processes were severely disrupted when the Trinity River was dammed in 1964 as part of the Central Valley Project in California, a gargantuan water scheme used primarily for irrigated agriculture. Trinity Dam drastically reduced annual high flows on the river (Figure 2-8) while diverting up to 90 percent of the river's flow into the Sacramento River basin.[54] Although this level of flow depletion may seem excessive or extraordinary, many of the West's rivers have been similarly exploited, with more than 75 percent of available surface flow now being consumed by human activities in most of the West's large river basins. More than 80 percent of that water goes to irrigated agriculture.[55]

The Trinity River's creatures were soon to feel the effects of flow reduction. The once-deep river pools used by adult salmon quickly filled with sand. Without annual high flows to keep it in check, riparian vegetation rapidly encroached upon the river's exposed margins, narrowing the river by as much as 60 percent in some areas and thereby greatly reducing aquatic habitat.[56] Under a natural flow regime, the dynamic and complex river channel included large, shallow areas where young salmon could

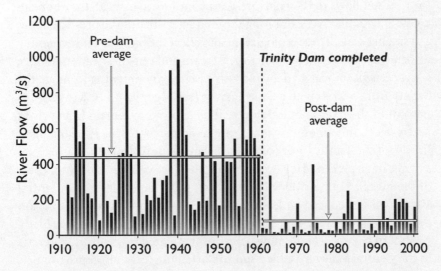

FIGURE 2-8. Dam-Induced Changes in Trinity River High Flows. Following construction of California's Trinity Dam, high flows were drastically reduced.

hang out in slower-moving currents that most predators could not access. Yellow-legged frogs deposited their eggs in these channel margins. Without channel-carving high flows, the river became a simplified, fast-moving, narrow canal without hiding places for juvenile salmon and other small aquatic organisms. Chinook salmon stocks quickly plummeted to one-fifth of their original numbers.[57]

For thousands of years, Hoopa and Yurok tribes used the fish, plants, and other animals along the Trinity for subsistence, cultural, ceremonial, and commercial purposes. The diminishment of these ecosystem services, along with federal listing of the chinook salmon as a threatened species, led to the formation of the Trinity River Restoration Program in the 1990s. Scientists from many federal and state agencies and academic institutions contributed to studies that culminated in 1999 with publication of the Trinity River Flow Evaluation Study. The study recommended five different dam release schedules, based on five "water year types" ranging from critically dry to extremely wet years.[58] Each of these release schedules was designed to support numerous ecosystem functions: forming and cleaning spawning gravels, scouring river pools, providing adequate water temperatures throughout the year, controlling riparian vegetation, and transporting young salmon to the sea.

The scientists working on the Trinity do not expect their prescription for restored flows to re-create pre-dam conditions. Instead, they hope to create a dynamic river exhibiting the characteristics of the pre-dam river, at a smaller scale. These ecological goals reflect the political and economic difficulties inherent in rebalancing instream and out-of-stream uses once a river has been heavily depleted—in essence, the intent is to move the Trinity from a Class D to a Class C river (see Figure 2-5). In wet years, 35 percent of the river's natural flow will be allowed to remain in the river; in dry years, this amount will increase to 80 percent. This rebalancing of the use of the Trinity River will reduce water exports from the basin by an average of 28 percent. However, because the Trinity River is only one part of the overall Central Valley Project, total water deliveries to the Central Valley will be reduced by less than 4 percent. Although this restoration program was officially approved by former Secretary of the Interior Bruce Babbitt in late 2000 and is now being implemented, agricultural interests in the Central Valley have filed suit to curtail the restoration program.

High-flow pulses are being reinstituted on other rivers for a variety of ecological purposes, particularly for the improvement of native fisheries.[59] A number of flow restoration efforts in Africa, for example, have been designed to recover endangered fish populations through the provision of high pulses to stimulate spawning. Spawning flows are being provided in the Groot River in South Africa for small-scale red fin minnows; in the Pecos River in New Mexico for the Pecos bluntnose shiner; and in the Columbia River in Washington to improve the survival of salmon smolts. In Zambia, high flows are being restored to benefit the Kafue lechwe, a wetland antelope. Removal of a dam on the Chipola River in Florida returned natural flow pulses to the system, leading to an increase in fish diversity from thirty-four to sixty-one species.

RESTORING FLOODS

Floods are bountiful times in the lives of fish and other creatures living in large rivers and estuaries. Fish and other mobile riverine organisms are able to move upstream, downstream, and out into floodplains or flooded wetlands to access additional habitats such as secondary channels, backwaters, sloughs, and shallow flooded areas. These usually inaccessible habitats become a food bazaar for fish during floods. Shallowly flooded areas are typically warmer than the main channel, and full of nutrients and insects that fuel rapid growth. Ecologists working in large rivers have coined this phenomenon the "flood pulse subsidy." Many fish species inhabiting large rivers spawn only, or far more prolifically, in shallowly flooded areas.

The fertile floodplain of the River Logone in central Cameroon supports a spectacular wealth of wildlife, including large herds of giraffe, elephants, lions, and various ungulates.[60] Flowing from the Adamoua plateau, the river once inundated about 6,000 square kilometers during its annual floods, nurturing a vast wetland area including Waza National Park. Prior to damming, the Logone floodplain stirred with reproductive activity each year as millions of fish moved in during the flood pulse.

This productive fishery was the primary or sole source of income for most of the Kotoko people, who could earn $2,000 (U.S.) in just four months each year. The Kotokos also depended heavily upon the floodplain as pasture for their sheep and goats, and for growing floating rice, a staple of their diet.

The Logone River was dammed in 1979, forming Lake Maga to supply water to the Semry II rice irrigation project. Flooding of the Logone floodplain was greatly reduced, and fish yields fell by 90 percent. Annual economic losses mounted to more than $550,000 in fishing, $930,000 in grazing, and $31,500 in flood recession agriculture. However, the developers of the Semry rice project soon realized that they would not be able to use the full volume of water being stored in Lake Maga, triggering discussions about the possibility of restoring some semblance of natural flooding to the Logone floodplain. Pilot flood releases were undertaken in 1994 and 1997. Although it is too early to assess the benefits of the restoration program in full, the return of fishing, grazing, and farming activities on the Logone floodplain is an important indicator of success.

Similar flood restoration efforts are now under way on other dammed African rivers utilized for subsistence farming and fishing, including the Hadejia in Nigeria and the Phongolo River in South Africa.[61] In the United States, flood restoration projects designed to improve the condition of floodplain vegetation have been implemented on the Rio Grande River in New Mexico, the Colorado River in Arizona, and the Truckee River in Nevada. Similarly, floods are being released from dams on the St. Mary River in Alberta, Canada, to restore cottonwood forests, and on the Murray River in Australia to restore river red gum forests. In a major new demonstration project supported by the European Union, floods are now being restored to the River Cole in Oxfordshire, England, for biodiversity benefits.

Many of the presumed or hypothesized benefits of flow restoration projects do not appear for many years. But gratification came almost immediately in cottonwood restoration efforts on the St. Mary River in Canada and the Truckee River in Nevada.[62] By releasing prescribed floods of sufficient size and at the right time, and allowing the flood to recede from the floodplain at an appropriately slow rate, thousands of new cottonwood seedlings sprouted along these rivers following flood releases.

LESSONS FROM THE COLORADO PIKEMINNOW

Three million years ago, when woolly mammoths, American mastodons, and saber-toothed cats roamed the grassy plains of the American West, a giant minnow probed the turbid waters of the ancient Colorado River and its tributaries. This powerful, torpedo-like predator ate nearly everything it could get its jaws around—mussels and snails, other fish, and even the occasional rodent or rabbit swept into the channel by the river's floods. Its heavy diet fueled its yearly long-distance migrations between winter haunts and vernal spawning grounds.

Known later as the Colorado pikeminnow, the giant fish keyed its life cycle to the river's natural flow pattern.[63] When snowmelt from the Rocky Mountains caused the river to flood during the spring, this behemoth minnow—up to 1.3 meters long and 30 kilograms in weight—knew to begin its long annual migration, traveling nearly 1,000 kilometers to spawn.[64] Rushing floodwaters carried tons of cobbles and gravels downstream, depositing them in constricted canyons, thereby forming perfect cradles for pikeminnow eggs. At the same time, the floodwaters flushed away sand and silt that otherwise would have smothered the newly deposited eggs. When tiny fish emerged from the spawning beds a couple of weeks later, the river's flow was still high enough to carry them into flooded backwater areas, where they fed and grew rapidly in the warmer, shallow waters swarming with aquatic insects. By synchronizing its reproduction with reliable annual floods, the minnow optimized its reproductive success, enabling thousands of offspring to be born each year. Floods large enough to create ideal conditions for the minnow did not occur every year, but they occurred often enough to enable the fish to give rise to a million generations.

Roving thousands of kilometers of river canyon and mountain stream, the Colorado pikeminnow was king of the river's food chain for millennia. The Pleistocene ice age came and went, and woolly mammoths, mastodons, and the large cats disappeared. But the pikeminnow endured. At the beginning of the twentieth century, the fish was so abundant that farmers pitchforked them out of irrigation canals to prevent the water from overflowing. Western settlers caught them by the truckloads and so enjoyed their savory meat that they nicknamed them "Colorado salmon." But by the late twentieth century, after 3 million years on earth, the Colorado pikeminnow was an endangered species, a creature on the brink of extinction.

The pikeminnow's nemesis came in the form of massive dams and irrigation works—the infrastructure that opened the western United States to widespread settlement. This infrastructure radically changed the river's natural flow patterns and water temperature, as well as the movement of river sediments that shape pikeminnow habitats. These modified conditions also enabled numerous introduced, nonnative fish species to proliferate, to the great detriment of native species including the pikeminnow.[65]

Hoover Dam, completed in 1935, effectively separated pikeminnow populations in the upper basin from those in the lower (Figure 2-9). In the 1960s, six more big dams were built on the Colorado River and its major tributaries as part of a grand public works scheme called the Colorado River Storage Project. In 1962, Flaming Gorge Dam on the Green River in Utah and Navajo Dam on the San Juan River in New Mexico cut off the pikeminnow's access to the upper reaches of those rivers and altered habitat conditions for many kilometers downstream. Glen Canyon Dam, which began to form Lake Powell on the Utah-Arizona border when its gates were closed in 1963, further shortened the pikeminnow's downstream forays. As other dams were erected, the pikeminnow lost access to upper reaches of the Gunnison, the Dolores, the Duschesne, and the White. Cut off from ancestral spawning grounds and other habitats essential to their life cycle, the pikeminnows left stranded below Lake Powell and above the dams on the upper Colorado and its tributaries soon disappeared, confining the pikeminnow's distribution to only 25 percent of its original range.[66] The last of the wild pikeminnow found themselves incarcerated between impassible concrete walls. In 1967, with life-giving floods no longer pulsing through much of their remaining stronghold between the dams, this 3-million-year-old species was formally listed as endangered.

When a species like the pikeminnow gets really good at playing the game of evolution—tightly hitching its life cycle to nature's cycles—and then humans fundamentally change the environmental conditions essential to its existence, the special adaptations that served the species so well for so long suddenly become liabilities. The pikeminnow's dependence on annual floods, which helped it proliferate, was the seed of its undoing when those floods were tamed. The process of evolution gives favor to characteristics in species that enable them to reproduce more prolifically, to grow faster, and to live longer. Over many generations, the genetic makeup and behavior of a species like the pikeminnow becomes finely tuned to both favorable and stressful environmental conditions, especially when those conditions are as reliable as yearly snowmelt floods in the Rocky Mountains. These simple tenets of evolutionary biology explain many of the problems river species around the world now face. In more than two-thirds of the planet's large river systems, humans are now turning the knobs that govern the flows of water, nutrients, and sediments in ways that do not resemble the natural rhythms to which river species are adapted.

By the time the Colorado pikeminnow was listed as an endangered species in 1967, its remaining populations were in bad shape and the species teetered on the brink of extinction. The pikeminnow was the

FIGURE 2-9. The Upper Colorado River Basin.

focus of at least ten major research studies conducted between 1978 and 1989 in the upper Colorado River basin.[67] In 1992, the U.S. Fish and Wildlife Service issued a Biological Opinion under the federal Endangered Species Act, concluding that operations of Flaming Gorge Dam jeopardized the continued existence of pikeminnow and three other endangered fish species.[68]

The Service's Biological Opinion included a number of ecological models and a set of flow recommendations designed to rebuild the populations of endangered native fish in the Green River downstream of Flaming Gorge Dam. This flow prescription reflected the leading edge of river science at the time. It considered the needs of native species and the river ecosystem as a whole. It was developed by an interdisciplinary group of scientists familiar with the biology of fish, aquatic insects, and riparian plants, as well as the physical habitat-forming processes of the river and its water quality.

The prescription addressed low flows as well as floods of varying sizes. Most important, the Biological Opinion called for a five-year experimental program (1992–1996) to test and refine the flow prescription, marking the onset of an adaptive management program for the Green River.

Due to the vagaries of climate and to flooding concerns expressed by riparian landowners, targeted flood levels were not attained in all five years of the program. However, average-sized floods were released in three of the five years from 1992 to 1996, and recommended summer and autumn low flows were met in all years. But the pikeminnow did not respond as anticipated. Had the scientists gotten it all wrong?

After exhausting deliberations, the scientists reached some new conclusions and refined their models. In particular, they came to understand that a mix of big and small floods was needed—similar to what the natural flow regime had provided prior to construction of Flaming Gorge Dam. They hypothesized that big floods are needed to transport the cobbles and gravels needed to form the spawning bars required by the fish. They also speculated that the big floods knock back the populations of nonnative fish like red shiner that prey on young pikeminnow.[69] However, big flood years are not ideal for pikeminnow reproduction, because too many young fish are swept away by the torrent. But if the big flood years are followed by years with smaller floods more conducive to spawning and juvenile growth, the scientists predicted that pikeminnow should reproduce prolifically.

Based upon these hypotheses, the scientists working in the recovery program offered a new set of flow and water temperature recommendations in 1998. It called for greater variability in flood sizes, and a return to more natural low flow conditions. In at least one-third of the years, floods would need to be considerably bigger than the scientists had originally recommended in 1992. Once every ten years, the floods would need to be 60 percent bigger. The 1998 flow prescription moved a step closer to the natural hydrograph conditions.

Coincidentally, nature produced a lot of water in the Green River in 1997 and 1998, and as a result the fish got bigger floods. Preliminary results suggest that the pikeminnow are responding favorably. Although it remains far too early to tell whether the pikeminnow is on its way to recovery, these early signs of success are heartening.

How much water does a river need? The pikeminnow, the frogs, and the trees will tell us, now that we are learning how to listen. The bigger question now is, will society be willing to give them the water they need?

∽

CHAPTER THREE

The Policy Toolbox

At a gathering in London in November 2000, former South African president Nelson Mandela captured the essence of the new challenge ahead for societies in their relationships with rivers. The occasion was the release of the final report of the World Commission on Dams, the first-ever independent global review of the effectiveness of large dams in promoting sustainable human development. "It is one thing to find fault with an existing system," Mandela said. "It is another thing altogether, a more difficult task, to replace it with an approach that is better." Surely no one knows this better than Nelson Mandela.

Society's existing approach to managing rivers clearly is not working. Numerous indicators—from the rates of species imperilment, to the decline of fisheries, to the drying up of river flows—show that rivers are at risk. Now that scientists have devised methods of determining how much water a river needs, society is confronted with a clear call to action: will we ensure that those water needs are met?

Many of the conflicts over water use and management that have erupted in recent years reflect the mounting tension between those who wish to heed this call to action and those vested in protecting the status quo. Within the United States, disputes have broken out in recent years over water allocations between "offstream" uses of rivers (e.g., irrigation) and "instream" uses (e.g., protection of endangered species) in the Klamath River basin of California and Oregon; the Snake River basin of Idaho; the Truckee-Carson river system of Nevada; the Apalachicola-Chatta-hoochee-Flint river basin of Georgia, Alabama, and Florida; and the

Shepaug River system of Connecticut—to name just a few. Similar con-
flicts are arising around the world in river basins large and small, from
Southeast Asia's Mekong to South America's Paraguay to southern
Africa's Okavango.

Striking a more optimal balance between human water uses and those
of rivers themselves will require adjustments. But they need not be
wrenching ones, and in the end they will produce a more lasting set of
benefits from rivers. A significant portion of society is coming to understand more deeply that human welfare is tightly hitched to the health of
the ecosystems around us—that protecting rivers also protects ourselves.
Moreover, there is no single, static optimum allocation of water between
people and nature. Just as our scientific understanding is evolving about
how much water a river needs to be healthy and well-functioning, so is
our collective sense about the levels of protection rivers need to be given.

It is now clear, however, that securing the freshwater flows needed to
conserve biodiversity and safeguard critical ecosystem services will
require governments to reshape laws and policies that were crafted in an
earlier time—one concerned with controlling rivers for economic
advancement, not with protecting their ecological health for this and
future generations. Recasting the rules of river use and management will
not be easy. But it is necessary. As Thomas Jefferson wisely observed in
1786, "laws and institutions must go hand in hand with the progress of the
human mind."[1]

ALLOCATING WATER FOR ECOSYSTEM SUPPORT

The life-forms within each river and the ecological roles they play have
evolved over thousands of years in synchrony with the river's naturally
variable pattern of flow—its highs and lows, its floods and dry spells. Protecting freshwater biodiversity and ecosystem services therefore requires
establishing an allocation of water for ecosystem support. That eco-support allocation will vary depending upon whether society chooses to
maintain a river in excellent ecological health or to allow some deterioration in its health in order to satisfy human needs for water and energy. In
either case, however, a sustainability boundary is defined for the river.
That boundary, in turn, implies a limit on how much water can be
extracted from the river, as well as on the degree to which its natural pattern of flow—its natural hydrograph—can be altered.

Scientists express this eco-support allocation as a flow prescription, as described in Chapter 2. That prescription specifies how much water a river needs at specific times of the year in order to meet certain ecological goals. If a river is to be sustained in a very healthy condition, for example, its eco-support allocation needs to protect its natural flow regime from harmful modification in the future. For rivers already dammed for flood control or hydropower, but that still retain most of their water, the eco-support allocation will show the degree to which dams, levees, and other infrastructure may need to be operated differently, or perhaps removed altogether, in order to restore ecological flows. Finally, for rivers that have had their flows both heavily dammed and diverted, the eco-support allocation suggests how much water needs to be returned to the river to satisfy its quantity requirements, as well as how its managed flow needs to be modified to approximate its natural historical pattern.

Although the eco-support allocation is a simple concept, it represents a marked departure from current policies and practices in most countries. It might seem, at first glance, like an unwelcome barrier to economic growth, but it is perhaps better perceived as a valuable safeguard against ecologically harmful growth. Designating water for ecological support is no more radical a notion than suggesting that the bricks comprising a building's foundation not be pulled out and used to construct the fourth or fifth story. Economic growth that destroys ecological support systems is neither sustainable nor truly progress.

Moreover, a scientifically based limit on river flow alterations is the key to optimizing the total array of benefits that society derives from rivers. The eco-support allocation safeguards ecological health, biodiversity, and ecosystem services, while at the same time creating a strong incentive to increase the productivity of human water uses. As water withdrawals from a river approach the ecologically sustainable limit, for instance, water managers and users will turn to conservation and efficiency measures to reduce per-capita water use in cities and towns, per-hectare water use on farms, and per-product water use in industries. Just as improvements in labor productivity—output per worker—are beneficial to an economy, so are improvements in water productivity—output per liter or gallon.

Cities, industries, and farms in various parts of the world have shown that cost-effective conservation and efficiency measures can reduce water use by 25–50 percent or more, saving money and energy while at the same time protecting rivers and groundwater systems.[2] Capping flow modifications at the sustainability boundary encourages water users not only to use their existing water supplies more efficiently, but also to share and trade water with one another. It also unleashes the power of technical innovation to create new ways of satisfying human needs that are less water-intensive—including, for instance, drip irrigation, native landscaping, wastewater reuse, and new industrial process designs. Especially in developing countries, where populations and economies are growing rapidly, building conservation into agricultural and urban infrastructure from the start allows the needs of more people to be satisfied within the sustainability boundary. Likewise, energy efficiency measures can help meet expanding electricity needs with fewer or smaller new hydropower dams, or enable dam operations to accommodate ecosystem-sustaining flows.

In short, an allocation of water for ecosystem support implies a limit on human water use and river modifications, but not on economic or social progress. Ideally, each eco-support allocation would sustain every river at a high level of health and functioning. In a world of 6 billion people with increasing material aspirations, however, this is simply not realistic. Some degree of river health will need to be sacrificed in order to achieve other social and economic goals. But the process of setting a boundary makes society more conscious and clear about its choices—which rivers are being protected, which are being degraded, and why.

For a system like this to work, it must be applied broadly. It will do little good for the world's freshwater ecosystems if each time a river basin reaches its ecological limit, water managers begin to divert additional supplies from a neighboring river that has no sustainability boundary in place. That approach would lead to a domino effect of degradation, yielding little if any net protection of ecosystem health over time.

The idea of allocating to rivers the flows they need to sustain their health and functioning—and making this allocation a priority—is beginning to surface in various forms on the national and international scene. Among the seven principal recommendations of the independent World Commission on Dams is that of "sustaining rivers and livelihoods." According to the Commission, "releasing tailor-made environmental flows can help maintain downstream ecosystems and the communities that depend on them."[3] At the December 2001 International Conference on Freshwater in Bonn, Germany, delegates from 118 countries developed recommendations for action at the 2002 World Summit on Sustainable Development in Johannesburg, South Africa, one of which said that "the value of ecosystems should be recognised [*sic*] in water allocation and river basin management," and that "allocations should at a minimum ensure flows through ecosystems at levels that maintain their integrity."[4]

The European Union, which to date has focused primarily on water quality concerns, issued a directive in late 2000 establishing a new framework for water policy that includes a focus on river flows. A key feature of the directive is the establishment of criteria for classifying the ecological status of rivers (and other water bodies) as high, good, moderate, poor, or bad, depending upon how much the river's ecological characteristics deviate from a natural or undisturbed condition. (This classification approach is similar to that used in South Africa, as described in Chapter 2.) Member countries are then to take measures to ensure that at least a "good status of surface water and groundwater is achieved . . . and that deterioration in the status of waters is prevented."[5] Each member country has responsibility for translating the Directive into legislation and for adopting implementation measures, which are likely to include controls on water withdrawals and flow alterations. Importantly, the Directive establishes criteria for classifying the ecological status of rivers, including river flow and channel characteristics.

It is too early to judge the effectiveness of this new European policy, but on paper it offers great promise for protecting and restoring ecological flows for Europe's rivers. It has already provided new standards against which organizations and agencies can judge proposed water projects and plans. For example, opponents of the large-scale river diversions that are part of Spain's national hydrological plan have pointed out that the plan—for which Spain is seeking European Community funding—is at odds with the principles and objectives established by the new European water policy directive.[6]

In Australia and South Africa, where scientists have advanced new methods for setting environmental flow requirements, policymakers have taken great strides toward translating the concept of allocating flows for ecosystem support into actual policy and practice. Together the initiatives of these two countries are in large part responsible for the marked shifts in river management philosophy that are increasingly evident internationally. Because they are at different stages of economic and water development, these two countries and their pioneering experiences offer some useful lessons for others. Among them is the importance of establishing ecosystem-support allocations as early as possible in the course of river development—preferably before human water use surpasses ecological limits. They also show the importance of working at the river basin or watershed level, and of involving scientists, policymakers, and stakeholders in the process of setting appropriate boundaries on flow modifications.

We examine these two sets of policy initiatives, and then explore the state of river-flow protections in the United States, which, by contrast, has no overarching vision or policy to secure ecosystem-sustaining flows. Within its complex patchwork of federal and state regulatory and legal authorities, however, are some promising possibilities for progress. After looking at the policy venues in these three countries, we briefly describe some economic tools and ethical precepts that are also important instruments in the toolbox for water reform.

SOUTH AFRICA PIONEERS THE WATER "RESERVE"

Few opportunities arise in the life of a country to completely rewrite the constitution, laws, and policies that govern it. South Africa was given such an historic opportunity after the collapse of apartheid in the early 1990s and the election of a new majority democratic government headed by President Nelson Mandela. The new leadership effectively wiped the governing slate clean, and crafted a new set of principles to take the nation forward. Reform of the nation's water laws and policies was an important part of this process, and the result—which is still evolving—is an entirely new approach to valuing and managing rivers. Though conceived under unique circumstances, this groundbreaking policy design offers much for other countries to learn from and perhaps to emulate.

The public trust doctrine is the foundation of South Africa's new water law. The basic precept of the public trust is that governments hold certain rights and entitlements in trust for the people and are obliged to protect those rights for the common good. As a legal principle, it traces back to A.D. 530, when Roman Emperor Justinian assembled his top scholars and asked them to collect and put in writing all the laws of the Empire. Among this body of Roman civil law, known as the Institutes of Justinian, is a provision that states, "By the law of nature, these things are common to mankind—the air, running water, the sea, and consequently the shores of the sea."[7] Later referred to as the public trust, the doctrine lived on through the centuries as Roman law was incorporated into the canon law of the medieval church, gave inspiration to Renaissance philosophers, and was adopted as the basic law of many European countries as well as territories within the British Empire, including Ceylon (now Sri Lanka), Scotland, and South Africa.[8]

For the architects of South Africa's post-apartheid water governance structures, the adoption of the public trust as a grounding principle signaled that "South African law will return to its source and adopt a broad purposeful understanding of the public's rights. . . . To make sure that the values of our democracy and our Constitution are given force in South Africa's new water law, the idea of water as a public good will be redeveloped into a doctrine of public trust which is uniquely South African and is designed to fit South Africa's specific circumstances."[9]

Even more than the formal adoption of the public trust, the translation of this guiding principle into policy stands out as a pathbreaking development. The water law's framers did not work behind closed doors. They actively sought public comments over a two-year period and held consultations with citizens and interest groups in all nine provinces. In 1996, some of them also attended a workshop for the Sabie-Sand river system that included aquatic ecologists working on the rivers of Kruger National Park, as well as scientists who had developed the Building Block Methodology for assessing environmental flow requirements. The legal team came away from the workshop convinced that the new scientific methods for determining how much water a healthy river needs were sufficiently solid to meet legal requirements.[10]

South Africa's National Water Act, passed in 1998, is a landmark in international water policy.[11] It integrates public trust principles, recognition of ecosystem service values, and the natural flow paradigm for conservation of river health in a way that could revolutionize that society's relationship with rivers. Specifically, the law establishes a water allocation known as the "Reserve," which consists of two parts. The first part is a nonnegotiable allocation to meet the basic water needs of all South Africans for drinking, cooking, sanitation, and other essential purposes. The second part of the Reserve is an allocation of water to support ecosystem functions in order to conserve biodiversity and secure the valuable ecosystem services they provide to society. Specifically, the Act says, "the quantity, quality and reliability of water required to maintain the ecological functions on which humans depend shall be reserved so that the human use of water does not individually or cumulatively compromise the long term sustainability of aquatic and associated ecosystems."

Importantly, the water determined to constitute this two-part Reserve has priority over all other uses, and only this water is guaranteed as a right. The use of water for purposes outside the reserve, including, for instance, irrigation and industrial uses, has lesser priority and is subject to authorization[12] (see Table 3-1).

One year after passage of the new water act, the government issued guidelines describing in detail how the Reserve should be determined.[13] Many of the river scientists in South Africa are now engaged in quantifying the flow allocations that will constitute the ecological component of the Reserve in each major watershed. Besides setting flow requirements that are scientifically credible and legally defensible, a major challenge to the political viability of South Africa's new water policy is likely to come in river basins that are already over-allocated—where part of the task is to return some water to natural systems in order to satisfy the Reserve.

If imitation is the best form of flattery, South Africa's new approach is already winning accolades. In its Vision for Water and Nature, IUCN (the World Conservation Union), one of the largest conservation organizations in the world, incorporates the idea of the Reserve into its guiding principles: "Respecting the intrinsic values of ecosystems, and the benefits they provide, implies leaving water in ecosystems to maintain their functioning. This water, together with the water that is needed to meet basic human needs, is a reserve that has priority above all other water uses. Only water resources in excess of these basic needs should be thought of as 'available' for allocation to other uses."[14]

Together, the adoption of the public trust as the guiding ethic of its water laws and the establishment of the Reserve as a way of carrying out its trust obligations place the South African government in a unique and pioneering role in twenty-first-century water governance. As with any policy, its value lies in its implementation—and there are many hurdles to overcome. But the architects of South Africa's new law and policies have mapped out a promising path for rebalancing water allocation to better meet the water needs of both people and ecosystems.

AUSTRALIA OVERHAULS WATER POLICY AND TRIES A "CAP"

As the driest inhabited continent on earth, Australia has its share of water challenges. Over the last century, the nation has invested heavily in engi-

TABLE 3-1 Water Allocation under South Africa's National Water Act

Water Allocation	Purpose of Water	End Objective	Mode of Allocation
Water for Basic Human Needs	To support basic human needs (i.e., drinking water, cooking, and sanitation)	Meet human survival needs	Nonnegotiable
Water for the Ecological Reserve	To sustain a certain state of the ecosystem (e.g., subsistence fishing and recreation)	Social and economic growth and well-being	Negotiated through ongoing stakeholder dialogue and consensus around trade-offs
	State of the ecosystem associated with a specific range of goods and services	Use of goods and services support a range of benefits	
Water for Licensed Use	To support activities that rely on water as applied outside of the ecosystem (e.g., irrigation)	Social and economic growth and well-being	Negotiated through ongoing stakeholder dialogue and consensus around trade-offs
	Activities lead to a range of benefits		

SOURCE: van Wyk et al., 2002.

neering infrastructure to capture and store water for irrigation, industrial expansion, and urban growth. Australia is estimated to have more reservoir storage capacity per person than any other country in the world.[15] With just over 19 million people and 486 large dams, Australia has constructed one large dam for every 39,500 persons, compared with one large dam for roughly every 43,200 persons in the United States, for every 57,500 persons in China, and for every 250,000 persons in India.[16]

Under the Australian Constitution, the Commonwealth (or federal) government has limited authority over water matters. Primary responsibility rests with the states and territories. Growing concern during the last two decades about the increasing scarcity and deteriorating quality of fresh water and the widespread degradation of rivers and aquatic ecosystems led the Commonwealth and state governments to reshape the principles and policies governing water management and use.[17] The resulting Council of Australian Governments (COAG) Water Reform Framework, signed in 1994 by all the state premiers, recognized the need to move toward sustainable use of water and greater protection of freshwater ecosystems.[18]

A key piece of this reform package calls for states to recognize the environment as a legitimate user of water and to allocate water specifically to freshwater ecosystems. To assist the states in doing this, the Agriculture and Resource Management Council of Australia and New Zealand, along with the Australian and New Zealand Environment and Conservation Council, developed a set of "National Principles for the Provision of Water for Ecosystems." These principles were revised in 2001 to incorporate lessons from the states' implementation efforts up to that time. The stated goal of these principles is "to sustain and where necessary restore ecological processes, habitats and biodiversity in water-dependent ecosystems."[19] Among the twenty principles—which cover issues ranging from assessing ecological flow requirements to accountability and community involvement—is one stating explicitly that environmental water provisions should be legally recognized. Another says that when environmental water allocations are not sufficient to prevent significant ecological harm, extractions of water from that river basin "should be capped."

Within the last few years, all eight Australian states have passed new water laws to reflect the agreed-upon COAG goals, and they are now in the process of setting environmental flow requirements for their rivers.[20] In the state of Western Australia, for example, the Water and Rivers Commission has established a water allocation policy that gives ecological flow requirements top priority. First, water is reserved to support ecosystem health; then the remainder can be licensed for use. Since Western Australia's rivers generally are not yet overallocated, the setting of this ecosystem support allocation early on should help prevent the kind of ecological damage that has occurred to rivers elsewhere in the country.[21]

In the state of Queensland, where a new water act was passed in 2000, advice on environmental flows is being provided by panels of scientists from a variety of different disciplines. These panels employ the "benchmarking methodology" for setting environmental flows, a method that uses rivers already degraded by dams and flow regulation to help predict the impacts of future flow alterations. Just as South African scientists have adopted the DRIFT methodology as particularly useful for their situation, Australian scientists consider this method—which is relatively new and still evolving—a valuable approach. In this process, environmental flow limits are defined as "the level of change beyond which there is an increased risk of unacceptable environmental degradation." These limits help determine how much water should be dedicated to maintaining ecosystem health, and are fed into the state's water allocation and management planning process.[22]

As in South Africa, the presence in Australia of a strong scientific community that has worked on criteria and methods for establishing environmental flows for rivers—and the willingness of scientists to interact with the policy and legal communities—greatly increases prospects for the implementation of Australia's reforms. Angela Arthington, a professor at Griffith University in Queensland and a pioneer in environmental flow methods, sums up progress to date: "In one decade in Australia we have seen the concept of in-stream flows progress from vague notions of 'compensation flows' for riparian users and 'the environment,' and 'minimum flows' to provide habitat for a few species of fish, to the definition of flow regimes to sustain biodiversity and the key ecological processes linking rivers, their floodplains and associated terminal waterbodies, including inland lakes, wetlands, estuaries and coastal waters."[23] Arthington points out, however, that because the COAG can only issue goals and guidelines, the states will determine their own implementation strategies—and these may vary considerably. A more overarching national policy, she points out, might increase the chances of success.[24]

Alongside these state water reforms, another progressive river policy experiment is taking place in Australia's Murray-Darling basin—the placement of a cap on water extractions. The largest river system in Australia, the Murray-Darling catchment covers most of the inland southeast region, includes much of the nation's best farmland, and supplies water to about 3 million people (see Figure 3-1). With more than a tripling of water withdrawals between 1944 and 1994, flows in the lower Murray River have dropped dramatically: median annual flows from the river to the sea are now just one-fifth of predevelopment flow levels. Severe low flows now occur in the lower Murray in 60 percent of years, compared with 5 percent under natural conditions. Classic signs of deteriorating river health are apparent—including reduced areas of wetlands from the decrease in flooding events, declines in native fish populations from the disappearance of flows that trigger spawning, and increases in salinity levels and the frequency of algal blooms.[25]

Spanning parts of four states (New South Wales, Queensland, South Australia, and Victoria) and the whole of the Australian Capital Territory, the river is managed cooperatively with the aid of the Murray-Darling Basin Commission (MDBC). Basinwide decisions are made by a Ministerial Council consisting of the resource ministers from each basin state or territory, plus the Commonwealth. Council resolutions must pass unanimously to become effective.

In the early 1990s, worsening ecological conditions in the river system led the Ministerial Council to call for an audit of water use in the basin. Released in 1995, the audit found that water consumption had climbed by 8 percent between 1988 and 1994 and could increase by an additional 14.5 percent under the existing management rules. These rules had evolved during a time when water managers were encouraging development and use of the basin's rivers, and they were not oriented toward protecting river health. Confronted with these realities, the Council determined "that a balance needed to be struck between the significant economic and social benefits that have been obtained from the development of the Basin's water resources on the one hand, and the environmental uses of water in the rivers on the other."[26] In mid-1995, the Council placed an interim cap on diversions from the Murray-Darling basin, and then made the cap permanent in 1997.

As originally established, the cap is not designed to reduce diversions from the basin's rivers, but rather to prevent them from increasing. It is defined as "the volume of water that would have been diverted under 1993/94 levels of development."[27] The actual formula for determining the cap is rather complicated. It is not the volume of water that was actually extracted in 1993/94, but rather the volume of water that would have been

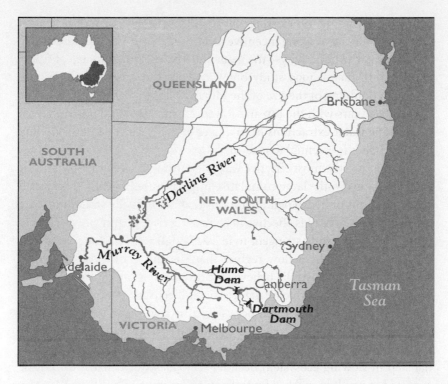

FIGURE 3-1. The Murray-Darling River Basin.

used that year under climatic and hydrologic conditions similar to the year in question. The actual diversions allowed under the cap will therefore vary from year to year, but as a long-term average should not rise above the 1993/94 level. An annual independent audit of water use in each basin state determines whether or not the states have met their respective caps for that year.[28]

The cap's political palatability is due partially to its being promoted not just as a way of arresting the decline in the Murray-Darling's health but also as a way of securing the water supplies of existing consumers in the basin. In times of drought or when the river system cannot meet all the demands made upon it, water users share the pain of rationed cutbacks. By preventing new diversions, the cap therefore helps ensure that existing users will get their full allotment more of the time. Officials also promoted the cap as a restraint on diversions, but not on new water uses or on economic development. New water demands can be met through conservation and efficiency improvements, as well as through the marketing and trading of existing allotments.[29] As designed, the cap is expected to create a strong incentive to improve water-use efficiency and to raise water productivity—the value derived per cubic meter of water extracted. In fact, a 1999 study on Water and the Australian Economy projects a doubling of the size of the Murray-Darling basin economy over twenty-five years with the cap and water reforms in place.[30]

Limiting water extractions from a river in the way the Murray-Darling basin cap does is essential to creating a flow regime that protects a river's health. It is also the most effective way of guarding against the "tyranny of small decisions"—the large cumulative impact caused by numerous small river diversions or hydrologic alterations that individually would not raise much concern.[31] A cap is effective in protecting river health, however, only if it is both sufficiently stringent to leave enough water in the river and if it is accompanied by a flow regime that sustains ecological functions. Many scientists in Australia believe that the existing cap on Murray-Darling diversions will need to be made stricter if ecosystem health and functions are to improve. As a number of scientists wrote in 2000: "The Cap was originally set at a level of water extraction that contributed to the current degradation of the river system, and while the Cap is seen as an essential step in slowing ecosystem decline, ecologists warn that it cannot be expected to result in marked improvements in riverine health."[32]

To our knowledge, the cap is the only serious attempt in the world, not just in Australia, to limit extractions from a large multi-state river basin that is already oversubscribed. It seems likely that additional water will need to be returned to the Murray if an adequate flow regime is to be achieved. Even so, work is now under way among scientists, resource managers, and communities in the basin to establish environmental flow requirements and to design an adaptive approach to the management and operation of the river.[33] Although far from perfect, the attempt in the Murray-Darling basin to limit diversions and to prescribe a pattern of flow that will sustain ecosystem functions makes it an important test case worth watching.

U.S. POLICY LACKS FOCUS ON ECOLOGICAL HEALTH

With each passing year, the need for greater protection of river flows in the United States becomes more apparent. Two centuries of dam building, levee construction, and straightening of river channels have left very few river segments in anything close to their natural state: only 2 percent of U.S. rivers and streams remain free-flowing.[34] Conflicts over the allocation of water between human needs and ecosystem needs have been intensifying across the country, from west to east and north to south. Freshwater life in running waters is increasingly at risk.

Many western U.S. rivers are oversubscribed, leaving little or no flow to meet ecosystem requirements. Similar signs of stress are apparent now in the eastern portions of the country, areas long thought immune to the water predicaments of the naturally drier West. Nearly 500 kilometers of Vermont's rivers are impaired due to flow alterations and heavy withdrawals.[35] The Ipswich River in Massachusetts now periodically runs dry during the summer months because heavy groundwater pumping for suburban lawn irrigation is depleting the river's base flows.[36] Excessive water withdrawals and diversions have impaired the flow of numerous Connecticut rivers, including the Shepaug, the subject of a citizens suit brought before the state's Supreme Court. In the rapidly growing Southeast, Georgia, Alabama, and Florida have haggled for more than a decade over sharing the waters of the Apalachicola-Chattahoochee-Flint river basin, an ecosystem seriously threatened by rapidly increasing water extractions and flow modifications.

Despite widespread degradation of its river systems, the United States has no overarching vision or goal to secure the flows that rivers need to support the diversity of freshwater life and to sustain ecological functions. Historically, the U.S. government has deferred to the states in matters of water allocation, use, and management. This acquiescence, however, is a matter of choice. The U.S. Constitution makes clear that when state law conflicts with federal, the latter trumps the former. In the area of water allocation, this notion was upheld in the landmark 1899 decision in United States v. Rio Grande Irrigation Co., which effectively subordinated state-authorized water uses to federal powers over commerce and public land. According to University of Colorado water-law scholar David Getches, early cases also made it clear that federal preemption of state water law did not require any special legislative action.[37]

In practice, however, federal authorities have rarely interfered with state systems of water rights and allocation, and so the states have called most of the shots. Each state has a body of water law that derives from its constitution, legislative acts, and court decisions. The eastern and western states abide by different legal doctrines, which reflect in part their dissimilar climatic, historical, and economic circumstances. Most eastern states apply the "riparian" doctrine of water law, according to which parties adjacent to rivers and streams can make reasonable use of those waters. Under the riparian system, individuals do not own rights to water. The state permits the use of water bodies, often accompanied by conditions or requirements that ensure such uses do not cause unreasonable harm to others.

By contrast, most western states abide by the "prior appropriation" doctrine, often encapsulated by the motto "first in time, first in right." Those who made the earliest claims on a river have the highest priority rights to its water. Once granted, water rights become the private property of their holder. These rights are what lawyers call "usufructory" rights: they are rights to use water, not to own it outright—hence the other motto that has characterized western water law, "use it or lose it." Along with a specified volume, each water right comes with a date that determines its ranking in the allocation hierarchy. In times of drought, the holder of a more senior water right—one with an earlier date—will get all of his or her water before a more junior rights holder gets any. State agencies administer the applications for and granting of water rights, and any legal challenges are typically handled by state courts.

Federal authorities over rivers take place within the context of these state legal systems. These include federal laws, such as the National Environmental Policy Act (1969), the Clean Water Act (1972), and the Endangered Species Act (1973); case law derived from federal court decisions; as well as authorities granted under the U.S. Constitution, such as the commerce, property, and supremacy clauses. These overlapping and at times competing federal and state authorities would almost certainly not be the policy framework of choice for water management today if, like South Africa, the United States had the opportunity to start over with a blank slate. But it is the system that is in place, and so the challenge lies in interpreting, enforcing, and where necessary, amending these authorities such that they collectively do a better job of balancing human uses of water with the protection of aquatic ecosystems. Our review of the relevant federal and state laws and policies shows a great deal of potential for the protection and restoration of river flows, but most of it so far is unrealized.

FEDERAL OPTIONS

At the federal level, there are at least nine categories of actions or measures that agencies could take to improve river flows (see Table 3-2). Each

TABLE 3-2 Federal Authorities for Protecting River Flows in
the United States

Action or Measure	Principal Agents
Revising management of federal dams built for irrigation, flood control, water supply, hydropower, and navigation	Army Corps of Engineers Bureau of Reclamation Department of Energy Tennessee Valley Authority Bonneville Power Administration Western Area Power Administration
Licensing nonfederal hydropower dams	Federal Energy Regulatory Commission
Listing freshwater species as endangered	Fish and Wildlife Service Marine Fisheries Service (for salmon)
Protecting habitat for species listed as endangered	Secretary of the Interior Fish and Wildlife Service Marine Fisheries Service (for salmon) All federal agencies impacting rivers
Gaining federal "reserved" water rights through state legal systems	National Park Service Forest Service Fish and Wildlife Service Bureau of Land Management Indian tribes
Establishing federal "nonreserved" water rights	Forest Service Bureau of Land Management
Protecting water quality and overall river health	Environmental Protection Agency Army Corps of Engineers
Controlling activities on public lands that would impact streamflows	National Park Service Forest Service Fish and Wildlife Service Bureau of Land Management
Designating rivers as "wild and scenic"	U.S. Congress Secretary of the Interior upon state request

of these measures has succeeded in preserving or restoring flows in some cases—establishing all as viable policy tools—but none has been applied broadly enough to significantly improve river flows on a wide scale. Although existing laws and powers seem to give federal agencies the authority to limit flow modifications in order to safeguard river health, this action has not been taken.

The most powerful federal authorities over river flows derive from the commerce clause (Article I, Section 8) of the U.S. Constitution and the Clean Water Act of 1972. Under the commerce clause, the federal government has the power to regulate commerce among the states and with other nations. Because waters may be used for commercial navigation, it gives Congress some authority over water management. Initially, this authority was interpreted narrowly to cover only activities causing an obstruction to navigable waters. Over time, however, federal courts expanded the definition of "navigable" and the range of activities to which the commerce clause applied. As David Gillilan and Thomas Brown write in their analysis of instream flow protection measures in the western United States, "Eventually the courts determined that rivers did not actually have to be navigable for the Congress to assert its commerce powers. By the time Congress passed the Clean Water Act in 1972, the courts had allowed the federal government to assert jurisdiction over all the waters of the United States, including rivers, lakes, streams, estuaries, and even wetlands."[38]

The federal Clean Water Act (CWA) offers the broadest and clearest mandate to the U.S. Congress to protect river health. Coupled with powers granted under the commerce clause, it leaves little doubt that the federal government has all the authority it needs to protect and restore the flow of rivers. The expressed goal of the act is "to restore and maintain the chemical, physical, and biological integrity of the Nation's waters." During three decades of implementing the act, however, Congress and the federal agencies administering it have focused primarily on protecting chemical integrity through the setting of water quality standards, pollution control requirements, and best management practices. They have done little explicitly to regulate the quantity and timing of river flows to protect the physical and biological integrity of rivers.

Several events and court decisions during the 1990s extended the reach of the CWA to river flows. So far, however, these have been relatively isolated cases that demonstrate the act's potential potency but that have so far not led to broader protections. In 1990, for example, William K. Reilly, administrator of the Environmental Protection Agency, used his authority under the CWA (Section 404) to veto the construction of Two Forks Dam, which would have flooded Colorado's scenic Cheesman Canyon on the South Platte River in order to increase water supplies for Denver. Reilly cited as his main reasons for the veto the loss of a valuable trout stream and recreation area, the destruction of valuable wildlife, and the availability of less-damaging alternatives to meet Denver's water supply needs.[39] With scientists now in wide agreement that restoring more natural flow patterns to rivers is essential to safeguard their ecological integrity, a logical extension of activities under the CWA would be a joint federal-state program to establish ecological flow prescriptions for the nation's rivers.

In the absence of a broad initiative of this type, public servants charged with protecting rivers can nonetheless make progress using a number of other federal authorities. Among the most underused measures is the acquisition of "reserved" water rights by federal agencies that oversee public lands. This authority derives from a 1908 legal decision, Winters v. United States, in which the U.S. Supreme Court said that in establishing an Indian reservation for two Montana tribes in 1888, the U.S. government had "impliedly" reserved for the tribes enough water to carry out the purposes for which the reservation was created. For more than half a century, these newly identified "reserved" water rights were thought to apply only to Indian reservations. But in a 1963 ruling, the U.S. Supreme Court decided in Arizona v. California that reserved water rights could apply to any federal land reservations, not just Indian lands. This meant that designated national parks, forests, wildlife refuges, and other federal land reservations, as well as Indian reservations, could claim reserved water rights to the extent those rights were necessary to carry out the purposes for which the federal reservations were established. Moreover, the priority date of the federal reserved rights would not be the date the rights were first claimed, but rather the date that the federal lands in question were established—which was often in the late nineteenth or early twentieth centuries. This would give the newly established federal reserve rights a more senior priority than many existing private water rights.

Despite their sweeping potential to reallocate river water for ecological purposes, few reserved rights designations have been fought for and won. Federal agencies are required to go before state courts to adjudicate their reserved rights. Many have been reluctant to do this, and when they do, state courts have been reluctant to grant them rights. To date, for example, no court has ever granted the U.S. Forest Service an implied reserved water right for the protection of instream flows.[40] This is despite the fact that the 1897 Organic Act specifically cites "securing favorable conditions of water flows" as a purpose of the national forests, and that more than a third of national forest lands have been identified as important to the protection of aquatic biodiversity.[41] The courts have granted federal reserve rights most readily to national parks, which have as a primary purpose conserving "the scenery and the natural and historic objects and the wild life therein," as well as leaving these attributes "unimpaired for the enjoyment of future generations."[42] In a case decided in Colorado courts in 1993, for example, Rocky Mountain National Park received federal reserve rights to all of the unappropriated water in the park.[43]

To date, the federal Endangered Species Act (ESA) has spurred the greatest protection of river flows for ecological purposes. Passed in 1973, it requires the Department of the Interior to identify species at risk of extinction, and prohibits all federal agencies from taking any actions that would jeopardize the continued existence of a listed species. The power of the ESA first became evident in the now infamous case of the snail darter, a minnow whose only known habitat at the time was a river in Tennessee. The snail darter's listing as endangered held up the federal Tennessee Valley Authority (TVA) from finishing the Tellico Dam on the Little Tennessee River, which would have inundated the snail darter's habitat. In TVA v. Hill, the Supreme Court decided that the congressional intent in passing the ESA (and specifically Section 7) was to give the protection of endangered species priority even over the legitimate missions and functions of the federal agencies.[44]

The ESA thus has great influence on water policy and management. In recent years, ESA requirements have led to the shutting off of irrigation water to farmers in the Klamath River valley straddling the California-Oregon border; calls for operational changes in the large hydroelectric dams that have decimated salmon populations in the Columbia River basin, including pressures to breach four major dams on the lower Snake River; and revisions in the operating procedures for Flaming Gorge Dam on Utah's Green River, to name just a few examples. Even the prospect of a lawsuit under the ESA by a coalition of conservation groups was sufficient to induce three irrigation districts to agree to keep a minimum flow of water in the Walla Walla River of eastern Oregon and Washington in order to protect bull trout, which was listed as threatened under the ESA in 1998.[45]

As a tool for broad protection and restoration of freshwater habitat, however, the ESA has several major drawbacks. First, it targets individual species for protection rather than overall ecosystem health. This narrow focus can lead to remedial measures designed to increase the population of a particular species but that do little or nothing to restore and protect the diversity of species and processes that comprise the ecosystem as a whole. The construction of fish ladders to help endangered salmon migrate past dams is a good example. Second, the act's influence has been more reactive than proactive: it kicks in mainly when a conservation group files a lawsuit against the government. And third, the ESA often takes effect too late in the trajectory of ecological decline. Species are typically listed as endangered because their habitat has been too diminished and degraded to sustain them. As a result, ESA protections often prove to be too little, too late.

Another option that offers great potential for restoring river flows is the design of new management criteria for federal dams. The federal government owns and operates some 1,932 dams—many of them very large ones—across the United States (see Figures 3-2 and 3-3). The operating procedures for these dams still largely reflect the twentieth century priorities of providing inexpensive water, power, and flood control to encourage settlement and economic growth. Only minimally, if at all, do they

FIGURE 3-2. Federal Dams in the United States.

incorporate protections for freshwater ecosystems. Moreover, the agencies overseeing these dams—principally the Army Corps of Engineers, the Bureau of Reclamation, and several region-specific authorities such as the Bonneville Power Administration in the Pacific Northwest and the Tennessee Valley Authority in the Southeast—are not required to conduct periodic reviews to assess the dams' costs and benefits, which can change markedly over the multi-decade life of a dam. As Steve Malloch, formerly of Trout Unlimited, points out: "Federal taxpayers have an investment worth hundreds of billions of dollars in federal dams and water projects. No rational investor would make that kind of investment and then forget to manage it. We should bring these dams into line with current needs."[46]

Each of these dams has a set of operating rules that determine how much water gets released from their reservoirs and when those releases occur. Adding the protection of river health to the list of beneficial purposes served by a dam—such as hydropower, irrigation, and flood control—would require a change in the schedule of flows released from the reservoirs in order to re-create important components of the river's natural (pre-dam) flow regime. A few dam reoperations of this sort have already

FIGURE 3-3. Gavins Point Dam, managed by the U.S. Army Corps of Engineers, has become the focus of flow restoration discussions on the Missouri River. (Photo by Harry Weddington, U.S. Army Corps of Engineers, Omaha District.)

occurred. In March 1996, federal officials opened the floodgates of Glen Canyon Dam on the Colorado River in order to generate a spring flood sufficient to rebuild key elements of the river's habitat through the Grand Canyon (Figure 3-4). The results of this experiment were mixed, but within the context of adaptive management and learning-by-doing, they have led scientists, conservationists, and river managers to propose two more sets of experimental releases to benefit the river ecosystem, one each in 2003 and 2004. The Secretary of the Interior has not yet decided whether to carry out the proposed plan.[47] Further upstream in the Colorado system, the Bureau of Reclamation is changing the operation of Flaming Gorge Dam on the Green River in Utah, a major tributary to the Colorado, in order to protect critical habitat for four endangered native Colorado River fish. The recommended schedule of reservoir releases would create a flow pattern much more similar to the river's natural flow regime. An adaptive management program is now under way (see Chapter 2).[48]

With nearly two thousand dams under federal control, a requirement that federal agencies update their operating instructions by specifically incorporating flow releases that benefit the river ecosystem itself could do a great deal to improve river health, restore native fish populations, and conserve biodiversity. One small but significant step in this direction was taken in July 2002, when the U.S. Army Corps of Engineers entered into a partnership with The Nature Conservancy, a large private conservation organization, to examine how releases from thirteen dams operated by the Corps might be changed to benefit the river environment. If fruitful, this partnership could serve as a springboard for broader reform of federal dam operations nationwide.

In a similar way, a federal requirement that the efficiency of water use in federal irrigation projects be improved could do much to restore flows in heavily depleted western rivers. Consumption of water now exceeds 75 percent or more of surface runoff in much of the West, and most of this is attributable to irrigation. The Bureau of Reclamation has built more than 190 projects and supplies about one-third of the surface water used for irrigation.[49] The implementation of conservation projects to improve the productivity of irrigation water use could help restore flows to depleted rivers without harming crop production or rural economies.

Yet another promising avenue for federal action is the relicensing of nonfederal hydroelectric power dams. The Federal Energy Regulatory Commission (FERC) licenses some 1,800 hydroelectric facilities across the country that collectively account for nearly half of total U.S. hydroelectric

FIGURE 3-4. A controlled flood release from Glen Canyon Dam on the Colorado River in 1996 highlighted the potential to restore degraded river ecosystems by modifying dam operations. (Photo by Bill Jackson, National Park Service.)

generating capacity.[50] These licenses usually have thirty- to fifty-year terms, and when they expire the dam owners must apply to FERC for a new license. By evaluating the environmental effects of these dams more thoroughly and either requiring operational changes as a condition of license renewal or deciding not to renew a license when the environmental harm is too great, FERC could aid in the rebalancing of river management between human and ecosystem purposes. In 1994, FERC issued a policy statement making clear that it had the authority to deny an application for license renewal, as well as to order a dam to be removed if such action served the public interest. FERC acted on this authority three years later, ordering the decommissioning of Edwards Dam on Maine's Kennebec River.[51] A small stone and timber structure built in 1837, the Edwards Dam produced a tiny share of the power used by the state capital of Augusta while blocking the migratory routes of several legendary fish runs, including Atlantic salmon, alewife, and shad. Upon signing the landmark agreement clearing the way for the dam's removal, Secretary of the Interior Bruce Babbitt heralded a new day when he said it was "a challenge to dam owners and operators to defend themselves—to demonstrate by hard facts, not by sentiment or myth, that the continued operation of a dam is in the public interest, economically and environmentally."[52]

POWER TOOLS FOR THE STATES

With states effectively having primary responsibility for water allocation and management, they have considerable leverage to secure environmental flows for rivers. As with federal authorities, however, the application of state powers has been patchy, inconsistent, and so far mostly ineffective at protecting the ecological integrity of rivers. Many state efforts still focus on establishing minimum flow requirements, which may keep water running in rivers but not necessarily at the volumes or times that the ecosystems need. Many are also oriented toward safeguarding flows for anglers, boaters, and other recreationists, but not for the ecosystem itself.

A number of policy tools for restoring healthy flows to rivers are available to the states. Although their applicability and practicality vary from state to state, these options include legislating the establishment of environmental flows for rivers, using permit programs to enforce basinwide limits on flow modifications, granting or transferring water rights for instream purposes, setting conservation goals and requiring conservation programs, and, as legal cases arise, applying judicial protections, such as the public trust doctrine.

The ability most states have to grant, deny, and set conditions on permissions to extract water from state water bodies (often surface water and groundwater) gives them substantial potential to protect river flows. To be used effectively, however, state permitting programs need to be directly keyed to the maintenance of ecological flow regimes such that the sum of all flow modifications in a river do not exceed the threshold defined for that place and time. A "percent-of-flow approach" used by the Southwest Florida Water Management District comes close to this idea. In 1989, the District, which is one of five such geographic districts responsible for managing Florida waters, began limiting direct withdrawals from unimpounded rivers to a percentage of streamflow at the time of withdrawal.[53] For example, cumulative withdrawals from the Peace and Alafia rivers are limited to 10 percent of the daily flow; during periods of very low flow, withdrawals are prohibited completely. The District is now considering using percentage withdrawal limits that vary among seasons and flow ranges in order to better protect the ecological health of rivers under its jurisdiction.

Importantly, this mechanism preserves the natural flow regime of rivers by linking water withdrawals to a percentage of flow—specifically, by ensuring that a major percentage of the natural flow is protected every day. If a new permit application would cause total withdrawals to exceed the threshold, denial of the permit is recommended unless the applicant can demonstrate that the additional withdrawals will not cause adverse ecological impacts. This provision allows for flexibility, but places the burden of proof on potential water users to show that their withdrawals would not harm the ecosystem.

A number of New England states have also taken some positive steps in recent years. In July 2000, Vermont revised its water standards to recognize the need to adjust human-induced flow alterations in order to protect aquatic habitat. The New England office of the U.S. Environmental Protection Agency is working hand in hand with states in the region to encourage the adoption of standards more protective of environmental flows. It has also funded the Connecticut River Joint Commission to examine ways to improve policies affecting flows in the upper Connecticut, New England's largest river.[54]

In western states that apply the doctrine of prior appropriation, the challenge is to establish instream water rights that are sufficient to sustain ecological flows for rivers. None have done this adequately, but many have taken steps either to reserve a portion of flows for instream purposes or, more commonly, to establish minimum streamflows, although these are usually geared toward protecting certain fish species rather than whole ecosystems. Perhaps more importantly, all the western states have criteria for evaluating requests for new appropriative water rights and changes to existing ones, and nearly all (Colorado and Oklahoma are the exceptions) require that new appropriations serve the public interest. Early on, the public interest tended to be equated with economic development, but increasingly public interest criteria are being used to protect river flows from further depletion or modification.[55]

As a result, water rights dedicated to ecosystem protection can now often enjoy the same legal status as rights used for irrigation or other extractive purposes. A major drawback to instream flow water rights designations, however, is that they often have such a low priority date that they do not offer much protection to rivers. To rectify this, some states allocate funds for the purchase of existing higher-priority water rights and then convert them to instream rights. Another important limitation of instream water rights is that they are usually quantified as constant year-round or monthly values that do not come close to approximating a river's naturally variable pattern of flow; they therefore often do little to protect or restore ecosystem health (see Figure 3-5).

One intriguing idea proposed in recent years is that of turning these conventional instream water rights upside down. Instead of prescribing flows for ecosystem support, and implicitly allocating all remaining flows for extractive or other economic purposes, so-called "upside-down instream flow water rights" are defined by turning the question around and asking instead: how much can a river's natural flow pattern be modified in order to meet irrigation, hydropower, and other water development demands and yet still meet the flow needs of the river ecosystem itself? This degree of water development is then specified, and all the remaining flows are allocated to protection of ecosystem functions and

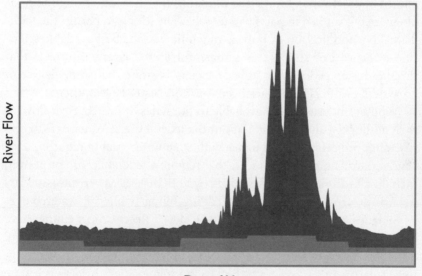

Day of Year

■■■ **Natural hydrograph**
■■■ **Variable minimum flow water right**
■■■ **Steady minimum flow water right**

FIGURE 3-5. Conventional Instream Flow Water Right. A conventional instream flow right defines a fixed amount of water to be left in a river. Such rights are usually expressed as a single minimum flow level, sometimes varying by month, to be protected. Because the remaining water is available for other uses, this approach provides little protection for the natural flow regime. (Adapted from Silk et al. 2000.)

services (see Figure 3-6). Attorneys Nicole Silk and Robert Wigington of The Nature Conservancy, along with Jack McDonald of the Northwestern School of Law at Lewis and Clark College, make a strong case for legal recognition of upside-down instream flow water rights either as federally reserved water rights in relation to national parks, forests, or other public lands; or as appropriative rights under state law.[56] These rights may be most applicable, they note, on rivers not overly developed and may work best when implemented with a precautionary approach: that is, reserve only a modest amount of water for development initially, and add more incrementally as scientists develop clearer delineations of where ecological harm will occur.

In essence, upside-down instream flow water rights are a way of implementing the shift toward ecologically compatible water development within the context of the appropriative water rights system in the western United States. In many ways it is similar to the "benchmarking methodology" being applied in parts of Australia. The idea is to permit the withdrawal or modification of only as much flow as the best available scientific evidence can support as unharmful to the river's health. If that threshold is exceeded, then at least society is aware that some degree of ecosystem health is being sacrificed for more water development.

Another underused tool available to the states to protect river flows is their authority (under Section 401 of the federal Clean Water Act) to certify water projects for compliance with state water quality requirements. This authority applies to projects that require a federal license or permit, including hydropower licenses issued by FERC as well as permits issued by the Army Corps of Engineers for dredging, filling, or altering watercourses or wetlands (under Section 404 of the CWA).[57] Recent court rulings have made clear that states can use this certification authority to powerful effect. In a key 1994 decision (PUD No. 1 of Jefferson County v. Washington Department of Ecology), the U.S. Supreme Court held that a state could impose flow conditions on a FERC-licensed project if necessary to protect the state's designated uses of the river. The Court swept away any notion that the CWA applies only to water quality and not to water quantity, stating that this is "an artificial distinction," since in many cases "a sufficient lowering of the water quantity in a body of water could destroy all of its designated uses. . . ."[58] The Court said the state of Washington was permitted to set flow requirements in its certification of a hydroelectric facility on the Dosewallips River, because the flows were needed to maintain the designated uses the state had established for the river.

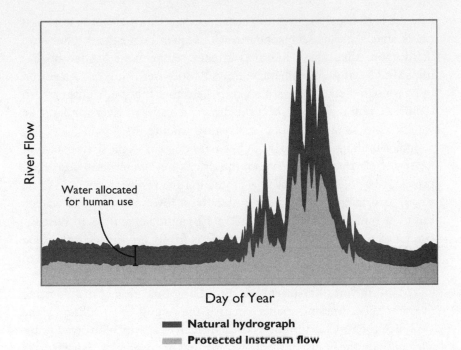

FIGURE 3-6. Upside-Down Instream Flow Water Right. In the upside-down approach for protecting instream flows, the allowable human use is a fixed constant. On any given day, this amount is "shaved" from the natural river flow. By limiting withdrawals to a fixed level, much of the river's flow variability is protected. (Adapted from Silk et al. 2000.)

The full effect of this ruling could prove substantial. It has already influenced the licensing of the largest hydroelectric facility in New England, the Fifteen Mile Falls project on the upper Connecticut River. In 1996, the project's owner began a collaborative FERC-relicensing process that included federal, state, and local agencies, as well as environmental organizations. It resulted in a negotiated agreement, signed by all the parties in 1997, that calls for operational changes at the three project dams— including flow releases to improve downstream habitats. It also set up a fund to mitigate past and ongoing environmental damage, with monies going toward wetland restoration, creation of riparian buffers, and other river restoration activities.[59] In the Pacific Northwest, the conservation organization American Rivers and the regional Environmental Protection Agency have urged the states of Idaho, Oregon, and Washington to take the high court's ruling into account when listing rivers as impaired under state water quality standards. Consequently, the three states have listed more than three hundred stream segments as "water quality impaired" because of inadequate flows.[60] Moreover, a July 2002 decision by Washington state's Supreme Court held that the state's authority to require certain flows to protect the designated uses of rivers under state water quality standards applies to existing water rights.[61]

Judicial rulings based on the public trust doctrine—the same common law principle that underpins South Africa's new water law—also have proven to be potent tools for flow protection and restoration within some states. As originally applied, the public trust involved only tidal waters, but some states have broadened this interpretation over time. In Wisconsin, for example, where the public trust is firmly grounded in the state constitution, the courts have expanded the definition of the trust to include wetlands and non-navigable streams.[62]

To date, the most far-reaching application of the public trust doctrine to water allocation and management is the August 2000 ruling by the Hawaii Supreme Court in the Waiahole Ditch case, which involved water allocation on the island of Oahu. Noting that the people of Hawaii "have elevated the public trust doctrine to the level of a constitutional mandate," this decision could spawn substantial reform of Hawaiian water policy in favor of river protection. In some ways similar to South Africa's approach, the Hawaiian Court defined three constitutionally protected public trust uses of water—ecosystem protection, domestic use, and preservation of the traditional and customary rights of native Hawaiians. These public trust uses are to take priority over private commercial uses in water allocation decisions. According to the Court, "If the public trust is to retain any meaning and effect, it must recognize enduring public rights in trust resources separate from, and superior to, the prevailing private interests in the resources at any given time. Underlying every private diversion and application there is, as there always has been, a superior public interest in this natural bounty." The Court emphasized that the state's first step toward fulfilling its trust obligations is to establish instream flow standards for Hawaii's rivers and streams.[63]

Similarly, court rulings in both Connecticut and Michigan have hinged on public trust responsibilities that are explicitly recognized in state statutes. Michigan's 1970 Environmental Protection Act, for example, prohibits the destruction or impairment of the state's trust resources. Historically, the Michigan courts have not used the statute to limit water diversions, but in a 1998 ruling the state Supreme Court defined "impairment" broadly, and a trial court has ruled that state approval of a diversion for a golf course violated the public trust.[64]

Connecticut's environmental protection act provides that the state's natural resources, including water, are a public trust. This recognition played an instrumental role in a February 2000 ruling protecting flows in the Shepaug River, prized for its recreational, ecological, and aesthetic values. The central issue in the case was whether the city of Waterbury was diverting so much water from the Shepaug as to constitute an "unreasonable impairment" of the public trust. The court found that impairment of the river had indeed occurred (see Box 3-1), and that the impairment was unreasonable because management practices were readily available that could lessen damage to the river—notably water conservation measures.[65] A subsequent reversal of this decision by the state Supreme Court, however, shows how the public trust doctrine's adaptability to changing times can be undercut by anachronistic laws or standards. The higher court ruled in June 2002 that a water flow standard established in 1979 by the state Department of Environmental Protection was the only standard that could be used to define "impairment" of the river, even though department officials themselves had testified that the 1979 standard had no ecological basis and was insufficient, according to current science, to protect the river's health.[66]

In the western states, where many rivers and streams are already overallocated, the public trust doctrine is highly controversial because of the threat it poses to existing water rights holders. If insufficient quantities of water remain within a river system to safeguard a feature of the public trust, then a court might rule that existing water rights need to be altered or revoked in order for the state to fulfill its trust obligations. Not all states recognize the public trust doctrine, but in those that do, it is a potentially powerful tool for returning water to natural systems.[67]

That potential first became clear in a 1983 decision involving California's Mono Lake, a beautiful water body on the eastern side of the Sierra Nevada. The city of Los Angeles had been granted water rights by the state to divert most of the flow from four of Mono Lake's five feeder streams. Several decades of these diversions caused the lake's level to drop 13.7 meters and its volume to shrink by half. In 1979, the National Audubon Society, the Mono Lake Committee, and other groups filed suit, claiming that Mono Lake was protected by a public trust. The case eventually went before the state Supreme Court, which ruled in 1983 that the public trust

BOX 3-1 Connecticut's Shepaug River and Impairment
of the Public Trust

The role of natural river flows in sustaining habitats in the Shepaug River and a determination that a deviation from natural flows constituted an "impairment" of the river—a public trust resource—were critical in this case decided in Connecticut Superior Court in February 2000, as the following excerpts from Judge Beverly J. Hodgson's decision show. The state Supreme Court reversed this decision on the grounds that "impairment" should have been defined, not according to the best available science, but rather a 1979 state water standard (see text for discussion).

"The Shepaug River has areas along its length which the various expert witnesses characterized as riffles, runs and pools. Riffles are the portion of the stream interrupted by boulders; runs are areas of relatively flat running water over either smoother or deeper stream beds than riffles; and pools are places where water exists in greater depth and with less flow.... At times of high flow, the water may cover the boulders in the stream bed so that more of the river can be characterized as runs; in low flow, the boulders may protrude from water barely deep enough to wet the feet of a person walking in the stream bed. From bank to bank across, the stream bed varies in width. Full or overflowing at high flows, it can be a narrow, shallow stream running in a narrowed course between exposed boulders at low flows....

"The conduct that the defendants characterize as unreasonable impairment in the case before this court is the diversion of particular quantities of water from the west branch of the Shepaug River. The defendants allege that this diversion impairs the river itself by reducing its summer flow and altering its natural condition. They also assert, apparently both as instances of the consequences of reduced flow and as separate impairments of natural resources, that Waterbury's diversion of water harms the fish population and the 'benthos,' a term used to refer to the population of such organisms as caddis flies, May flies, and stone flies, which are part of the ecology of a river and which, along with other roles, supply food for fish. The defendants also assert that the diminishment of flow impairs the suitability of the river for recreational uses and diminishes its appearance and aesthetic properties.

"The conclusion is inevitable that the erection of a dam across a river alters that river. Instead of having a natural flow, including natural seasonal variations in the amount of flow, a dammed river is affected by the storage function of the dam, which operates to hold some of the water from periods of high flow for use in some manner during periods of low flow.

"This court concludes that the ordinary meaning of the word 'impairment' is best adhered to by considering whether the summer flow of water in the river is reduced below its natural flow in the months of May through October.... [T]he natural flow of the river is diminished by about thirty-five percent in August and up to seventy percent in June. Such a diminishment constitutes a substantial 'impairment.'"

SOURCE: State of Connecticut Superior Court, 2000.

did indeed apply. Moreover, the court essentially said that the public trust doctrine can trump appropriative water rights when the two are in conflict. Specifically, it said that the "public trust doctrine and the appropriative water rights system are parts of an integrated system of water law. The public trust doctrine serves the function in that integrated system of preserving the continuing sovereign power of the state to protect public trust uses, a power that precludes anyone from acquiring a vested right to harm the public trust and imposes a continuing duty on the state to take such uses into account in allocating water resources."[68] Ultimately, the city of Los Angeles was required to greatly curtail its withdrawals from Mono Lake's tributaries.

So far, courts in other western states have been reluctant to follow in the footsteps of the California court. Some have even reversed earlier support for the public trust doctrine. Idaho's Supreme Court, for example, decided that the doctrine did not apply in the adjudication of water rights in the Snake River basin after earlier ruling that it did apply to waters of the state. The Idaho legislature then topped this off by prohibiting application of the public trust doctrine in matters of water rights and appropriations.[69] Although its ultimate utility in rebalancing flows between human demands and ecosystem needs remains unclear, the public trust doctrine has evolved over time to reflect changing public values and interests and will likely continue to do so.

FEDERAL-STATE PARTNERSHIPS

Two of the largest freshwater ecosystem restoration efforts currently under way in the world—the Everglades and the San Francisco Bay-Delta—are the result of partnerships between the U.S. government and the relevant states. A unique global treasure, the Everglades in south Florida have shrunk by half over the last century because of manipulations to the natural hydrological regime that sustained this famed "river of grass," coupled with rapid population growth and pollution from agricultural fields. A $7.8 billion plan to restore freshwater flows and ecosystem processes within the Everglades has begun, with funds coming from both the state of Florida and the federal government.

Similarly, a federal-state partnership known as CALFED is aimed at restoring the vast delta where the Sacramento and San Joaquin rivers join before reaching San Francisco Bay. This delta region is the heart of California's water system, supplying some 20 million Californians and large areas of irrigated land. Most of the fresh water that historically flowed through the delta and into San Francisco Bay is now captured and diverted for cities and farms. The resulting habitat destruction has decimated fish populations and driven the delta smelt toward the brink of extinction. As with the Everglades, restoration of this unique and biologically rich ecosystem is certainly warranted, but it is an expensive, complicated process that will take decades.[70]

In addition to federal and state agencies, each of these initiatives also involves a broad range of stakeholders and scientists, and they may well yield some useful new models of collaboration and cooperation. Such unconventional approaches often serve as useful incubators and trials of new ideas, which can later be incorporated into broader water reforms. As much as possible should be learned from these opportunities.

Most fundamentally, however, the Everglades and Bay-Delta schemes are expensive rescue efforts that would never have been needed had existing laws and policies done a better job of protecting the aquatic environment in the first place. Most ecosystems at risk do not have the public visibility or political champions needed to get such major restoration efforts orchestrated and funded. More than anything, they doubly underscore the need for stronger legal and institutional mechanisms to prevent such devastation of freshwater ecosystems from occurring.

ECONOMIC TOOLS FOR SECURING RIVER FLOWS

Once water authorities have established ecological flow requirements for rivers and a corresponding limit on water use and flow alterations, the challenge is to sustain jobs, livelihoods, and overall economic progress without overstepping this limit. This requires improvements in water productivity through conservation, recycling, increased efficiency, and the reallocation of water among different users. In some cases, water saved through these measures will need to revert to instream purposes in order to meet the ecosystem's flow requirements. In other cases, the savings will be needed to meet new water demands so that total water use remains within that river basin's sustainability boundary. Economic incentives, especially effective water pricing and the creation of water markets, can be useful tools for boosting water productivity. Water markets also provide opportunities for conservation groups, government agencies, or others to purchase water or water rights specifically to enhance river flows.

Virtually all water authorities have the ability to price water or water services, yet many do not use this tool effectively. Most governments, for instance, heavily subsidize irrigation water, with the result that farmers in many countries pay less than 20 percent of the real cost of their water supplies. Such low prices discourage farmers from investing in efficient irrigation practices, as well as growing crops that are appropriate to the local climate. In many cases, charging the full cost of water will not be feasible, but it is nonetheless possible to implement pricing or payment structures that strongly encourage efficient water use.

One idea now being tried on farms in California, for instance, is a three-tiered water rate structure. The U.S. Congress mandated this pricing policy as part of the 1992 Central Valley Project Improvement Act, which aimed at improving fisheries, wetlands, and river flows within the vast Sacramento–San Joaquin river basin, the main source of water for this large federal irrigation scheme. Under this pricing structure, irrigation districts pay the same rates they were previously paying, plus a fixed surcharge, for up to 80 percent of their contracted water volume. If their usage equals 80–90 percent of their contract allotment, however, they pay substantially more per cubic meter for that additional 10 percent, and if their usage goes as high as 90–100 percent of their contract amount, they pay even more for that last 10 percent increment—in some cases, nearly three times more than the base level.[71] Irrigation districts therefore have an incentive to reduce their water use in order to avoid paying the higher unit costs for the last 10 or 20 percent of their contracted allotment. One irrigation district that implemented a similar pricing scheme in the late 1980s saw its average water use decline by 19 percent within a few years. In areas such as the western United States, where irrigation is the dominant consumer of water, incentive pricing strategies similar to this one could potentially free up large quantities of water for the restoration of river flows.

In the small subset of countries and regions where water rights are held as private property and may be sold or traded, a more varied tool kit of economic options exists. Chile and Mexico are the only countries that have established formal systems of tradable water rights at the national level. Some Australian states and many western U.S. states also have such systems. Under Chile's 1981 water code, the government grants property rights to both surface water and groundwater that the owners may then sell to anyone for any purpose at an agreed-upon price. As a water-scarce developing country, Chile is using water markets and transfers primarily to help satisfy growing water demands. Water trading, for instance, has enabled some Chilean cities to purchase water from farmers rather than constructing a dam at greater economic and environmental cost. The city of La Serena bought 28 percent of its water rights from nearby farmers, postponing the need for a new dam. Likewise, the city of Arica has met a portion of its water needs by leasing groundwater from farmers.[72]

An interesting feature of Chile's system is that water rights are defined volumetrically but revert to proportional rights (a share of river or reservoir water) when the available supply is not sufficient to fully satisfy all the volumetric rights.[73] In this way, users in a given basin share the pain of shortages rather than some getting a full allotment while others get none (as is the case in much of the western United States). This proportional rights provision would seem to allow for protection of environmental flows. Either the government or the water user associations responsible for enforcing water rights would have to decide to reserve fresh water for ecosystem purposes, and then, when necessary to secure those flows, proportionately reduce each water rights allocation accordingly. A similar option would seem to exist in Mexico, where water rights are defined volumetrically, but any deficits or surpluses are shared proportionately. The definition of a deficit could presumably be made to incorporate environmental flow protections.[74]

In Australia, water trading has only recently become an active part of river management. The 1994 Council of Australian Governments water reform agenda called for the introduction of water entitlement transfers, including cross-border trades. In addition, the setting of the cap on diversions for the Murray-Darling basin has spurred an active water market within that watershed. "Cap-and-trade" is essentially the guiding management philosophy in the basin now. With a lid on extractions, new water demands are met through conservation, efficiency improvements, and water trading.

Indeed, the ability to trade water licenses is a key to the cap's workability, since reallocation of water becomes critical when the total supply is not increasing. The volume of water traded in the Murray-Darling basin after the cap's institution in the mid-nineties was more than five times greater than the volumes traded in the early nineties. Most of these were temporary sales between water users in the same state, but permanent transfers are increasing as well.[75] In recent years, for instance, highly profitable cotton growers have paid about $560 per thousand cubic meters for permanent water licenses.[76] Web pages now exist to facilitate water trading on the Internet, and brokers at newly established water exchanges are competing for water-trading business. If the cap is made more stringent, as scientists believe is necessary to improve the health of the ecosystem, trading will become even more active.

The use of water markets and trading directly for the restoration of river flows is more common in the western United States than anywhere else. Without a regulatory instrument comparable to the Murray-Darling basin's cap or South Africa's reserve, the transfer of offstream consumptive water rights to instream purposes is one of the few options available to return water to rivers. All western states now recognize the validity of an instream water right (albeit to varying degrees), but because most western rivers already are overappropriated for human uses, granting new rights for ecological purposes does little good in most places. Such rights would have such a low priority under the appropriation system that they would be ineffective at protecting ecosystem health. However, the purchase of existing higher-priority consumptive use rights and their conversion to instream flow rights can accomplish some ecological goals. The quantities of water involved will generally be too small to restore anything close to the river's natural flow regime. But such transfers can improve a river's base flows and perhaps provide higher flows of limited duration, both of which may improve habitat conditions.

A variety of water transfer options exists, including (1) short-term leases or temporary transfers of water; (2) longer-term but still temporary leases (e.g., five, ten, or even thirty-year contracts); (3) purchase of water or water rights from a central water bank, if one exists; (4) dry-year options (also sometimes called interruptible supply contracts, drought insurance contracts, or water supply options), in which a private or public entity buys an option to interrupt an existing rights-holder's use of water under certain conditions—for example, when a drought creates dangerously low flows or when extra flows are needed to meet important habitat requirements; and (5) permanent transfers of water rights.

Only in the case of permanent sales does ownership of water rights change hands. But even temporary transfers, when used strategically, can improve river habitat at critical times. For instance, during the cold Idaho winter of 1988–1989, ice formed in a fork of the Snake River and blocked trumpeter swans from getting to critical food supplies. The Nature Conservancy and the Trumpeter Swan Society each purchased just under 4 million cubic meters of water from the upper Snake River water bank. This water was then released, along with an additional 12.3 million cubic meters donated by a local water district, to break up the ice.[77]

Between 1990 and 1997, a total of 2.94 billion cubic meters of water—a volume equal to 16 percent of the average annual flow of the Colorado River—was leased, purchased, or donated for the purpose of enhancing river flows in the western United States. The vast majority of this transferred water was in the form of leases; less than 6 percent were permanent purchases of water rights. Of the nearly $62 million spent on these transactions over the seven-year period, $33.5 million was paid by federal agencies, $25 million by state authorities, and slightly more than $3 million by private organizations.[78] Most of the federal acquisitions were made by the Bureau of Reclamation, including programs in California, Idaho, Oregon, and Washington. The 1992 Central Valley Project Improvement Act, for instance, provided funding for water acquisitions in California, and requirements to protect habitat for endangered salmon in the Columbia River basin led to water leasing arrangements there. At the state level, the Washington Department of Ecology is among the agencies that are actively acquiring water rights for flow restoration, with a $6 million fund dedicated to this purpose. In late 2000, the agency agreed to pay $405,000 for rights to Walla Walla River irrigation water in order to enhance flows for endangered fish.[79]

Within the private sector, environmental organizations have become increasingly active in water markets. National groups such as Environmental Defense, Trout Unlimited, and The Nature Conservancy have been joined by conservation organizations at the state level, including the Oregon Water Trust, the Washington Water Trust, and Nevada's Great Basin Land and Water, as active participants in the acquisition of senior water rights for conversion to instream flow rights.[80] In some cases, private organizations work together with state agencies in effecting water rights transfers. In Colorado, for example, only the Colorado Water Conservation Board is entitled to hold instream water rights, so when a subsidiary of the Chevron Corporation donated to The Nature Conservancy some valuable water rights on the Black Canyon of the Gunnison River, the Conservancy turned those rights over to the state agency for conversion to an instream right.

Despite many promising uses of markets, the buying and selling of water rights have made only a small contribution to the very large task of reallocating water to natural systems. The private appropriation of fresh water has been allowed to proceed so far in the western United States that most rivers systems have 75 percent or more of their flow consumed by irrigation and other human activities. Apart from the revocation of water rights under the public trust doctrine or stronger enforcement of "reasonable use" provisions under state water laws, the only way to get significant restoration of flows in western U.S. rivers is through state and federal purchases of large volumes of existing water rights and their conversion to instream flow rights.

A promising approach called the Environmental Water Account (EWA), for example, is one of the incubator ideas emanating from the joint federal-state CALFED program in California. Supported by the Bureau of Reclamation and the California Department of Water Resources, the EWA operates much like a water bank for ecosystem protection. It buys or leases water from willing sellers and uses that water for habitat improvement. In 2001, the EWA purchased some 475 million cubic meters and paid sellers between $60 and $250 per thousand cubic meters ($75–$300 per acre-foot), depending on the location and source of water. The Bureau of Reclamation operates a similar program instituted under the federal Central Valley Project Improvement Act. Called the Water Acquisition Program, it is currently spending about $10 million a year on water purchases for wetland restoration.[81]

Water markets have the greatest role to play where water has been heavily appropriated by private interests. State and federal agencies could make more effective use of this tool by adding a small fee to each water trade and using the proceeds for water rights acquisitions or other flow restoration measures. The transfer fee, which might be a small share of the value of the water trade, would be a fair way of slightly shifting the allocation of water between human uses and ecosystem needs, in particular to restore base flows during the dry season. Markets, trades, and transfers, however, can accomplish only a small part of the large challenge of rebalancing water allocation between human uses and ecosystem support. They are not a substitute for a broader legal or regulatory mandate to designate flows for the health and functioning of freshwater ecosystems.

ETHICS IN RIVER POLICY

Do rivers and the life within them have a right to water? In most modern-day legal systems, the answer is no. Water is typically the property of the state, and rights to it are conferred by governments to individuals, cities, corporations, and other human enterprises. Allocations for fish, mussels, and rivers themselves are made only if agents of government deem such allocations socially beneficial, or necessary to fulfill any trust obligations that may exist.

The ethical dimensions of society's water use and management choices could conveniently be ignored as long as those choices did not kill other living things. With freshwater life being extinguished at record rates, however, this is clearly not the case today. Our water management decisions have serious ethical implications, and yet these rarely enter the debate over water plans, projects, and allocations. This may not be surprising given that governments have failed even to provide safe drinking water to all people, which results in several million human deaths each year. Yet our moral obligations both to our fellow human beings and to other life-forms implore us to begin injecting these other ethical implications into our policy choices—to manage water as the basis of life for all living things, rather than as a commodity for the benefit of some.

The fact that rivers have no right to water, and that portions of them may be held as private property fits into an ethical code grounded in prevailing socioeconomic philosophies, but one that is neither universal nor unchanging. The American conservationist Aldo Leopold viewed the extension of ethics to the natural environment as "an evolutionary possibility and an ecological necessity."[82] More recently, Harvard biologist Edward O. Wilson notes in his book *Consilience* that, historically, ethical codes have arisen through the interplay of biology and culture. "Ethics, in the empiricist view," Wilson observes, "is conduct favored consistently enough throughout a society to be expressed as a code of principles."[83]

In a practical sense, an ethic serves as a guide to right conduct in the face of complex decisions we do not fully understand but that may have serious consequences. Scientists are making clear that the health and life of rivers depend upon a naturally variable flow pattern. As scientists and economists quantify more of the ecosystem services at risk, societies will come to see that the protection of ecosystems is not only an ethical action, but a rational one: acts of stewardship and economic self-interest will converge. But rates of species extinctions and ecosystem decline are too rapid to wait for this convergence to take place. We need some ethical precepts to guide us wisely through this time of risk and uncertainty, and toward actions that preserve rather than foreclose options for this and future generations.

The principle of the public trust offers a good foundation for a code of water ethics in the twenty-first century. Making it a practical guide, however, requires some pragmatic rules and tools. An important one is the ecosystem support allocation, which we have already described in some detail. Another is the precautionary principle, which essentially says that given the rapid pace of ecosystem decline, the irreversible nature of many of the resulting losses, and the high value of freshwater ecosystem services to human societies, it is wise to err on the side of protecting too much rather than too little of the freshwater habitat that remains. It operates like an insurance policy: we buy extra protection in the face of uncertainty.

Applying the precautionary principle to the protection of river health would mean dedicating a large enough share of natural river flows to ecosystem support to accommodate scientific uncertainty over how much water the river system needs. The Benchmarking Methodology that scientists are using to set environmental flow requirements for rivers in Queensland, Australia, takes a precautionary approach by identifying the levels of flow modification beyond which there is increased risk of unacceptable ecological damage. Under Hawaii's new water policies, the state must apply the precautionary principle as a guide for allocating water in fulfillment of its public trust obligations. And in what is perhaps the strongest recognition of the precautionary principle by an international water institution, the International Joint Commission (IJC) adopted it as a guiding principle for protecting the Great Lakes, which straddle Canada and the United States. In a 1999 report to both governments, the IJC cites the precautionary approach as one of five principles, noting: "Because there is uncertainty about the availability of Great Lakes water in the future— . . . and uncertainty about the extent to which removals and consumptive use harm, perhaps irreparably, the integrity of the Basin ecosystem—caution should be used in managing water to protect the resource for the future. There should be a bias in favor of retaining water in the system and using it more efficiently and effectively."[84]

New scientific knowledge about the importance of healthy rivers and the flows required to sustain them has placed upon us new responsibilities. The establishment of ecosystem flow reserves for rivers is essential to protect the diversity of life and to preserve options for future generations. The scientific, legal, policy, and economic tools exist to make these reserves a reality. A basic code of ethics requires that we act.

CHAPTER FOUR

Down to the River

As both the science and policy of flow restoration advance, a growing number of jurisdictions are now grappling with the challenge of securing ecological flows for rivers. Local communities, conservation organizations, and governments at all levels are working to restore degraded rivers and their beleaguered species by re-creating some semblance of natural flow patterns. A working database compiled by The Nature Conservancy identifies planned, ongoing, or completed flow restoration efforts in more than 230 river basins in twenty countries (see Table 4-1).[1] At least 150 of these projects have been implemented, and a third have involved the removal of one or more dams.

In most cases, the primary motivation for restoration has been to benefit fish. But many of these efforts have been directed at broader societal goals, including improvement of recreational opportunities or aesthetic enjoyment. Many projects in developing countries have been designed to revive activities that depend on natural ecosystem services, including floodplain farming and grazing or subsistence fishing.

The strength of the science underpinning these restoration projects varies considerably. Unfortunately, only a small share of these efforts includes the kind of monitoring and data collection needed to verify results and quantify benefits. However, some clear and hopeful trends are evident. Increasingly, ecological goals are addressing the health of whole river ecosystems rather than just single species. Interdisciplinary scientific investigations of ecological flow needs are becoming standard practice. And financial supporters of restoration are beginning to require moni-

TABLE 4-1 Sampling of River Flow Restoration Efforts

River Location	Type of Flow Restoration	Ecological Purpose
Baraboo River, Wisconsin	Dam removal	Numerous dams removed to restore free-flowing condition to improve water quality and spawning access for numerous fish species
Buck Hollow Creek, Oregon	Reduction of agricultural water usage	Restored spring and summer flow to benefit salmon and steelhead populations
Cole River, Oxfordshire (England)	Modified dam operations	Restored flooding to improve aquatic and floodplain habitats
Colorado River, Arizona	Modified dam operations	Released controlled flood to rebuild river beaches and deepen backwater and eddy habitats
Coosa River, Alabama	Modified dam operations	Increased low flows to benefit endangered snail and native fish populations
Groot River (South Africa)	Modified dam operations	Released high flows to induce spawning in endangered minnow
Gwydir River, New South Wales (Australia)	Modified dam operations	Extended high flows and increased low flows to benefit nesting water birds and migrating fish
Itchen River, Hampshire (England)	Reduction of municipal water usage	Flows increased to benefit salmon and trout fisheries
Kafue Flats (Zambia)	Modified dam operations	Provided flood releases to benefit an endangered antelope and improve overall biodiversity
Kennebec River, Maine	Dam removal	Dam removed to restore free-flowing condition and spawning access for numerous fish species
Kissimmee River, Florida	Meander restoration	Re-created natural flow routes to improve overall biodiversity
Lachlan River, New South Wales (Australia)	Modified dam operations	Restored natural flows to benefit fish and breeding birds, and to flush salinity and blue-green algae

(*continued on next page*)

TABLE 4-1 (*continued*)

River Location	Type of Flow Restoration	Ecological Purpose
Little Piece Meadows, New Jersey	Wetland restoration	Restored flood storage capacity of wetlands to improve wildlife habitat
Logone River (Cameroon)	Modified dam operations	Provided flood releases to restore floodplain ecosystem and subsistence uses
Upper Mississippi River, Minnesota	Modified lock-and-dam operations	Restored low water levels to improve floodplain vegetation
Mun River (Thailand)	Opened dam gates	Free flow restored for two years to recover swamp forest and fish migrations, and to reduce salinity
Murrumbidgee River, New South Wales (Australia)	Modified dam operations	Restored natural flow variability to improve wetlands and aquatic habitats
Pamehac Brook, Newfoundland (Canada)	Dam removal	Restored free-flowing condition to enhance rearing and spawning of brook trout and salmon
St. Mary River, Alberta (Canada)	Modified dam operations	Increased low flows and reduced rate of flood recession to facilitate cottonwood recruitment
Theodosia River, British Columbia (Canada)	Modified dam operations	Reinstated natural flow patterns to restore salmon populations and overall ecosystem
Vienne River (France)	Dam removal	Provided passage for spawning salmon

SOURCE: The Nature Conservancy.

toring of ecosystem responses to the actions taken, thereby creating the opportunity for adaptive management.

Australia and South Africa have advanced the integration of science and policy significantly during the last decade, while agencies and organizations at various geographic scales in the United States are beginning to explore practical ways of incorporating ecological flows into the management of particular rivers. Very few accounts of flow restoration for ecological purposes have emerged so far from Central and South America or Asia. Here we describe the ongoing efforts in six river basins—three in the continental United States (the Missouri River, the Green River in Kentucky, and the San Pedro River in Arizona); the Brisbane River in Queensland, Australia; the Sabie River, running through South Africa's Kruger National Park; and the Espíritu Santo on the Caribbean island of Puerto Rico. We have selected these examples not necessarily because they are the best or most successful ones, but because they represent a diverse set of hydrological conditions, ecological goals, human contexts, and policy settings. As such they offer some useful lessons and insights for taking up the challenge of rebalancing the management of water for human and ecosystem needs in other locations.

A COMEBACK CHANCE FOR THE MISSOURI?

On May 14, 1804, Meriwether Lewis and William Clark departed St. Louis and began a remarkable journey up the Missouri River, the longest river in the coterminous United States (see Figure 4-1). President Thomas Jefferson had charged them with exploring the western expanses of North America, and shortly before they began their journey, he purchased the Louisiana territory from France. Lewis and Clark and their band of explorers traversed the entire Missouri River from mouth to source, except for a 29-kilometer portage around the impassable Great Falls. By the time they reached the Missouri's headwaters in the Rocky Mountains of Montana in late July 1805, they had acquired not only many fascinating tales to tell, but also a meticulous set of records of the plants and wildlife they saw along the way—including 122 species or subspecies of animals and 178 species of plants.[2] Many of these plants and animals were already known to the Indians who had long lived in the region. But the Lewis and Clark journals revealed for the first time for a young United States the biological bounty of the Great Plains and the northwestern interior.

As the nation prepares to celebrate the two-hundredth anniversary of that historic expedition, the Missouri River ecosystem and much of its biological richness is gravely at risk. As it turned out, the Lewis and Clark expedition's findings unveiled great potential for westward expansion of commerce and economic development—setting into motion changes that eventually brought great harm to the river. In typical twentieth-century fashion, the Missouri was transformed by a series of dams, reservoirs, and levees from an ecologically healthy river doing nature's work to

FIGURE 4-1. The Missouri River Basin.

an ecologically impoverished river working almost exclusively for the human economy. Within just the last few years, however, there has emerged some hope that at least portions of the Missouri River system may be revived. Scientists, conservation organizations, water managers, and regional river interests are engaged in a laborious, often acrimonious, and as-yet unresolved attempt to see if the use and management of this great river can be rebalanced enough to restore some of its ecological health and to give its nonhuman communities a chance to bounce back.

Like many large rivers in Europe, Australia, the United States, and other industrialized countries, the Missouri has been altered substantially from its natural state. The lower third of the river, a total of 1,212 kilometers, is no longer connected to its floodplain at all: engineers have deepened and straightened its channel to enable barges to run to and from the ports at St. Louis, where the Missouri joins the Mississippi. Instead of the naturally variable flow of the river, this channelized stretch now gets a discharge controlled by upstream reservoirs. Naturally low flows from August through January no longer occur, because barges need a water depth of at least 2.7 meters. The Missouri's middle stretch, a length of 1,233 kilometers, is now controlled by six large federal dams. Fort Peck, the most upstream of these, was completed in 1939—a federal response to the terrible drought and economic depression of the 1930s. Five other dams were completed between 1952 and 1963 under a plan known as Pick-Sloan, a joint endeavor of the U.S. Army Corps of Engineers and the Bureau of Reclamation. With a combined storage capacity of 90.6 billion cubic meters, these dams and reservoirs constitute the largest reservoir system in North America.[3] The upper third of the river is by far the least altered stretch, but four relatively small dams and reservoirs prevent even this section from flowing freely.[4]

The dams, levees, and other engineering works built on the Missouri, impressive for their time, completely altered the natural flow regime of the river and the habitat for much of the life that evolved in its watershed. This natural flow pattern had three key attributes—big floods in March–April caused by snowmelt in the Great Plains, somewhat smaller floods in May–June caused by melting of the Rocky Mountain snowpack along with spring rains, and then a period of relatively low flows from August through January (see Figure 4-2). Operation of the mainstem dams and reservoirs has flattened the river's flood flows, raised its low flows (although some of this is due to higher rainfall levels in the post-dam period), and greatly reduced its variability in flow throughout the year and over time.

These flow modifications, in turn, have caused major changes in fresh-water habitats. Fish and other organisms can no longer access flood-plains. Sandbars and shallow-water habitats that are critical to fish, birds, and riparian vegetation have disappeared. Flows that provided vital life-cycle cues no longer occur. As a result, numerous species within the Missouri River ecosystem are now at risk: federal or state agencies have listed as endangered, threatened, or rare a total of sixteen species of fish, fourteen birds, seven plants, six insects, four reptiles, three mammals, and two mussels.[5] Of sixty-seven native fish species living along the Missouri mainstem, fifty-one are now judged to be rare, uncommon, and/or diminishing in number across all or part of their ranges.[6] The pallid sturgeon and two bird species—the least tern and the piping plover—are on the federal endangered species list. Production of mayflies, caddis flies, and other benthic invertebrates—a key part of the river's food web—has dropped approximately 70 percent in unchannelized portions of the river.[7] By most measures, the Missouri ecosystem is in seriously declining

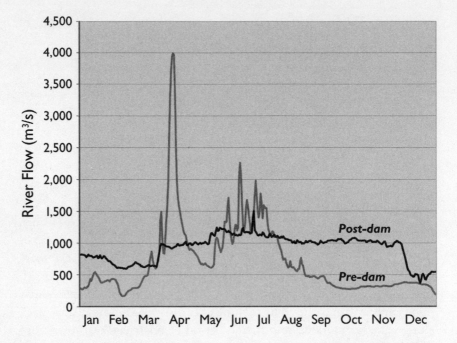

FIGURE 4-2. Missouri River Flows Before and After Regulation by Dams. Natural river flow patterns in the Missouri River were considerably different from the dam-regulated flows of today, as shown by this comparison of typical pre-dam and post-dam hydrographs.

health. It topped American Rivers' list of the most endangered rivers in the United States in both 2001 and 2002.[8]

The elimination of the spring flood pulses and the disconnection of the river from its floodplain have been especially harmful to the ecosystem's functioning. The yearly floods distributed plant seeds, organic matter, and nutrients throughout the river and floodplain, thereby sustaining the system's biological productivity. They replenished floodplain pools and backwaters. They spurred the growth and reproduction of cottonwoods, willows, and other streamside plants and trees. They served as a cue for fish to spawn and for insects to emerge from the water phase of their life cycle. And they enabled fish and other organisms in the channel to move onto the floodplain to breed, feed, and grow—and then return to the channel as the floodwaters receded. In many ways, the flood pulse and the mosaic of river-floodplain habitats it created were the keys to the ecosystem's productivity, biodiversity, and overall health.

Yet another important job historically performed by the annual floods is the transport and distribution of sediment throughout the river system. Before completion of the Pick-Sloan dams, the Missouri carried on average some 142 million tons of sediment a year past Sioux City, Iowa—earning the river its nickname, The Big Muddy. After closure of the dams, the sediment load dropped by 97 percent.[9] Much of it was trapped behind dams upstream, and less sediment was mobilized overall because of the curtailment of the high-velocity flood flows. Erosion and deposition of channel sediments are what make a river meander. In the case of the Missouri, this lateral movement across the floodplain is critical to the regeneration of riparian vegetation and to the creation of sandbars where the endangered plovers and terns build their nests. An adequate sediment supply is also needed to maintain the physical integrity of the river channel. Without new sediment to replace what is eroded, the river channel deepens, which makes it harder for the river to overtop its banks and spread onto its floodplain. This channel deepening also lowers the adjacent floodplain water table, because the two are hydraulically connected. This in turn drains water from wetlands, pools, and oxbow lakes—eliminating critical habitat.

Although less well documented, the low-flow periods of late summer and autumn were also vitally important to maintaining the ecological health of the Missouri. They exposed sandbars for nesting birds and channel-bank sites for nesting turtles. Sturgeon and other fish found ideal nursery conditions in the shallow waters along sandbar margins and in braided channels. In autumn, migrating shorebirds would stop over on exposed mudflats to fuel up on insects and worms during their long-distance flights from the northern plains to the Gulf of Mexico and South America.[10]

The importance of these natural processes to the overall health of the Missouri ecosystem has led a recent panel of scientists commissioned by the National Research Council (NRC) to conclude that "degradation of the Missouri River ecosystem will continue unless some portion of the hydrologic and geomorphic processes that sustained the pre-regulation Missouri River and floodplain ecosystem are restored—including flow pulses that emulate the natural hydrograph, and cut-and-fill alluviation associated with river meandering."[11]

In a nutshell, therein lies the challenge of reviving the Missouri. Can enough of the natural flow pattern, floodplain habitat, and channel structure be re-created in a large enough portion of the river to restore ecological health and revitalize populations of threatened species? The challenge involves altering dam and river operations in order to satisfy some specific ecological goals, which were not on the radar screen a half century ago when the initial management objectives for the river were established. Because society's needs, values, and scientific knowledge have changed substantially since then, a change in river operations is essential to optimize the total social and economic benefits derived from the river.

The U.S. Army Corps of Engineers serves as the master regulator of the Missouri. Under the Pick-Sloan scheme, the Corps has authority to control the operation of the mainstem dams to serve the primary purposes of the plan—namely flood control, irrigation, navigation, hydropower, industrial and domestic water supply, and wildlife and recreation. Enacted in the mid-1940s during the heyday of the U.S. reclamation era, the plan for the Missouri was focused squarely on optimizing use of the river for economic growth, agricultural development, and commerce. Only much later came the federal environmental mandates—including requirements to assess the environmental impacts of federal projects (under the 1969 National Environmental Policy Act), to meet water quality standards (under the 1972 Clean Water Act), and to avoid further jeopardizing species at risk of extinction (under the 1973 Endangered Species Act). The meshing of these early economic goals with later environmental goals has proven complicated and contentious in the Missouri, as it has in many river basins.

Army Corps engineers operate the Missouri River dams according to procedures spelled out in a handbook referred to as the Master Manual, which was first developed in 1960. Protection of the Missouri River's health and ecosystem services does not directly appear in the list of objectives. The manual ranks the provision of benefits to recreation, fish, and wildlife lowest—and says this function should not interfere seriously with meeting the other higher-priority objectives. This ranking was developed by the Corps at its own discretion; the U.S. Congress gave no weighting to these objectives in the 1944 act establishing governance procedures for the river. Each year, the Corps prepares a detailed plan for operating the dams and reservoirs. The timing and volume of actual water releases on a daily or hourly basis are determined by staff at the Corps' Reservoir Control Center in Omaha, Nebraska.

In the late 1980s, the Corps came under pressure to update the Master Manual (which had last been revised in 1979) to better reflect contemporary social values and concerns about habitat preservation, species conservation, recreational enjoyment, and other environmental benefits. The agency's decision during a serious drought to maintain flows sufficient for navigation rankled upper-basin states, which suffered economic losses from reduced reservoir recreation. The Corps was also under pressure to revamp river operations as a result of the issuance of a jeopardy opinion by the U.S. Fish and Wildlife Service under the Endangered Species Act. In response, the Corps began a process of revising the manual that—at the time of this writing nearly fifteen years later—is still not complete. The large differences of opinion voiced by the wide range of groups with a stake in the final outcome have resulted in gridlock.

In their 2002 report on prospects for recovery of the Missouri River, the NRC committee called for a moratorium on the manual revisions until they incorporate a scientifically sound adaptive management approach to improving the Missouri's condition—a clear departure from past practice. The committee also recommended that, in light of the river's poor condition, actions to begin restoring its health get under way and not be delayed by the moratorium on revising the manual. The NRC committee felt that the learning-while-doing approach of adaptive management could enable constructive progress to be made toward restoring the river even while a new operating strategy for the dams and reservoirs is worked out.

Fortunately, the compass direction for restoring the Missouri is clear. It points toward re-creating to some degree the river's natural high and low flows, as well as allowing a portion of the Missouri to meander again. These actions obviously involve trade-offs among the competing uses of the river. A more natural flow regime will likely increase economic benefits from recreation, for instance, but may reduce those from navigation. Moreover, many of the economic uses of the river are measured in dollar terms, whereas the benefits of ecosystem services and conserving freshwater species typically are not.

Nonetheless, the trade-offs may be less murky for the Missouri than they appear at first glance. Due largely to the expansion of railroads, barge traffic on the lower Missouri never reached the levels anticipated when the river initially was channelized. Today, commercial shipping traffic is less than half what it was at its peak twenty-five years ago. Annual net benefits from commercial navigation on the Missouri total about $3 million.[12] Moreover, as the NRC report points out, any lost navigation benefits would likely be more than compensated by increased recreation and hydropower benefits, because more water would be stored in reservoirs

during the summer months rather than released to raise water levels for
a small number of barges. To these benefits would be added valuable but
unquantified benefits to endangered species and from ecosystem services
—upping the net benefits to society even more.

Of the various alternatives developed by the Army Corps of Engineers
for revising the Master Manual, the most likely to restore river health and
protect at-risk species is one referred to as GP2021. Many river scientists
and conservation organizations favor this alternative because it gives the
Corps the flexibility it needs to operate the Missouri dams in a way that
more closely mimics the river's historical flow pattern. Specifically, it
would allow for a spring rise to mimic historical patterns, as well as for a
late summer low closer to natural historic lows.

This alternative is intended to provide a flow trigger to stimulate fish
spawning, increase sandbar habitat for endangered least terns and threatened piping plovers, increase shallow-water habitat for native fishes, and
augment recreational benefits. From an ecosystem perspective, however,
it is far from perfect. The proposed spring flow rise would occur later than
the natural spring flood and earlier than the natural early-summer
floods. The proposed spring rise would be only slightly larger than is currently being provided, and only a tiny fraction of what would have
occurred naturally. Moreover, the Corps would create this late-spring rise
only once every three years on average, whereas naturally it would occur
in two out of every three years. In terms of economic trade-offs, it would
require curtailing navigation during a portion of the low-flow period in
summer, but barge traffic could remain at normal levels during the spring
and fall, when most agricultural goods are shipped. With this option, the
Corps anticipates no significant impact on flood control benefits and a
small increase in hydropower benefits.[13]

A decision on operational revisions is expected in 2003. If the spring-
rise alternative is adopted, an adaptive management program to monitor
and assess the impacts will be critical, since some scientists fear it will not
be a sufficient mimicking of the natural flow regime to significantly
improve ecosystem health or habitat. Nonetheless, adoption of this alternative may be just the springboard to get operational changes under way,
with the understanding that revisions will be needed as more is learned
about how the ecosystem is responding. If the Corps adopts the NRC's
recommendation to not revise the Master Manual until a scientifically
based adaptive management program is developed, then implementation
of the spring-rise alternative may provide useful information to feed into

this process. One thing is certainly clear: with no changes to dam and reservoir operations, the river will continue its downhill ecological slide.

Some actions are already under way or planned to revive the Missouri. In May 2002, the Corps had planned to release higher and warmer spring flows from Montana's Fort Peck Dam to attempt to provide hydrologic and temperature cues for the endangered pallid sturgeon. Unfortunately, an upper-Midwest drought caused the Corps to delay this test, probably for at least two years. Scientists are now gathering background information in preparation for a later test.

Mother Nature also has provided some impetus for restoration. Heavy midwestern precipitation caused record flooding in the lower Missouri in 1993, 1995, and 1996. As the river breached levees in various locations, it reconnected with its floodplain—affording researchers an opportunity to observe how habitats, species, and ecosystem dynamics might recover if such a reconnection was made more permanent. They found that a variety of plants and animals immediately took advantage of the river-floodplain reconnection. For example, after the flooding, sixty-one different fish species occupied wetlands that were connected to the river channel, while only twenty-six species were found in unconnected areas. The variety of plants and aquatic insects was also richer in connected versus isolated zones.[14]

Overall, these recent flooding events suggest that a return to a more natural flow regime would benefit a wide variety of species by creating a richer mosaic of habitats and by reestablishing conditions that are critical to their life cycles. In addition to changes in dam operations, this requires dedicating more land adjacent to the river as working floodplain. The 1986 Water Resources Development Act authorized the Corps to create habitat on 7,365 hectares of existing federal and state land on the floodplain, as well as to purchase 12,100 additional hectares from willing sellers. After the mid-nineties flooding, a number of property owners became interested in selling, and so far 9,530 hectares have been acquired. A 1999 federal water act authorized acquisition of an additional 48,000 hectares over the next thirty-five years, but to date no funds have been appropriated for the estimated $750 million cost of these purchases.[15]

The U.S. Fish and Wildlife Service has also purchased floodplain land as part of The Big Muddy wildlife refuge. In one meander bend, the river had breached levees a dozen times between 1943 and 1986. Finally, after irreparable damage from the 1993 flood, the agency acquired the land for the river's use as active floodplain. A major secondary channel has formed at this site, and in 2000, scientists located pallid sturgeon larvae there—the first such find in the lower Missouri in decades—and a clear sign of hope. The Big Muddy refuge now contains 6,730 hectares and the Fish and Wildlife Service has proposed expanding it to more than 24,280 hectares through purchases from willing sellers. Added to Corps and state acquisition efforts, this expansion would bring the total area of restored floodplain to 12 percent of the total floodplain area in the state of Missouri—within the range of what scientists estimate is necessary to maintain the health of the ecosystem over the long term.[16]

Despite these and other important initiatives, a coordinated, strategic, and sufficiently large-scale plan based on sound science has not yet emerged. Scientists have established that the integrity of the Missouri ecosystem depends on restoring more natural flow patterns, reconnecting the river with its floodplain, and widening the river's channel to allow it to braid and meander. The revision of the Master Water Control Manual that guides the Corps' operation of the six major dams, along with renewed interest in converting riverside properties back to active floodplain, have opened a great window of opportunity to breathe new life into the Missouri. With political leadership, citizen and scientific advocacy, and appropriate funds, perhaps the great river Lewis and Clark explored two centuries ago stands a chance to regain some of its river-ness.

RESTORING THE BRISBANE RIVER OF AUSTRALIA'S GOLD COAST

The early history of human interaction with the Brisbane River is embodied in the lore of the Jagara, an aboriginal tribe known as the watershed's earliest human inhabitants. Little is recorded about their culture and experiences because these were handed down through ceremonies, dance, and stories, rather than the written word. But the Jagara clearly relied on and greatly respected the river. Says Neville Bonner, a modern-day tribal elder, "our priorities were to hunt, gather food and only take what was needed for the day."[17]

Although the priorities of later settlers in the watershed were more demanding of the river, there is today renewed interest in restoring some of the Brisbane's damaged natural features and lost ecological functions. Beloved by visitors and residents alike for its graceful course through Queensland's capital city, the Brisbane River is a major waterway along

Australia's famous Gold Coast. Its watershed extends from the Great Dividing Range to Moreton Bay, a shallow inlet protected from the South Pacific seas by a pair of barrier islands (see Figure 4-3). There, some eight hundred dugong, a large herbivorous marine mammal, graze on tasty seagrasses. Moreton Bay also supports an important commercial and recreational fishery, with the latter alone bringing in more than $225 million a year.[18]

Only 14 percent of the entire land area in the Brisbane River catchment remains uncleared. The upper portions are mostly farm, forest, and grazing lands; the lower portion is urbanized. More than 1 million people live in the catchment, with the greatest concentration downstream in the city of Brisbane, where the population continues to grow quite rapidly.[19] The lowest 80 kilometers of the river are tidal—a stretch where the river's intimate connection to the sea is plainly evident.

Over the last century, the Brisbane has come under increasing regulation for irrigation, water supply, flood control, and electric power generation. A variety of engineering works—including several large dams, many weirs, and numerous small dams—have altered the natural flow patterns of the river and its tributaries. Among the major developments was the completion in 1955 of Somerset Dam on the Stanley River, a major tributary to the Brisbane, and the construction of Wivenhoe Dam on the mainstem. Completed in 1985 for water supply and flood control purposes, Wivenhoe's operation has largely disconnected the middle stretch of the Brisbane from the upper part of the river and watershed. Further downstream from Wivenhoe, Mt. Crosby weir regulates outflows to supply the city of Brisbane and a power station.[20]

With passage in 1994 of a major package of water reforms by the Council of Australian Governments, the states were called upon to recognize ecosystems as legitimate users of rivers and to allocate water specifically to their health and protection (see Chapter 3). In 1996, as part of this effort, the South East Queensland Water Board commissioned a study of the environmental flow needs of the Brisbane River.[21] Carried out by a team of researchers at Griffith University, the study aimed to determine the flow regimes required to protect biodiversity, ecosystem functions, and fisheries productivity in Moreton Bay. The research team also made concrete suggestions for altering existing reservoir and water supply operations so as to meet these environmental flow requirements.[22]

After determining the historic flow pattern of the river prior to dam construction, a key challenge was to assess the ecological impacts associ-

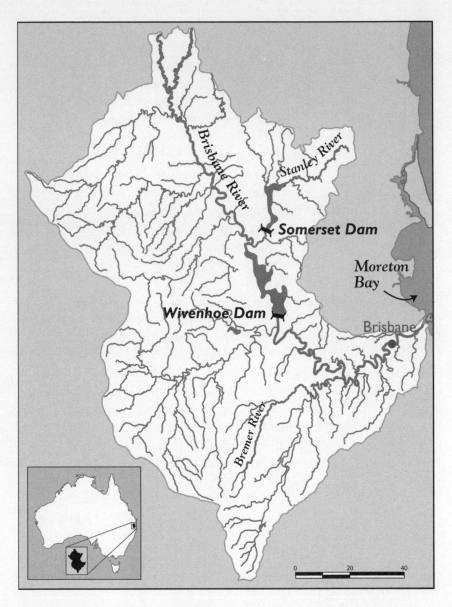

FIGURE 4-3. The Brisbane River Basin.

ated with the operation of Wivenhoe Dam, which strongly regulates flows downstream of it. The team identified many important alterations of the river's flow pattern, channel form, habitat diversity, and other attributes. These included disruption of sediment transport, loss of critical riffle habitat, reduction in the frequency of channel-maintaining floods, and a general flattening of the river's hydrograph due to the artificial raising of low flows and suppression of peak flows. These alterations, in turn, were seriously impacting freshwater life in the river, as well as in Moreton Bay (see Box 4-1).

BOX 4-1 Sampling of Ecological Effects from Alterations of the Brisbane River's Flow Downstream of Wivenhoe Dam

---

Dams and weirs have reduced sediment supply to downstream areas.

Wivenhoe Dam blocks the upstream movement of eels, mullets, Australian bass, and other fish species.

The elevation of low flows has greatly reduced critical riffle habitat and the variety of habitats overall.

Elevated low flows may damage breeding of turtles and lizards, which bury their eggs in the riverbank.

The frequency of flood flows that flush and maintain the channel has dropped.

Changes in streamside vegetation may be interfering with shading and temperature controls, in turn increasing the incidence of algal blooms and lowering dissolved oxygen levels.

Flow alterations and changes in streamside vegetation may reduce the availability of food from terrestrial as well as aquatic sources. Terrestrial insects and plants, for instance, figure importantly in the diets of rainbowfish, smelts, blue-eyes, olive perchlets, purple-spotted gudgeons, and Australian bass.

Loss of invertebrate diversity and numbers may reduce food availability for fish, platypus, and other river species.

Reduction in the frequency and magnitude of high flow events is likely to reduce catches of fish and crabs in Moreton Bay.

Reductions in species diversity may affect food webs, energy flows, and the productivity of higher-level consumers, such as water birds.

SOURCE: Adapted from Arthington et al., 2000.

Based on these findings, the team then developed a set of flow thresholds for meeting specific ecological goals. For example, they determined that flows greater than 30 million cubic meters per day are needed to inundate floodplain and backwater areas and to provide floodplain habitat for fish spawning and feeding. Flows in excess of 40 million cubic meters per day are required to cue Australian bass to migrate downstream and to stimulate recruitment of fish and crabs at the river's mouth and in Moreton Bay. In addition to the volume of flow, the duration, frequency, timing, and other attributes of the flow regime were defined as well. By linking flow thresholds—stair-stepping from 500,000 cubic meters per day up to 100 million cubic meters per day—with the ecosystem and biodiversity functions those flows help sustain, the team was able to come up with a series of environmental flow scenarios. These scenarios were then incorporated into the model used for managing the Brisbane River dam-and-reservoir system in order to determine the effect of providing environmental flows on the system's water supply yield and reliability—the bottom line for water managers.

In some sense the results were sobering. The research team determined, for instance, that re-creating the very low flows (less than 500,000 cubic meters per day) that were part of the natural flow regime is not possible with the current infrastructure and water delivery arrangements. The absence of these very low flows has reduced critical riffle habitat and may have damaged the breeding of turtles and lizards, which bury their eggs in the riverbank. But restoring those low flows is not a simple matter. Large urban demands are met by sending water from Wivenhoe Dam downriver to the Mt. Crosby weir, from which water is supplied to south Brisbane. Reservoir releases less than 500,000 cubic meters per day would not get enough water to Mt. Crosby to meet these water demands. Nonetheless, with a change in water-delivery mechanisms—for instance, using pipes or canals (instead of the river) to deliver water from Wivenhoe to Mt. Crosby—or with an alternative source of supply for Brisbane, it might be possible to restore the natural low flows downstream of Wivenhoe Dam. These options, moreover, would become more feasible if urban conservation and demand reduction measures were implemented simultaneously, because less water would then need to be transported to Brisbane.

Similarly, restoring the very high natural flows needed for habitat diversity and ecosystem purposes would require changes in the use of automobile bridges spanning the river downstream of Wivenhoe Dam. Currently, the law says that bridges cannot be inundated for more than five to seven days. Releasing flows to mimic the river's natural highs would flood bridges for a longer period than this. As with the restoration of low flows, however, there are options to consider. The law could be changed to allow bridges to close for more days at certain times of the year. Engineers could modify the bridges to allow flood flows to pass without disrupting traffic. Officials could also develop alternative traffic routes. With both the restoration of natural low flows and of natural high flows, public officials would need to weigh the costs and benefits of the various alternatives, including the full range of environmental and economic effects. Some of these costs and benefits could be quantified in monetary terms, but some could not.

In general, the research team concluded that the Brisbane's natural flow pattern could partially be restored by letting all inflows in excess of 500,000 cubic meters per day pass through the Wivenhoe reservoir. However, this would reduce the system's water supply yield by 60 percent in 2031 (the chosen reference year for future projections)—almost certainly an unacceptably high reduction. Another option less damaging to the provision of urban water supplies would be to let the first flow event of each month that exceeds 8 million cubic meters per day pass through the dam and reservoir. While this would likely provide some meaningful ecological benefits, it would not mend the harm done to species and ecosystem components from the lack of low flows.

This conflict between managing the Brisbane for human purposes versus meeting the river's own needs for water is one that arises on virtually any regulated river. Always, the task is one of rebalancing management goals to reflect previously neglected values of ecosystem health and biodiversity conservation, as well as new scientific knowledge. Complete restoration of the Brisbane's natural flow regime likely would cause too much disruption to landowners and water users to be publicly acceptable. But if authorities are amenable to developing other water delivery options for urban residents and to redesigning use of bridges or traffic patterns, possibilities open up for restoring some semblance of the natural flow patterns of the Brisbane (see Box 4-2). A core recommendation of the research team is that procedures for storing and releasing floods be changed so as to reduce the dampening effect of current reservoir operations and restore a more natural volume and duration of flood flows. Finally, to assess the benefits of any actions taken, the team recommended that physical and ecological conditions be monitored both prior to and after any changes in reservoir operations.

BOX 4-2   Sampling of the Environmental Flow Recommendations
for the Brisbane River, Queensland, Australia

For August Through November (the natural low-flow season) below Wivenhoe Dam

Maintain flows as low as possible within operational constraints of the system.

Do not permit average daily flow to drop below the natural average daily flow.

Do not allow flows to completely cease.

Maintain daily variability of low flows by allowing naturally occurring freshes
and small spates to pass through the dam. The duration (rates of rise and fall)
of these pass-throughs should mimic natural duration rates for similar volumes.

Distribute monthly flows to approximate the unregulated flow pattern and
the variability of that flow pattern among years.

For December Through July (the natural high-flow season) below Wivenhoe Dam

Allow naturally occurring small and moderate floods to pass along the river.

Maintain the natural frequency of small flood events from December
through March, when upstream movements of fish are likely.

Allow floods to pass through the dam with a natural peak volume and duration rather than an attenuated hydrograph, whenever possible.

Attempt to match the natural variation in daily flows in each month.

Provide flood flows greater than 43,000 megaliters per day between March
and July in order to cue Australian bass to migrate downstream to spawn.

Maintain daily variation in low flows by allowing naturally occurring freshes
and small spates to pass through the dam.

Provide temporal variability in flows by maintaining a reasonable frequency of
periods when flows are kept as low as possible within operational constraints
of the system. This variability is critical for maintaining habitat diversity.

SOURCE: Adapted from Arthington et al., 2000.

Queensland water officials are now using the researchers' findings to
help set environmental flow targets for portions of the Brisbane River,
as well as for the estuary, where emphasis is on sustaining fisheries in
Moreton Bay. In addition, both the ecological assessment and flow
restoration methodologies used in the Brisbane case are now being
applied in other parts of Australia, including river basins in Tasmania
and Western Australia.[23]

GROUNDWATER PUMPING AND
THE FUTURE OF THE SAN PEDRO

A chronicle of Spanish explorer Francisco Vásquez de Coronado's six-teenth-century expedition through Mexico and the American Southwest includes the following words: "I have always noticed, and it is a fact, that often when we have something valuable in our possession and handle it freely, we do not esteem or appreciate it in all its worth, as we would if we could realize how much we would miss it if we were to lose it."[24] Originally written in old Castilian Spanish, these words could not apply more appropriately today to one of the rivers Coronado's team likely followed during its journey—the San Pedro.

Much less well known than the region's bigger rivers, the Rio Grande and the Colorado, the San Pedro is one of the last remaining free-flowing rivers in the American Southwest. In this dry region, the mere existence in the twenty-first century of a significant river absent any dams is remarkable. Yet a major threat to the San Pedro's flow exists nonetheless: it is not a dam or surface diversion, but rather increased extractions of groundwater from the region's aquifer. The San Pedro underscores the importance that groundwater can play in sustaining a river's flow, as well as how uncontrolled groundwater pumping can threaten an entire river ecosystem. On the brighter side, the story of the San Pedro reveals the role that water conservation and demand management can play in protecting river flows, as well as the value of a collaborative partnership in the difficult search for solutions to sustaining a river and a local economy at the same time.

The San Pedro rises in the mountains of Sonora, Mexico, and then flows north across the border into Arizona—uninterrupted by dams all the way to its confluence with the Gila River. From there, its waters flow with the Gila into the lower Colorado River at Yuma, which then flows south back into Sonora, emptying what little water remains into the Gulf of California (see Figure 4-4). A 240-kilometer winding ribbon of green and blue, the San Pedro affords biological riches and ecological wealth far out of proportion to its size. It is one of North America's preeminent habitats for migratory songbirds: up to 4 million songbirds traverse the San Pedro's corridor each year as they journey between their wintering grounds in Central America and Mexico and their breeding grounds in the United States and Canada. Nearly 390 bird species—including 250 neotropical migrants—have been recorded within the San Pedro River valley.[25] More than 15 percent of the world's known population of western yellow-billed cuckoo breeds along the San Pedro corridor.[26] A portion of the ecosystem is designated critical habitat for the southwestern willow flycatcher, which is listed as endangered under the U.S. Endangered Species Act. Not surprisingly, birdwatching is a popular recreational and tourist activity in the area. Nonresident visitors to two key birding sites along the upper San Pedro spent an estimated $10–17 million in the local area in 2001, boosting total economic output by $17–28 million and generating 350–590 jobs.[27]

In addition to the great variety and number of birds, the San Pedro ecosystem is home to some eighty species of mammals—one of the richest assemblages of land mammal species found anywhere in the world—as well as more than forty species of reptiles and amphibians. Along with the southwestern willow flycatcher, two native fish species—the spikedace and the loach minnow—are federally listed as endangered, as are the Huachuca water-umbel and the jaguar.

The San Pedro is the healthiest, most intact river system of significant size remaining along the Mexican-U.S. border. As the Colorado, the Rio Grande, and other north-south rivers have increasingly been altered and degraded, the birds and wildlife that depend on these southwestern river habitats have come to rely more heavily on the San Pedro for survival. Migratory birds depend on the dense canopies of cottonwoods and willows in these river corridors for food, water, and shelter from predators. As these habitats are destroyed, more birds die of starvation and predation, unless they can find other hospitable habitats. In recognition of the San Pedro's unique and increasingly important status, the U.S. Congress in 1988 designated a 69-kilometer stretch of the river and parts of its watershed as the San Pedro Riparian National Conservation Area (SPRNCA). Several years later, in 1996, the Commission for Environmental Cooperation (formed under a side-agreement to the North American Free Trade Agreement signed by Canada, Mexico, and the United States) recognized the SPRNCA as an "Important Bird Area" in North America.

These designations reflect the San Pedro's increasing value, but also its increasing vulnerability. Over the last few decades, rising water demands in the basin have begun to threaten the continued health and productivity of the ecosystem. Flows in the San Pedro are mediated by a vast aquifer beneath the valley floor. The aquifer gets replenished by runoff from the surrounding mountains as well as by flood flows caused by summer thun-

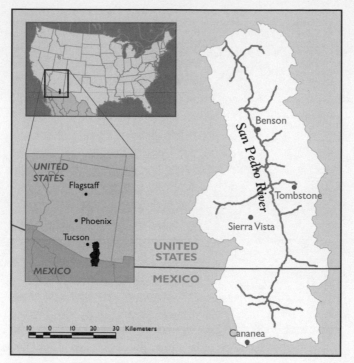

FIGURE 4-4. The San Pedro River Basin.

derstorms that soak through floodplain soils. This natural flow regime, in turn, helps maintain the rich diversity of floodplain species and the conditions needed for young cottonwood and willow trees to sprout and grow in the riparian zone. During the dry period of the year, typically April through June, it is the aquifer's job to feed the river and keep it flowing (Figure 4-5). These base flows are critical to the long-term survival of many of the ecosystem's plants and animals—including the migratory birds that depend on a healthy and productive riparian corridor.

The same groundwater that sustains the San Pedro ecosystem, however, is also the source of irrigation water for farmers and ranchers, of household and commercial water for the region's residents, and the water supply for a military base called Fort Huachuca. In recent decades, as the population and economy expanded rapidly in the area, groundwater pumping increased to satisfy rising demands. Between 1940 and 1997, annual pumping in the upper San Pedro basin climbed twelve-fold[28] (see Figure 4-6). By the late 1990s, pumping from the aquifer exceeded replenishment by nearly 9 million cubic meters per year—an annual deficit pro-

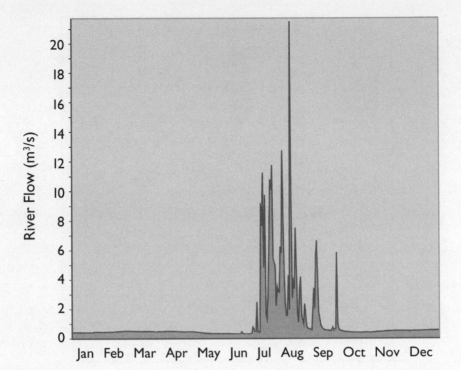

FIGURE 4-5. Typical San Pedro River Hydrograph. Thunderstorms cause the San Pedro River to rise frequently during the summer, but the river remains quite low during the rest of the year. In April through June, low flows in the river are sustained by discharge from the regional aquifer.

jected to grow to 15.5 million cubic meters by 2030 in the absence of remedial actions.[29] Models developed by the Arizona Department of Water Resources and others indicate that even current levels of pumping would diminish the San Pedro's baseflows, with groundwater discharge in one location estimated to fall 30 percent from normal levels.[30]

Because of the river's dependence on groundwater for its base flow, these trends threaten the integrity of the ecosystem in a fundamental way. Without sufficient baseflow, portions of the San Pedro that now flow year-round could begin drying up for parts of the year. This could set off a chain of harmful effects to aquatic wildlife, riparian vegetation, and the many bird species that depend on the riverine habitat. For example, Goodding's willow and Fremont cottonwood—two important canopy trees that provide shelter and shade for migrating birds—require shallow groundwater. As conditions become too dry, they are replaced by other species with deeper roots or greater drought tolerance. These vegetation shifts then sever other ecological connections that ultimately render the river corridor far less suitable for the native species that depend upon it. An interdisciplinary team commissioned by the Commission for Environmental Cooperation to study the San Pedro ecosystem concluded in 1999 that unless serious steps are taken, established water-use trends "will eventually jeopardize this natural asset which enriches the quality of life within this basin and the biodiversity of the entire hemisphere."[31]

The challenge in the San Pedro—as in so many other river basins we have described—is to rebalance the use and management of water so as to meet the ecosystem's needs as well as human needs. One advantage in the case of the San Pedro is that substantial damage to the ecosystem has not yet occurred, and so the challenge is more one of protection than restoration. Avoiding harm, however, will not be easy, and time to do so is short. If groundwater pumping continues at current rates and no mitigative measures are taken, aquifer levels and dry-season baseflows will continue to decline. Under this scenario, it would just be a matter of time before damaging effects on the ecosystem begin to unfold. Moreover, the expanding population in the region will add considerably to human pres-

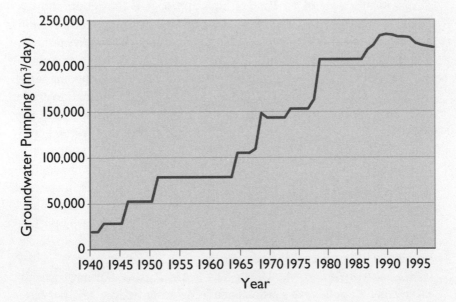

FIGURE 4-6. Estimated Groundwater Pumping in the Upper San Pedro Basin, 1940–1997. (Source: Goode and Maddock 2000.)

sures on the river and aquifer. Sustaining the river's baseflows in the face of these pressures will take substantial efforts to curb per capita water demands and to alter existing water-use patterns.

At the moment, hope lies with the Upper San Pedro Partnership, a consortium of twenty agencies and organizations working together to find solutions that protect both the ecosystems and the people in the watershed. The Partnership is developing comprehensive water conservation plans to ensure that "an adequate long-term groundwater supply is available to meet the reasonable needs of both the area's residents and property owners (current and future) and the SPRNCA."[32] The scientific objectives include maintaining groundwater levels and river flows within an acceptable range of variation in order to sustain the health of the ecosystem overall.

To date, the Partnership has developed a list of fifty-seven measures to consider for implementation. Among these are various options for conserving water, reusing wastewater in lieu of pumping groundwater, artificially recharging the aquifer, and augmenting the available water supply[33] (see Table 4-2). Ultimately, measures will be selected based on how much water they would yield, their unit costs, and their overall technical and political feasibility.[34]

A critical feature of the Partnership's approach is the adoption of an adaptive management framework that allows planning, conservation action, and scientific study to proceed together in an interactive fashion. Rather than a static document, the conservation plan is an evolving strategy that is revised periodically to incorporate the results of ongoing projects, update strategies, and build in the best technical information available. The results from ongoing scientific studies and monitoring inform the design of the conservation plans, helping ensure that research and action build upon each other. Moreover, the Partnership's approach is benefiting from one of the most underappreciated attributes of adaptive management—that it can allow work to get started before all the answers are in. By engaging in a process rather than implementing a single plan, the Partnership can proceed in a learning-while-doing fashion. The ecosystem can begin to improve right away, rather than being held hostage to delays caused by uncertainty.

Several members of the Upper San Pedro Partnership have already taken concrete actions to start balancing the water budget. Analysts have not yet quantified the expected savings from all of these measures, but the savings tallied so far are estimated to total nearly 7.2 million cubic meters

TABLE 4-2 Sampling of Water Conservation and Management Options under Consideration by the Upper San Pedro Partnership

Measure	Estimated Water Yield (thousand cubic meters per year)	Estimated Unit Cost (dollars per thousand cubic meters)
Recharge aquifer with wastewater	4,566	243
Restrict growth	1,357	162
Retire parcels of agricultural land	1,111	47
Eliminate existing golf courses	839	405
Regulate existing landscaping	605	81
Use wastewater for park, golf course irrigation	568	243
Restrict turf area in parks, golf courses	469	405
Institute conservation rate structure	284	162
Detect and repair leaks in water system	235	162

SOURCE: Upper San Pedro Partnership, 2002a.

per year, starting at the end of 2002. These savings alone will cut the area's net groundwater demand by half. Among the big-ticket items are the purchase and retirement by The Nature Conservancy, the U.S. Department of Defense, and the federal Bureau of Land Management of several parcels of irrigated farmland and grazing land. These acquisitions reduced agricultural water pumping by 1.4 million cubic meters in 2001. Fort Huachuca is recharging the aquifer with more than 1.2 million cubic meters of treated effluent each year—much of it strategically placed to mitigate the "cone of depression" formed in the aquifer by heavy pumping.[35] The city of Sierra Vista is also artificially recharging groundwater with treated wastewater, in this case through infiltration basins that allow the wastewater to seep through to the aquifer. Eventually this process is expected to return 4.9 million cubic meters to the aquifer annually.[36]

In addition, both the city and the military base are implementing a wide variety of measures to reduce water consumption. Fort Huachuca has replaced old water-guzzling plumbing fixtures with 350 waterless urinals, 1,500 water-saving showerheads, and other efficient fixtures. Sierra Vista prohibits the use of turf at new government, commercial, and industrial sites, and requires golf courses to use low-water-use turf and to limit turf area to no more than 5 acres per hole.[37] For several years, the city has required the installation of low-flow plumbing fixtures in new construction and more recently has introduced toilet retrofit and rebate programs for homeowners, a leak detection program to reduce waste, and a requirement that all new commercial facilities install water-less urinals.

Perhaps the most impressive attribute of the ongoing work in the Upper San Pedro basin is the collaborative manner in which it is being undertaken. Decisions on the use and management of water fundamentally affect the future quality and way of life in the region, and not surprisingly these questions have been heatedly debated by local residents. The Partnership, however, offers a mechanism to minimize conflict and foster cooperation—a very real institutional challenge in any basin needing to alter water use patterns to accommodate ecosystem needs.

The San Pedro experience also underscores the importance of sound science and good analysis in an adaptive management framework to help all involved understand what is at stake and to make informed choices among a range of options. While "no-regrets" conservation projects are being implemented, scientists will be determining more precisely the timing and volume of water needed by the vegetation lining the San Pedro corridor and by the fish and other aquatic organisms in the river system. They will also be updating the groundwater model and developing other decision-making tools. Through the twenty-member Partnership, there is a collaborative framework and process for all of this information to be brought to bear on the management actions that are taken at any given point.

Time will tell whether this promising process in the Upper San Pedro succeeds. As in so many places, population growth ultimately could undo any short-term progress made in reducing human pressures on this valuable ecosystem. Success, if it is won and lasts, will be evident not only in the bottom line of the region's water budget but in the brilliant colors and beautiful birdsongs of millions of migrants seeking respite in the San Pedro corridor as they fly across the hemisphere.

FLOWS FOR SHRIMP IN THE TROPICAL RIO ESPÍRITU SANTO

Early European visitors to Puerto Rico often referred to the island as "the land of many rivers." It is one of the wettest islands in the Caribbean, boasting some 1,300 streams—seventeen of them large enough to be called rivers. The island covers less than 9,000 square kilometers, but supports some 4 million people, giving it one of the highest population densities in the world. Increasing water demands over the last century have placed great pressure on Puerto Rico's rivers and streams. At least twenty dams were constructed between 1928 and 1956, by which time virtually every stream was in use. Aqueducts delivered water from reservoirs to cities and towns, and an extensive system of hydroelectric dams powered the island with electricity. In subsequent decades, many rivers were channelized to control flooding.[38] In short, this small island experienced in microcosm most of the pressures on and modifications of freshwater ecosystems taking place around the world.

Rivers located near metropolitan San Juan, the island's capital city and home to a third of its population, came under particular pressure. One of them is the Espíritu Santo, which rises in the Luquillo Mountains and flows through the Caribbean National Forest (CNF), located in Puerto Rico's northeastern corner (Figure 4-7). The CNF is the only tropical forest in the U.S. national forest system and it harbors the largest remaining parcel of old growth forest in the Caribbean islands. Valued for recreation, tourism, and ecological research, it was declared a Biosphere Reserve by the United Nations in 1976. Nine rivers, including the Rio Espíritu Santo, drain the forest. At least one dam has been constructed on the main channels of eight of them. Numerous water intakes are located on these rivers, both within the CNF as well as outside the forest boundary. On an average day, half of the river and stream water draining the CNF is captured and used for municipal water supplies.[39]

As a result, the Espíritu Santo has experienced a major change in its flow regime. Since the dams are small, and high flows can simply bypass the water intake structures, the flood events needed to maintain the channel, riparian communities, and other flood-dependent features still occur. But, on an average daily basis, the extensive diversion of water for urban supplies has altered greatly the volume, depth, and flow of water in the Espíritu Santo and other rivers of the CNF. Protecting the ecological health of these rivers in the face of mounting water supply pressures now presents a major challenge to resource managers.[40]

Until recently, most of the information available to those charged with managing tropical aquatic ecosystems came from studies of temperate rivers. Recent scientific work in Puerto Rico and other tropical regions, however, has begun to reveal unique features of these aquatic systems that are critical to efforts to conserve the biodiversity and ecological processes that underpin their overall health.[41]

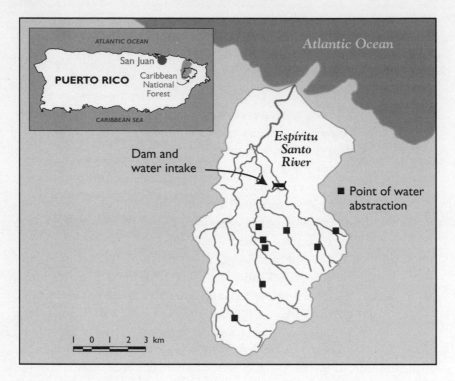

FIGURE 4-7. The Espíritu Santo Basin.

In many tropical stream systems, certain freshwater species—such as fishes and shrimps—control the structure of the aquatic community. In the mountain streams of Puerto Rico, for instance, shrimps are the dominant animal type by weight and they perform critical ecological roles— from processing leaf litter and assimilating fine organic matter to reducing sedimentation and influencing nutrient cycling. At least nine species of freshwater shrimps live in the Espíritu Santo (Figure 4-8). Besides being critical to the health and functioning of the river ecosystem, these shrimps are considered delicacies and are an important source of protein for rural island residents.[42]

All of the shrimps must migrate to complete their life cycle, but their migratory patterns differ substantially from those of the more familiar anadromous salmon species of the northwestern United States, which spend most of their adult lives at sea and migrate upstream to freshwater sites to spawn. Shrimps in the Espíritu Santo and other Puerto Rican rivers have what is called an amphidromous life cycle, in which they spend most of their lives in fresh water. Adult females release their larvae into the river. The larvae then drift with the current downstream to the river's brackish estuary. Reaching this saltier environment appears to be necessary for the larvae to molt into their next life-form. The young shrimp will linger for some seven to sixteen weeks in the estuary as they metamorphose into juveniles. They then migrate back upstream, where they will spend their adult lives.[43]

From detailed studies on the Espíritu Santo, researchers at the University of Georgia's Institute of Ecology and the International Institute of Tropical Forestry in San Juan discovered that large water withdrawals from the river, along with a small dam, were having a serious impact on the shrimps. They found that 42 percent of the shrimp larvae migrating to the sea were killed as they became entrained in the water intake structures; when the river was at very low levels, virtually all of the shrimp larvae were sucked into the intakes. Combining their field data with a thirty-year record of river flows, the research team estimated that long-term shrimp mortality averaged 34–62 percent depending upon how much water was being withdrawn.[44] In addition, for juvenile shrimps heading upstream from the estuary, the Espíritu Santo dam created an artificial

FIGURE 4-8. Freshwater shrimp are key to the healthy functioning of the Rio Espíritu Santo. (Photo by James March.)

predation trap: fish would eat some of the shrimps before they could crawl around the dam structure and continue their journey upstream.[45]

It was close observation of the timing and manner of the shrimps' downstream and upstream migrations that allowed the researchers to make specific recommendations to water managers for improving shrimp survival. It turns out that the shrimp are much more active at night than in the day. Females release their offspring at night, and so larvae drift downstream under cover of darkness—likely an evolutionary adaptation to visual predators. The peak period of larval drift occurs between 1900 and 2200 hours.[46] During these three hours, the rate of larval mortality due to entrainment into the water intakes could exceed one thousand individuals per second, compared to a nighttime average of 233 per second.[47] In addition, juvenile shrimp migrate back upstream at night. If they encounter an obstacle, whether natural or human-made, they crawl around the wetted margin of whatever is blocking them. The research team observed that water flow appeared to be an essential cue for this crawling behavior. When no water is flowing over a dam, the juvenile shrimps do not get a cue to go around the barrier and continue heading upstream; instead, they remain below the dam. If even a small volume of water is flowing over the dam, however, the juveniles will move around it and keep migrating up the river.

Armed with this detailed ecological information, the researchers were able to recommend some specific water management changes that would better balance human uses of the river with the shrimps' flow requirements. They found that if water managers stopped withdrawing water for five evening hours spanning the peak period of larval migration, shrimp deaths due to water-intake entrainment could be reduced to 20 percent or less. Maintenance of some minimum flow over the dam, along with upkeep of a fish-and-shrimp ladder, would also boost shrimp survival.[48] Moreover, these management changes could be made with little detrimental impact on municipal water supplies or other human needs of the river.

For biologist James March of Washington and Jefferson College, "the rewarding aspect of this research is that regulators and water resource managers listened to the message." Some permits for new dams in Puerto Rico now have written into their terms that water cannot be taken during peak periods of larval drift. On the Mameyes River, the only undammed river draining the CNF, a new in-channel withdrawal system is being used to pump water directly out of the unmodified channel, in lieu of conventional dam and intake structures. The in-channel system appears to cause few if any shrimp deaths.[49]

Some important lessons emerge from this work on Puerto Rico's rivers within the CNF. First, it is critical to think not only about the downstream effects of dams and diversions, but about the upstream impacts as well. As University of Georgia ecologist Catherine Pringle notes, "alterations to streams and rivers in their lower reaches can produce effects in upstream reaches on levels from genes to ecosystems."[50] Second, understanding in some detail the life histories of the species living within an altered ecosystem may allow some simple management changes to be identified that better protect those species. And third, to the extent that scientists, resource managers, and water authorities work together, the likelihood increases that ecological findings will be translated into meaningful management reforms.

REDUCING IMPACTS OF FEDERAL DAMS ON KENTUCKY'S GREEN RIVER

A postcard printed in 1910 pictures the steamboat Chaperon docked at a river wharf, carrying hundreds of passengers up the Green River in Kentucky to visit one of the world's great wonders—Mammoth Cave. Women in long white dresses and men sporting straw boater hats hang from the boat's railings and bustle about on the wharf, excitedly anticipating their excursion to the longest cave on the planet. Earlier visitors had enticed them with tales of the "appalling spectacle" of the cave's "nether world," from which nitrous odors and eerie puffs of wind would emanate.[51]

But like most people of their day, these tourists were unaware that the navigation locks and dams which made possible their steamboat's passage up the shallow river were destroying one of the world's treasure chests of aquatic biodiversity. As has been the case with so many of the world's rivers, ecological crises occurring beneath the water's surface have escaped attention for long periods of time—in this case, for nearly a century. Fortunately, the Green River's story illustrates the growing role of science in heightening public awareness of what is being lost from river systems. It also demonstrates how the technical skills and ingenuity of water engineers can be harnessed in restoring rivers.

In 1906, just a few years before the photo of the steamboat Chaperon was taken, the U.S. Army Corps of Engineers had built a structure called

Green River Lock and Dam 6, at a point nearly 300 kilometers upriver from the Green River's confluence with the Ohio River and just downstream of Mammoth Cave (Figure 4-9). Steamboats had been operating on the Ohio since 1811, but only with Lock and Dam 6 in place were the big boats able to reliably make their way over the mussel-laden shoals of the Green to reach the cave. The new lock and dam backed up the river's flow and raised water levels in Mammoth Cave by nearly four meters, jeopardizing one of the world's richest and rarest assemblages of cave animals, as well as many more species in the Green River itself.

Mammoth Cave's origins date back 350 million years, to a time when the continents were all joined in one huge landmass called Pangaea. The warm waters of the Panthalassa Ocean teemed with corals, shellfish, snails, and other tiny organisms whose shells were made of calcium carbonate. As these creatures died, their shells accumulated on the floor of the ancient sea. Over 70 million years, the buildup of shells and muck created enough pressure to weld the mixture into limestone rock. Then, 280 million years ago, the sea level dropped and exposed the limestone, setting the stage for the formation of Mammoth Cave. Movements in the earth's crust caused the limestone to rise, buckle, and twist, forming cracks in the rock. Rainwater began seeping into the cracks, dissolving the limestone and forming tunnels, underground rivers, and huge caverns.

A rich variety of animals colonized the cave's unusual environs, in which the air temperature and humidity differed greatly from the outside world. More than two hundred animal species now occupy the cave. Some of the most extraordinary creatures include forty-two species of troglobites, animals that are adapted exclusively to life in the darkness and cannot live outside of caves. With no light in the cave's depths, many fish and crayfish evolved into eyeless beings with other highly developed sensory organs. With no need for camouflage or protection from the sun, many lost their skin pigment and turned white.

The Green River itself harbors one of the United States' most diverse assemblages of fish and freshwater mussels. More than 150 fish species and more than seventy mussel species have been found in the river. Many of their names sound fanciful, like fictional creatures out of a Dr. Seuss book—fish called the mooneye and the northern hog sucker, and mussels like the purple wartyback, elephant ear, sheepnose, and monkeyface. One does not have to use much imagination to know how the white heelsplitter got its name.

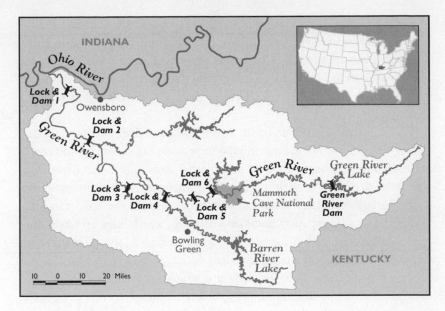

FIGURE 4-9. The Green River Basin.

Today, more than one-third of the fish species in the Green River are considered rare, threatened, or endangered at the state or federal level. Fourteen mussel species have disappeared from the river in recent decades. The Army Corps of Engineers itself attributes the loss of these mussel species to the lock and dam structures it owns and manages on the river.[52] The agency built three more of these structures after it completed Lock and Dam 6. However, Lock and Dam 4, located 250 kilometers upstream from the river mouth, collapsed in 1965 and all navigation above Lock and Dam 3 was discontinued in 1981. In 2001, the Corps proposed removing Lock and Dam 6 to restore ecological conditions in the Green River and Mammoth Cave. In its environmental assessment of the dam removal proposal, the Corps explained that the locks and dams had caused a shift in river habitats from cool, free-flowing conditions to slower-flowing, warm-water conditions, to the great detriment of many of the river's species. Riffle and shoal areas with sand and gravel beds were eliminated by the navigation dams, which replaced them with silty-bottomed artificial pools.

By removing Lock and Dam 6, the Corps can restore 27 kilometers of river habitat. In addition, the endangered Kentucky cave shrimp and innumerable other creatures in Mammoth Cave will likely benefit from the restoration of their habitats.

Removing Lock and Dam 6 is a critically important step in the ecological restoration of the Green River and Mammoth Cave. But in 2000,
at about the same time the Corps was preparing its proposal to remove
Lock and Dam 6, The Nature Conservancy conducted an analysis of its
own. Its study identified a much bigger problem with the river's hydrologic system.

Two hundred kilometers upstream of Lock and Dam 6 sits the Army
Corps' Green River Dam, built in 1969 to provide flood control and recreational benefits. Along with forty-seven other dams, the Green River Dam
was authorized by the national Flood Control Act of 1938 but was only
funded many years later, after a devastating flood hit the region in 1962.
Unlike the small navigation dams downstream, which back up water during low-flow periods but have little impact on floods, the 43-meter-high
Green River Dam completely plugs the river, stopping every drop of water
moving downstream. The Corps' dam operators then release water from
the dam through a concrete pipe 5 meters in diameter. Since 1969, the
Green River's flow has been completely under the control of the Corps.

The Nature Conservancy's analysis in 2000 of the dam's impacts on
Green River flows revealed that the Corps was releasing water from the
reservoir in a way that resembled natural flows during most of the year.
In most months, the Corps simply released water at the same rate at
which it entered the reservoir. But during portions of the spring and
autumn, flows were being altered substantially (Figure 4-10). These
changes in flow resulted from trying to manage the reservoir for both
flood control and recreational benefits. During summer, the reservoir was
maintained at a high level to maximize the surface area of the lake for
fishing and recreational boating. But during the winter, the lake was lowered by more than three meters to create space in the reservoir to store
winter floodwaters.

The transitions between these two reservoir levels were accomplished
during the spring and autumn. In spring, when trying to raise the level of
the reservoir to get ready for summer recreational use, much of the flow
of the Green River was captured in the reservoir, thereby reducing flows
downstream. Conversely, a considerable volume of water needed to be
released from the reservoir during the autumn in order to prepare to capture winter floods. The spring transition took four weeks, and the one in
autumn took ten, with most of the autumn release occurring between
October 16 and December 1. During those sharp transitions, the river
took a beating.

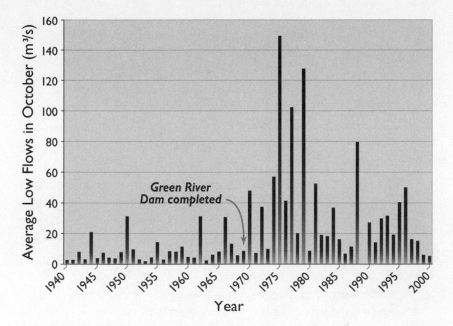

FIGURE 4-10. Alteration of Low Flows in the Green River. Autumn low flows in Kentucky's Green River were altered considerably following construction of the Green River Dam.

The Conservancy scientists believed that the flow alterations associated with the dam were causing serious problems for the Green River's mussels and fish. In particular, they were concerned about the autumn transitions. During a time when the river's flow would naturally have been low, the large dam releases in autumn created a sustained high flow in the river, nearly filling its channel. Figure 4-10 shows that in some years the dam-released October flows were five times higher than any of the pre-dam flows in that month. The Conservancy scientists were concerned that these prolonged, out-of-season high flows were harmful to fish spawning and mussel reproduction occurring during this time, perhaps even flushing some mussels and small fish downstream. They decided to discuss these issues with the Corps. A meeting with the Corps' Louisville District office was set for June 8, 2000.

On the day of the meeting, the Conservancy scientists met early to discuss their game plan. The group's hydrologist counseled the other scientists not to expect too much from the first meeting with the Corps. Their goal would be to gain a better understanding of the Corps' objectives, not to push for desired changes immediately. The scientists expected the Corps' engineers to describe their operating constraints—why the reservoir needed to be maintained at a certain level for recreation, why they needed ample flood control storage, and so forth. The scientists expected the engineers to be unyielding in maintaining the status quo. They were in for a big surprise.

After the scientists opened the meeting with some basic questions about the dam's operations, Bob Biel, the Corps' senior dam engineer in the Louisville District, asked a pointed question: What exactly did the scientists think the Corps was doing wrong? The scientists floundered for a moment, not anticipating such a direct query. Then they carefully began explaining how the river's plants and animals depend upon natural river flow conditions, and why the dam-altered flow patterns were problematic. They brought out their graphs depicting changes in river flows since the dam's construction, and suggested that they would like the Corps to modify their dam operations to alleviate some of the impacts.

Biel responded by explaining what the dam was built to do—control floods and provide for recreational uses. He further explained that marina owners had constructed their facilities in accordance with the expected summer reservoir level, and lowering that level would be very costly and contentious. Then, just as the scientists began to feel their pessimism resurface, Biel jumped out of his chair, went to the chalkboard, and began drawing a picture of how both organizations could get what they wanted.

First, Biel suggested that the winter reservoir level could be raised by a modest amount—about a meter or a little more. By reducing the difference between summer and winter reservoir levels, they would not need to capture so much water in the spring, nor release so much water in the autumn. Then, if they prolonged the transitions between high and low reservoir levels, they could further minimize the impacts. The scientists were elated. The engineers at the Corps expressed considerable interest in seeing whether they could make their dam operations more ecologically compatible, and were thankful that the scientists had taken the time to explain what they wanted. As the meeting came to an end, Biel said he wanted the scientists to use their expertise to design a monitoring program that could tell the Corps whether modifying their dam operations was making a difference for the river.

Bob Biel retired from the Corps six months after that meeting, ending a thirty-two-year career with the agency. He immediately went to work for the Conservancy under a contractual agreement to provide further assistance on modifying dam operations on the Green River, as well as helping the Conservancy to develop a broader relationship with the Corps. The Louisville District prepared various reports necessary to gain approval of the new plan within their agency and conducted public meetings to get input from landowners along the river. The Conservancy scientists collected extensive ecological data on the health of the river, providing them with an excellent baseline from which to compare ecological changes resulting from the revised dam operations. In autumn of 2002, the Corps began implementing the new plan, designed to be the first step in an adaptive management program.

The Corps and the Conservancy did not wait for the results of the Green River experiment before taking their partnership beyond the Louisville District. Both organizations were interested in seeing whether the same collaborative approaches applied at the Green River Dam might help them make improvements at some of the other 630 dams operated by the Corps in the United States. In 2002, the Corps and the Conservancy announced a national partnership called the "Sustainable Rivers Project." General Robert Flowers, Chief of Engineers at the Corps, reported that thirteen dams had been targeted for examination in the partnership, but he hoped it would soon spread to every dam they operate.

SHARING THE WATERS OF SOUTH AFRICA'S SABIE RIVER

With the fall of the apartheid system in the early 1990s, South Africans gained an extraordinary opportunity to reinvent their government and rewrite their laws. The South Africans passed a National Water Act in 1998 that has become a bellwether for water management in the twenty-first century, as we discussed in Chapter 3. But the toughest challenges still lie ahead, as the act's visionary language begins to be translated into day-to-day water management. As Kevin Rogers, a river ecologist and professor at the University of the Witwatersrand in Johannesburg, has put it: "Through our management of water we will learn what democracy is going to mean for South Africa."

As implied by Rogers' words, implementing the new water act is a social experiment with great consequences—ones that may even ripple far beyond the nation's borders. South African river managers are grap-

pling with a fundamental challenge confronting societies in many parts of
the world: there is simply not enough water to fully meet all human and
ecosystem needs. As the South Africans search for ways to solve this seem-
ingly intractable problem in a fair, just, and ecologically sustainable way,
the world is watching closely.

The Sabie River basin is in many ways a microcosm of water challenges in the developing world. The Sabie flows easterly through the
world-renowned Kruger National Park in South Africa before joining
the Incomati River in Mozambique, eventually emptying into the
Indian Ocean (see Figure 4-11). The river's importance as wildlife habitat is quite evident to park tourists as they drive over the long bridge
spanning the Sabie's wide, sandy channel. Crocodiles, hippos, hyenas,
buffalo, elephants, giraffes, baboons, marabou storks, and many other
animals can easily be seen from the bridge. The river system also supports
forty-five species of fish and a rich variety of riparian plant communities. This biodiversity and the waters of the river have been important
to tribal peoples such as the Ndebele and Shangaan clans for hundreds
of years.

Today, however, rapidly changing patterns of land and water use in the
Sabie basin upstream of Kruger park threaten the river's health, traditional river uses, and Kruger's spectacular biodiversity. Eucalyptus and
pine trees from Australia have been planted in industrial-scale forestry
operations. The trees consume far more water than the native grasslands
they replaced, causing the Sabie's average flows to drop by more than 15
percent.[53] Vast areas along the upper river have been converted into
banana and mango farms. Resort developers are building new hotels and
condominiums attractive to tourists. Resettlement villages are being
established to provide millet and maize farming areas for previously dis-
advantaged blacks moving back into their native homelands. Seven dams
have already been built on the Sabie's tributaries, and six others have been
proposed in the Sabie basin to provide domestic and irrigation water supplies for the growing population.

These changing water needs present some very difficult challenges
for residents and water managers in the Sabie basin. In 1985, human
water uses were consuming about 28 percent of the natural flow in the
basin. This water consumption was split evenly between citrus farms
and forestry plantations. By 2010, water consumption is expected to
grow to more than half of the basin's natural flow, with most of the
increase associated with population growth in the resettlement areas

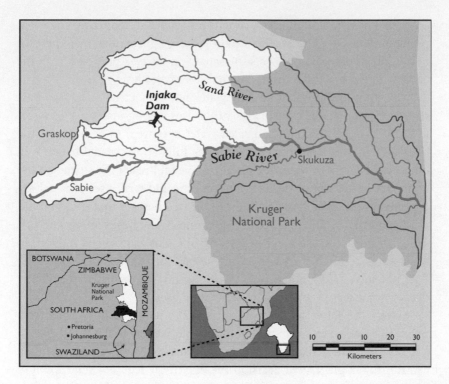

FIGURE 4-11. The Sabie River Basin.

and a shift in these areas from subsistence to small-scale commercial farming.[54] As the waters of the Sabie are further depleted, the growing needs and desires of the resettlement villages are increasingly coming into conflict with historic uses of water for citrus growing and forestry, and all of these human uses pose a growing danger to the health of the river ecosystem.

The National Water Act provides a powerful framework to guide water decision-making in the Sabie, but it does not solve all of the social problems posed by the limits of water availability. As we discussed in Chapter 3, the act calls for a two-part reserve. The first part reserves water to meet basic human needs—in other words, to provide a minimum amount of water to all South Africans for drinking, bathing, and cooking. In the 2010 water use projections for the Sabie, this would amount to only about 7 percent of the water available. The second part of the reserve is intended to protect the health of the river ecosystem and associated ecosystem services. An ecological flow assessment completed in 1997 concluded that protecting the Sabie ecosystem would require approximately 44 percent of the Sabie's natural flow.[55] In sum, satisfying the two-part reserve in the Sabie will require a little more than half the river's flow.

According to the water act, any water not protected in the two-part reserve may be made available for other uses through issuance of water licenses. If all existing and projected water uses were to be licensed, the river's water would be very close to being fully appropriated by 2010. In other words, human water uses in the Sabie will reach the sustainability boundary in less than a decade, yet domestic and farm uses of water are expected to continue growing in the Sabie well beyond that time. Should this future growth be curtailed abruptly once water limits are reached, or should historic uses of water in forestry or citrus growing be reduced to accommodate further growth in the resettlement areas? The water act does not solve these thorny social issues of how to prioritize the allocation of nonreserve water among competing uses.

Instead, the water act leaves these issues to new "catchment management agencies" to be composed of representatives of local interest groups and relevant national and provincial government agencies.[56] Rather than centralizing management decision-making in the federal Department of Water Affairs and Forestry (DWAF), the intent is to enable water governance to be shaped locally. The DWAF will provide funding and administrative support to help catalyze and sustain the local management authorities, but the composition and functionality of each authority will develop organically to address the particular circumstances and challenges in each river basin.

While it is impossible to predict what forms the new management agencies may assume, certain aspects of their functioning are becoming quite clear in the Sabie. In these rapidly changing physical and human landscapes, society's values and priorities for water management will certainly change as well. Thus, the catchment agencies will need to continually foster public participation in their decision-making. And the better this public dialogue is informed by ecological science, the greater will be the chances of sustaining healthy rivers. Hence, the catchment management agencies will need to build strong partnerships with the scientific community.

Kevin Rogers and others have suggested that public participation is particularly important in shaping a vision for the desired future condition of the river system.[57] In the Sabie, a nascent vision has taken form through a series of workshops in which the basin's residents, park managers, and scientists described their desire to meet their needs for water while not destroying the natural ecosystems they depend upon. The group coalesced around this vision for the Sabie catchment:

We are proud custodians of our rivers.
They sustain our economy and heritage.
We protect and manage them so that they can continuously bring benefits equitably to our people, the nation, and our neighbours.

Rogers calls this consensus approach "future building." Working with Rogers and other scientists, a diverse group of stakeholders in the Sabie River basin are making great initial strides toward building a vision for their future. Reflecting on this progress, Rogers says, "When I saw the citrus farmers and hotel developers sitting down to talk with tribal sangomas (shamans), I knew we were on to something."

Rogers says that this exercise of forming a shared vision can be time-consuming and difficult at times, but the outcome is worth every minute expended. He says that it is an essential first step in a coevolution of values and preferences, a process in which participants begin to walk away from their polarized, competitive positions and begin to understand each other's needs and desires—a shift of perspective from "me" to "us."

After reaching consensus on a shared vision, natural resource managers, scientists, and stakeholders were able to translate their vision statement into more detailed management objectives and targets.[58] These three linked components—vision, objectives, and management targets—are intended to provide a clear and durable road map for water management. The vision statement embodies the general values that stakeholders hold in common. The management objectives provide greater definition of the vision, providing managers, political leaders, and other decision-makers with a better sense of the intended outcomes of management activities (see Box 4-3). The management targets are numerical expressions of the desired condition for a suite of key ecosystem indicators, including desired river flows, thereby giving water managers something specific to shoot for (Table 4-3). The assumption is that by maintaining the ecosystem indicators within their targeted ranges, the objectives and overall vision will be realized. By monitoring the ecosystem indicators, scientists are able to tell managers whether their management strategies are succeeding.

BOX 4-3 Water Management Objectives Developed for the
Sabie River Basin, South Africa

Holistic and Integrated

A shared resource requires a common vision and coordinated action.

Cooperative Governance

Working partnerships must be created both vertically and horizontally.

Equity

There should be equity in access to the resource, and in the distribution of costs and benefits of using the resource.

Revenue should be generated from all who benefit from management of the resource (the river ecosystem) and not just water users.

Efficiency

Management and administration processes should work toward speedy and efficient service delivery.

Empowering Civil Society

Civil society should be informed and active.

The importance of a bottom-up approach, and grassroots sourcing of issues, must be recognized.

A sense of shared ownership and responsibility must be created.

Adaptive

Policies and process should be able to improve with experience.

The catchment management agency and all levels of stakeholder representation should be transparent, accountable, and open to challenge.

SOURCE: Personal communication with Kevin Rogers, University of the Witwatersrand, Johannesburg, South Africa.

The development of quantitative management targets has benefited greatly from scientific knowledge generated through the Kruger National Park Rivers Research Programme, initiated in 1989. This research program was formed largely in response to growing concern for the potential impacts of development on the health of the park's rivers, as well as increasing political pressure from neighboring Mozambique to ensure that the rivers would continue to support water needs downstream of the international boundary.

The inherent complexities of the Sabie River ecosystem present daunting challenges for scientists. The river flows through a complicated geologic setting, and as the river intersects different rock types it assumes fundamentally different forms. In some places it flows as a single channel through a broad, sandy floodplain. When it encounters highly resistant bedrock outcrops, it diffuses into many different channels, looking like

TABLE 4-3 Selected Ecosystem Indicators Used in Managing River Ecosystems Within Kruger National Park in South Africa

Ecosystem Indicator	Thresholds of Possible Concern (Management Targets)
River Flow: Baseflow in Sabie River during drought	When flow drops below 2.0–4.0 cubic meters per second, depending upon month
River Flow: Higher flows in Sabie River during drought	When flow drops below 5.0–8.0 cubic meters per second, depending upon month
River Channel: Channel types	When the area of sediment bars drops below 20 percent of the total river area, or when the area of pools drops below 15 percent or more of total area
Vegetation: Population structure of key species	When any riparian species fails to reproduce within any ten-year period
Fishes: Distribution of individual species	When the range of any individual species drops by 50 percent
Aquatic Insects: Species abundance	When population losses for any species exceed 50 percent
Birds: Habitat types	When any type is no longer represented (reed beds, mudflats, etc.)
Water Temperature	Any temperature outside a range of 8–25 degrees Celsius

SOURCE: Rogers and Bestbier, 1997.

water cascading over a cheese grater. Five distinctively different channel types have been identified along the Sabie.[59]

Each of the channel types, in turn, offers a heterogeneous mosaic of habitats—sandy areas, rocky outcrops, river pools, or rapids—that determine which plants and animals will be found there. For example, a reed called *Phragmites mauritianus* can be found adjacent to the sandy channels. Where the river is flowing through exposed bedrock, an ever-green tree called *Breonadia salicina* can be found clinging tenaciously to the rock. Similarly, the forty-five fish species in the Sabie basin are distributed according to the different aquatic habitats found in the various channel types. Some prefer fast-flowing water in bedrock rapids, some prefer deep pools with sandy bottoms, and others hang out in shallow areas along the river's edge or in backwater areas shaded by overhanging vegetation.

However, as discussed in Chapter 2, aquatic and riparian habitats can change radically as water levels rise and fall, and the rivers of South Africa are among the most variable in the world. During the dry season, the Sabie's baseflow averages 3–5 cubic meters per second, rising to 15–20 cubic meters per second during the wet season. Annual floods average 289 cubic meters per second, a ten- to hundred-fold increase over baseflow conditions. Mobile creatures like fish move around in the river to utilize a variety of areas to feed or spawn that become available as the river rises and falls. The overall mixture of plants and animals found in each channel type do not change a great deal from year to year as normal floods come and go. But every once in a while, large floods rearrange the physical template of the river system.

Understanding the diversity and temporal variability of a river ecosystem's habitats is essential in developing an ecological flow prescription adequate to protect its long-term health. The scientists working in the Kruger National Park Rivers Research Programme have learned a great deal from observing changes in the river since 1989. By watching how the river's plants and animals fare during droughts or following floods, they have learned what certain species can tolerate, and what they cannot. They have used their interdisciplinary expertise—spanning hydrology, geomorphology, fish biology, plant ecology, wildlife biology, and much more—to develop conceptual models of the Sabie's ecological workings. They have generated computer simulations to help them identify thresholds of change at which the natural ecosystem could start to come apart.

This knowledge has enabled them to specify management targets for river flows, channel changes, and populations of plants or animals that reflect the limits of acceptable change. As they gained these insights, they met with park managers and water resource planners to share what they were learning.

The Sabie is particularly vulnerable to development, they explained, because the majority of the river's water is generated in one part of the basin, and most of the sediment comes from other sub-basins. Most of the water (71 percent) is produced in the upper Sabie subbasin.[60] However, most of the sediment (70 percent) is delivered by the Sand River. This means that as river flows in the upper basin are reduced by human uses, the river will become unable to move all of the sediment being delivered to the middle reaches of the Sabie by the Sand. As a result, the lower Sabie is expected to gradually fill with sediment, eventually burying areas now dominated by exposed bedrock that support plants like *Breonadia*. These sand-filled areas would then be colonized by reeds, resulting in an overall loss of plant diversity in the river basin. The water reductions would impact the fish community as well, by giving competitive advantage to cichlids that proliferate during low water, slow-velocity periods and do not require floods for spawning.[61]

This scientific knowledge came into play during the design of the Injaka Dam, which was completed in 2001. Scientists warned that one of the options considered—called the "maximum use scenario"—would cause severe ecological impacts by substantially curtailing floods and causing the river to dry in places during droughts (Figure 4-12). They proposed an alternative "limited use scenario" that would reduce baseflows by 23 percent and peak flows by 16 percent, thereby staying within the recommended management targets.[62]

The Injaka Dam project highlights the critical importance of engaging scientists in the water development process to ensure that the ecological reserves determined under the National Water Act are duly considered and properly implemented. The scientists working in the Sabie River ecosystem do not expect their models to be perfectly right, nor do they want the numerical management targets they have set to be immutable. In fact, they refer to these management targets as "thresholds of possible concern," inferring that these targets should be revisited as scientific knowledge advances, and adjusted as needed to ensure that the management objectives and vision are being attained.

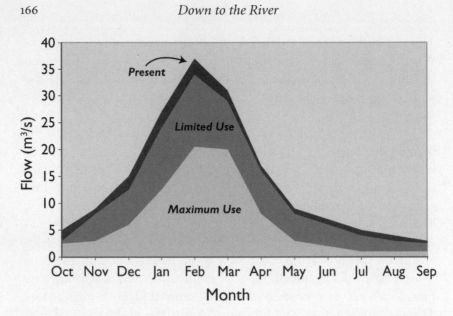

FIGURE 4-12. Potential Impacts of the Injaka Dam. The Injaka Dam could have considerable impact on Sabie River flows if the dam is managed for maximum water use. These impacts would be reduced greatly under a limited-use scenario. (Adapted from O'Keeffe et al. 1996.)

Only time will tell whether the water managers, scientists, and water users of the Sabie basin will be able to form a durable partnership, with mutual and enduring commitments to the visionary ideals of a water act that calls for meeting human needs while sustaining healthy rivers. If they succeed, they may find their model replicated in many other parts of the world.

CHAPTER FIVE

⌒

Building Blocks for
Better River Governance

In early May 2002, a front-page article in the *New York Times* opened with these provocative, full-of-promise words: "Scientists know what is ailing the great rivers of America. They also know how to cure it."[1]

A bit of hyperbole, perhaps. But in this piece focused on the Missouri River, journalist Blaine Harden reported on the scientific consensus that restoring some measure of a river's natural flow pattern can revitalize river health and resuscitate endangered fish and wildlife even in a heavily dammed and mechanized river like the Missouri. Reading on, however, the promise embedded in Harden's opening lines quickly fades as he describes how politics, not sound science, is likely to determine how the Missouri flows in the future.

To anyone familiar with the long history of water in the United States and much of the world, this outcome would hardly be surprising. An examination of any persistent conflict over water allocation or use almost always turns up two common ingredients: first, not everyone affected by the decision in question has had a say in making it; and second, the decision reflects the politics of power and influence rather than the broader public good.

Fundamentally, such decision-making represents a deep failure of governance to which the health of rivers and the diverse communities of people and species that rely on them are held hostage. The 3 million people in the "disaster zone" of Central Asia's Aral Sea basin are victims, like the sea itself, of decisions made by Moscow central planners into which they had no input and which did not properly account for how diversions upstream would affect their homes and livelihoods downstream. The destruction of indigenous fisheries following the construction of Pak Mun Dam on Thailand's Mun River spurred years of protest by villagers who relied on those fisheries for subsistence, but whose rights and needs were not adequately taken into account before the dam was built. And in the Colorado River Delta of northern Mexico, the native Cocopa Indian communities, which thrived in the region for many centuries, are now on the verge of disappearing. Neither their interests, nor those of the fish, birds, and wildlife that lived there with them, were adequately taken into account when the Colorado's flow was divided up decades ago among seven U.S. states and Mexico. In fact, more water was promised to the eight parties than the river usually carries, leaving the delta and its inhabitants bereft of water.

Governance is more than the sum of a community's policies and laws. It is about the process of getting to those policies and laws, including how decisions are made, who makes and enforces them, and what values and interests are reflected in them. Adding seats around the table where river decisions are made is a prerequisite to the equitable and sustainable use of rivers. But in most countries, the cards are stacked heavily against an inclusive and more balanced process. Patterns of governance for the most part still reflect the utilitarian mind-set of the twentieth century, which focused on the engineering challenges of bringing rivers under control for society's economic advancement. Whether in China, Egypt, India, or the United States, these decisions have largely been left to elite cadres of engineers with the technical know-how to get the job done. Decisions have flowed from the top down, with occasional provision for the broader public to comment on a particular project before it is built. In the worst cases, any kind of dissent is simply not tolerated. One Egyptian government official drew on a verse from Omar Khayyám's *Rubáiyât* to convey the degree to which those who questioned the wisdom of the Aswan High Dam fell into line behind President Gamal Abdel Nasser's decision: "When the King says it is midnight at noon, the wise man says behold the moon."[2]

Many countries governed in a less than democratic fashion continue quite obviously in the historic tradition of centralized and top-down decision-making. China's Three Gorges Dam and south–north river transfer projects, Libya's Great Man-Made River Project, and Egypt's Toshka project come readily to mind. Although less blatantly so, this hydraulic tradition is alive and well in the United States, too, largely in the form of powerful water bureaucracies such as the U.S. Army Corps of Engineers and the Bureau of Reclamation. University of Kansas historian Donald Worster, author of *Rivers of Empire*, has noted how difficult it will be for the western United States to free itself of these controlling influences: "For some time to come, the region will likely be ruled over by concentrated power and hierarchy based on the command of scarce water."[3]

These old styles of water governance, however, may be in for a shakeup. Much of the world is waking up to the problems of ecological decline, on the one hand, and to the promise of an economy more just and harmonized with its environment, on the other. From the local level to the global, groups of people are pioneering new ways of making better decisions about rivers and how they are managed. At the heart of these efforts is the simple idea that people affected by a major decision should have a voice in making it, and that the process of decision-making should be open, inclusive, and transparent. In the following sections, we describe some new initiatives and opportunities for improved river governance, which, if scaled up, could greatly improve prospects for protecting and restoring river health.

CAPTURING THE VALUE OF
ECOSYSTEM SERVICES

From this point forward, good river governance will require a way to incorporate ecological services in decisions about water allocation and management. As noted in earlier chapters, the failure to take stock of these benefits has resulted in more alteration of river flows than is socially optimal. Putting ecosystem services into the water management equation will tip the balance scale toward greater preservation of natural flows. The question is how to make those eco-service values tangible and visible, both to those who protect them and to those who benefit from them.

It bears repeating that many traditional cultures understood the value and importance of nature's workings to their well-being, and incorporated into their lives and societal rules the view that humans and nature are deeply interconnected. In the *dina* system of Mali, for example, different ethnic groups specialized in different livelihood activities in a way that made complementary use of the natural flood cycle within the Niger River Delta. One group fished in shallow waters, another in deeper waters. The Fulani specialized in animal herding, while others focused on particular crop cultivation techniques. The dina system included detailed rules of access for each of the productive components of the ecosystem. For instance, an opening date was specified for each major fishery, and rules would be established as to what fishing techniques could be used. A highly integrated approach to optimizing the myriad goods and services provided by the river-floodplain ecosystem, this traditional governance structure was formalized legally in the nineteenth century with the codification of different fishing, farming, and grazing territories and their allocation to different ethnic groups.[4]

For the modern world, several centuries of advancing our technological control over rivers have obscured our continued dependence on the natural services that healthy river systems provide. We have been so preoccupied with putting rivers to economic use—for hydropower, flood control, navigation, water supply, and irrigation—that we have paid little attention to the ecosystem values lost in the process. But as the supply of ecosystem services rapidly dwindles, their importance and value are gaining new recognition. The challenge lies in integrating this new knowledge into decisions about how rivers and watersheds are used and managed.

As a first step, most countries would benefit from an inventory of their natural freshwater assets, along with an assessment of the stream of ecosystem services those assets are producing. This work could be organized around major watersheds and be carried out by an interdisciplinary panel of scientists, resource managers, economists, lawyers, farmers, business representatives, conservationists, and others.[5] These inventories would fill critical information gaps and thereby enable society to make wiser choices about river and watershed management. They could build upon the ongoing Millennium Ecosystem Assessment, which aims to generate the first global appraisal of the condition of natural capital and ecosystem services.

Compared with other forms of capital, natural assets have the disadvantage of being much harder to measure, monitor, and value. Society still has much to learn about how natural capital works—how ecosystems do the work they do. Nevertheless, pioneering efforts around the world to value, protect, and in some cases actively invest in natural capital are demonstrating that ecosystem conservation can make economic sense. Scientists, economists, and policy analysts, often working together, have shown that preserving or restoring some degree of the natural flows in river systems and the natural functions of watersheds can provide greater net benefits to society than investing in the more conventional technological or development approach to water management. These results, moreover, have come from such diverse locations as Quito, Ecuador; the Catskills watershed of New York; the Western Cape of South Africa; and the floodplains of western Africa.

In a number of large river systems in Africa, people subsist along the river valley by practicing a mix of fishing, flood-recession farming, and animal grazing—all activities that depend on the river's natural flood. One such river system is the Senegal, which is shared by the three west African nations of Mali, Mauritania, and Senegal. In typical twentieth-century style, water planners and engineers decided to construct a large dam (called the Manantali) on the Bafing River, a major tributary to the Senegal, in order to expand irrigation, generate hydropower, and extend barge transportation on the river. They made no serious accounting, however, of the economic value of the highly productive flood-based system that downstream river valley inhabitants depended upon for their livelihoods.

To fill this gap, an interdisciplinary team of researchers from the Institute for Development Anthropology (IDA) in Binghamton, New York, undertook just such an assessment. First, they showed that the Manantali Dam would store enough water for both hydropower generation and for the release of a controlled flood to sustain the traditional subsistence uses of the river and floodplain. They also showed that when all the production activities were properly taken into account, the traditional flood-based practices yielded more benefits than were anticipated from the conventional irrigation option. According to IDA director Michael Horowitz, "the net returns per unit land from the total array of traditional production—flood-recession farming, herding, and fishing—actually exceed those from irrigation, without taking into account the latter's huge start-up and recurrent operating and maintenance costs."[6]

Based on this more complete analysis, a decision to operate the dam so as to provide an annual human-controlled flood would seem to be the clear winner—and, in fact, the Senegalese government endorsed the strategy. But the controlled flood option has not adequately been implemented, having fallen victim to power politics and financial interests in the three-nation river basin and its governing commission. Dam managers have provided only a meager two-week flood, and the small area of floodplain benefiting from it will likely shrink further now that hydropower production at the dam has finally begun and will usurp some of the water used to produce the flood. All in all, between five hundred thousand and eight hundred thousand people have lost access to the productive floodplains that had provided all or part of their livelihood.[7]

Meanwhile, the billion dollar Manantali Dam has not come close to delivering the benefits expected from it. Completed in 1987, it took some fourteen years to begin generating any hydropower. Construction of the irrigation network proved so expensive (some $25,000–40,000 per hectare) that less than 30 percent of the planned area has been readied for irrigation so far. Moreover, many valley farmers could not afford the seeds, chemicals, and other inputs needed for irrigated production, and mounting debts have forced some to sell off their livestock. In 1993, Germany's minister for development assistance reportedly called Manantali an "act of economic and environmental nonsense."[8] And an official appraisal report by the African Development Bank found that the absence or low level of an annual flood has "seriously disturbed the basin's ecosystems and disorganized its traditional economic activities, as a result of which the region became the poorest in all three countries."[9]

Clearly, had decision-makers heeded the researchers' findings on the benefits of the natural flood regime this situation could have been avoided, or at least greatly ameliorated. It is possible that a decision to provide an artificial flood sufficient to sustain the ecosystems and traditional livelihoods in the Senegal valley could still be forthcoming. But on economic and social grounds, the case of the Manantali Dam stands as an example of the value of preserving and investing in natural capital and its stream of goods and services.

The types of trade-offs highlighted by the Manantali Dam are common to many of the river valleys of Africa and Asia where people's livelihoods are keyed so closely to the ebb and flow of a river. As described in Chapter 1, researchers have made similar assessments for the Hadejia and Jama'are rivers of northern Nigeria and found that the net economic benefits provided by use of the natural floodplain exceeded those of proposed irrigation projects by more than sixty-fold. As in the Senegal valley, wetlands along the Nigerian rivers have shrunk greatly due to a combination of recurrent drought, dam construction, and irrigation expansion.[10] And yet, because of increased understanding of ecosystem services, more weight is now being placed on natural flood-based production systems than would have been the case even a decade ago. Indeed, the World Bank's 2002 draft water sector strategy identifies the Hadejia-Jama'are basin as an area ripe for water management reforms because of "the conjuncture of irrigation, urban water supply, and ecological flows for floodplain agriculture."[11]

In a remarkable turn of events, officials in Thailand opened the gates of Pak Mun Dam in 2001 in response to years of protest by local villagers who had seen their livelihoods decimated along with the Mun River's fisheries and floodplain productivity. The government agreed to open the dam gates for one year; then, based upon the results of commissioned studies, it would decide whether the gates should remain open permanently. Although the verdict is not yet in, the villagers have clearly benefited from a return to the more natural flow regime. They have greater food security, since they can again catch fish and cultivate crops along the floodplain. Local tourism has apparently benefited, and the villagers are again using the rapids and riverbanks for the Thai New Year festival and other ceremonies. Regional environmental groups report that 152 species of fish have returned to the Mun River, many of them migratory varieties that travel from the Mekong River to the Mun to feed and spawn.[12]

In the large river-floodplain systems of Europe and the United States, people are much less directly dependent on the natural flood cycle for their means of survival. But in these regions, the economic value of natural flood mitigation has been gaining greater recognition as well. During the 1990s, for example, the U.S. government initiated pilot projects and allocated several hundred million dollars for the removal of more than twenty thousand flood control structures. With a 65-35 federal-state cost-sharing formula, the program generated interest among more than one hundred communities in reactivating the work of natural floodplains. Activities can include buying floodplain properties, tearing down dikes, helping property owners to relocate, and enabling the river to reconnect with its floodplain.[13] The European Community has established a project called the "Wise Use of Floodplains"—a response both to the catastrophic damage caused by flooding in recent years, as well as to the 2000 Water Framework Directive, which places ecological health at the core of European water policy and management (see Chapter 3). The floodplain project involves six pilot case studies in England, France, Ireland, and Scotland, and is aimed at showing how the wiser use of river floodplains can contribute to sustainable water management.[14]

Although ecosystem services are clearly getting wider recognition, two barriers often stand in the way of incorporating them into river management decisions. First, rarely have their economic values been estimated for the location in question. Second, even if those values are known, there is usually no market, pricing, or funding mechanism to compensate the eco-service providers.

A common way of estimating the value of ecosystem services is by their "replacement cost"—that is, what it would cost to replace the naturally provided service with a technological or human-engineered solution. For some of nature's services, such estimates are readily at hand. For example, civil and environmental engineers are trained to calculate the cost of treating pollutant loads in treatment plants in order to achieve high-quality drinking water. If a healthy watershed is providing this clean water for free, its water purification value is equal to the cost of building and operating the treatment plant that would be needed if the watershed stopped functioning properly. The value of other services—such as the provision of fish and wildlife habitat or the delivery of freshwater flow to productive estuaries—may be more difficult to estimate and require other methods.[15]

Investing in nature's way of providing a service—whether it be flood control, water purification, or fish production—is often far less expensive than a technological approach. But if the providers do not benefit economically from sustaining the service, they will in all likelihood stop providing it. Fortunately, some new models for investing in natural assets and for linking the beneficiaries of ecosystem services with the providers are now emerging. To date, most of these deal with water supply and water purification services and primarily involve land-use decisions in watersheds. Since healthy watersheds can help protect river flows, and because these models may be applicable to the protection of other ecosystem services, they are worth a look.

New York City derives most of its drinking water from reservoirs in the Catskill Mountains in the central and northern part of the state. As this region has become more developed, the quality of the city's drinking water has begun to deteriorate. Faced with the prospect of having to build a $6–8 billion filtration plant that would require an additional $300 million a year to operate, the city has decided instead to invest on the order of $1.5 billion to restore and protect the watershed that had previously kept its water pure enough to drink. Using proceeds from an environmental bond issue, the city bought land in and around the watershed, improved local sewage treatment, and paid farmers $250 to $370 per hectare to forgo growing crops or grazing cattle right next to streams. As a result of these measures, farmers' incomes increased in some areas, and many watershed communities experienced improvements in their quality of life—significant side-benefits to investing in natural assets rather than technological ones. As the city's environmental commissioner remarked at the time of the decision: "All filtration does is solve a problem. Preventing the problem, through watershed protection, is faster, cheaper, and has lots of other benefits."[16]

Quito, the capital city of Ecuador, is working on a similar strategy to protect the watersheds that supply its drinking water. Parts of the watershed are situated in protected areas, including the Cayamabe-Coca Ecological Reserve and the Condor Biosphere Reserve, but overall the watershed lacks adequate protection from livestock grazing, agricultural practices, and other activities that can degrade the quality of water used by Quito and surrounding communities. In response, a coalition of government agencies, conservation organizations, and water users has created a watershed protection fund that is capitalized primarily through water-user fees. Initially, the Quito Municipal Sewerage and Water Agency is contributing to the fund 1 percent of its water sales, for an expected initial total of $305,000. The Quito Electric Utility, recognizing that it too benefits from reduced erosion and other improvements in the watershed, agreed to make an annual payment of $45,000 into the watershed fund. Because funding for watershed protection work comes from the interest-income generated by the fund, this level of capitalization is far from sufficient. But it is a start—and, most importantly, water users are beginning to pay for the important water quality services that the watershed is providing.[17]

A final example comes from the Western Cape of South Africa, where a rather unusual approach to watershed management is proving to be a cost-effective way to simultaneously restore streamflows, increase water supplies, and conserve biodiversity. The native *fynbos* (shrubland) watersheds of this region are part of the Cape Floristic Kingdom, the planet's richest area of endemic plant diversity and one of only six biogeographic plant kingdoms in the world. Besides its amazing variety of plants, the fynbos is very water-thrifty: it is well adapted to drought, and its low biomass requires relatively little water. With the invasion of Australian acacias and other nonnative trees and plants that consume considerably more water than the fynbos, runoff from the catchments has decreased markedly. These alien invaders thus pose a threat not only to the unparalleled plant diversity of the region, but also to freshwater ecosystems and the sustainability of the water supply.

As in the New York City situation, researchers assessed the ecosystem services provided by the fynbos watersheds with a broad landscape-level lens and found that it made sense on economic grounds alone for South Africa to invest in protecting the natural capital of these watersheds.[18] They analyzed the delivery of water supplies—a critical ecosystem service provided by the Western Cape watersheds—with and without the removal of the alien vegetation. They found that the catchment with the management of alien plants yielded nearly 30 percent more water than an equivalent-sized catchment without the removal of alien invaders. In addition, the unit cost of the water supplied by the managed watershed was 14 percent less than that of the unmanaged watershed—a clear economic endorsement for a program of alien plant removal. Through its Working for Water Programme, the South African government is doing just this: teams of South Africans have been hired to scour the watersheds and clear them of alien species. Not only is this activity putting water back into streams and increasing available supplies, it is creating jobs, conserving biodiversity, and helping sustain the flower and tourism industries that rely in part on the region's native plants.

What these examples have in common is recognition of the value of ecosystem services and the willingness to pay for them or invest in them. Numerous other ways of linking water use and development to ecosystem health are possible. In a river basin such as the Ipswich in Massachusetts, for example, heavy groundwater pumping for lawn irrigation is contributing to the depletion of baseflows to such a degree that the river actually dried up in 1995, 1997, and 1999. Scientists with the U.S. Geological Survey have estimated that in the absence of groundwater withdrawals the river would have baseflows of about 9,460 cubic meters per day during these low-flow periods, rather than running completely dry.[19] Sustaining the river therefore requires a mechanism for linking the damage caused by profligate lawn watering to the dead fish and dry channel of the Ipswich. In some communities, a substantial summer price surcharge on upper levels of water use might be sufficient to induce conservation and a switch to water-thrifty landscapes. But in high-income areas such as greater Boston, hefty water bills may not be enough: outright bans on lawn watering when river flows drop below ecological thresholds may be necessary to keep the river running and its fish alive.

Incorporating the protection of ecological services into river management decisions will require that stakeholders adopt the learning-by-doing philosophy of adaptive management. Because river systems are ecologically complex, the consequences of any action taken—whether it be the clearing of alien vegetation, an aggressive conservation program, the retirement of irrigated land, or a ban on lawn irrigation—cannot be known with certainty. Water users and the public at large need to allow scientists and river managers room for experimentation, monitoring, and course corrections; rarely will they "get it right" on the first try. For their part, scientists need to appreciate the practical realities that water managers and dam operators face—especially their need for reliability. Striking a better balance between ecosystem conservation and human use of rivers is like making a deal: each party needs to know what the other wants, what the other really needs, and to be ready to negotiate within those bounds to reach an accommodation.[20]

Together, adaptive management and the natural flow paradigm are powerful tools for improving river governance. The natural flow paradigm says, in effect: to save a river, it is not necessary to know exactly how sediment-dwellers keep the ecosystem's food web humming, or exactly what conditions riparian communities need for regeneration, or exactly how much water and at what time each river species needs to survive. Historically, the river's natural variation in flow took care of these critical elements. For its part, adaptive management says: there is no rational reason to stay in gridlock; actions to restore flows can get under way even in the face of some uncertainty.

Most rivers in the world that have had their flows altered for hydropower, irrigation, flood control, or water supply could provide more value to society in the form of ecological services if managed to restore, to some degree, their natural flow regime. Similarly, rivers slated for new dams and diversion projects will yield more overall value to society if an ecological flow allocation is incorporated from the start. The remaining sections of this chapter offer some guidance, examples, and ideas for achieving these goals through better river governance.

LESSONS FROM THE WORLD COMMISSION ON DAMS

In 1997, a pivotal gathering of some thirty water professionals in Gland, Switzerland, issued a mandate to the World Bank and the IUCN (World Conservation Union, a large private international conservation organization) to oversee the establishment of an independent panel to review one of the most controversial global issues of our time—large dams. The resulting World Commission on Dams (WCD) was specifically charged with assessing the "development effectiveness" of large dams, producing a framework for evaluating water and energy options in the future, and developing criteria and guidelines for planning, designing, constructing, operating, monitoring, and decommissioning dams. The WCD had no legal authority, and its findings and recommendations bind no one to a particular course of action. Yet the process that the WCD designed, and the way it conducted its affairs, reached its conclusions, and prepared its findings almost certainly constitute a watershed in global environmental decision-making. The WCD has greatly raised the bar for global environmental governance. It also has built the foundation and frame for a new architecture of river governance.

The WCD came on the heels of three decades of international commissions, conferences, and forums dealing with global environment and development issues. About a dozen in all, these included the Brandt Commission of the late 1970s, the Brundtland Commission of the 1980s, and separate world commissions on forests, oceans, and water during the mid- to late 1990s. Each of these endeavors raised public and political awareness on important issues, and some of them considerably advanced the process of global environmental governance. Following the path-breaking work of the Brundtland Commission, for instance, the holding of regional hearings to solicit input became common practice. The more recent commissions on forests and fresh water both followed this approach.[21] For the most part, these global commissions were composed of "eminent" persons with international name recognition—typically people with high-level experience in government or international agencies. This approach may have given them visibility and some clout, but it did not give them legitimacy with societal groups not represented on the commission. As a result, these commissions did not achieve a large-scale buy-in from the broad array of people potentially affected by their work.

By contrast, the makeup of the WCD was intentionally designed to be representative of the diverse set of groups and interests affected by its mission and findings. The twelve commissioners spanned the spectrum of stakeholders—from the dam-building industry to human rights groups actively campaigning against large dams. Not only did the commissioners themselves bring deep resolve and commitment to the WCD's work, but their presence helped achieve the broad buy-in that previous commissions had lacked. Perhaps more importantly, by interacting with and getting to know one another through the course of more than two years of work, the commissioners had a chance to understand the very different realities, concerns, and worldviews of their fellow commissioners. Göran Lindahl, chief executive of Asea Brown Boveri, one of the world's largest engineering firms, would arrive for a meeting at the WCD's headquarters in Cape Town, South Africa, on his private jet. Another commissioner, Medha Patkar, leader of an indigenous people's movement in India known as the Struggle to Save the Narmada River, would arrive weak from a hunger strike undertaken to protest the construction of large dams in western India's Narmada Valley.[22] Working together as commissioners, they had to search for an intersection of understanding and some common ground. Because of their roles in the wider world, however, they needed to remain accountable to their constituencies who viewed them as looking after their interests.

Another critical attribute of the WCD was its self-perception as a group charged with a much deeper mission than simply fact-finding and reporting on the global experience with large dams. The passion and life purposes of the commissioners was a key to this, but so was the resolve and philosophical bent of its chair, Kader Asmal, formerly South Africa's Minister of Water Affairs and Forestry and a human rights lawyer who spent the apartheid years in exile in Ireland. In introducing the final report of the WCD, which was released in November 2000, Asmal stated, "I assert that we are much more than a 'Dams Commission.' We are a Commission to heal the deep and self-inflicted wounds torn open wherever and whenever far too few determine for far too many how best to develop or use water and energy resources."[23] The Commission actively sought, in other words, a new mode of governance.

With this mission and makeup, the WCD embarked on a process that lived out the very ideals and practices it would end up proposing as solutions to the global stalemate surrounding large dams. That process was far from perfect, as any complex endeavor nearly always is. But it embodied through its activities the fundamental pillars of good governance that it would come to espouse and that were notoriously lacking in the historical approach to decision-making about dams—openness, inclusiveness, participation, transparency, and accountability. It demonstrated that a process grounded in these principles could actually be carried out and produce a set of recommendations that a wide spectrum of people could embrace. Most impressively, the WCD did not sacrifice leadership for consensus. Its findings and recommendations are not watered-down statements of little meaning. Rather, they offer a clear road map for moving toward more equitable and sustainable decisions on dams in the future. Among these recommendations is an endorsement of the idea of setting environmental flows in order to sustain river ecosystems and downstream communities (see Box 5-1).

Developing that road map was both time-consuming and labor-intensive. A major part of the work program was the generation of an exten-

---

BOX 5-1   Recommendations of the World Commission on Dams
for a New Policy Framework for Large Dams

Gaining Public Acceptance
Comprehensive Options Assessment
Addressing Existing Dams
Sustaining Rivers and Livelihoods*
Recognizing Entitlements and Sharing Benefits
Ensuring Compliance
Sharing Rivers for Peace, Development and Security

---

*Sustaining Rivers and Livelihoods
(text of recommendation)

Rivers, watersheds and aquatic ecosystems are the biological engines of the planet. They are the basis for life and the livelihoods of local communities. Dams transform landscapes and create risks of irreversible impacts. Understanding, protecting and restoring ecosystems at the river basin level is essential to foster equitable human development and the welfare of all species. Options assessment and decision-making around river development prioritizes the avoidance of impacts, followed by the minimization and mitigation of harm to the health and integrity of the river system. Avoiding impacts through good site selection and project design is a priority. Releasing tailor-made environmental flows can help maintain downstream ecosystems and the communities that depend on them.

SOURCE: World Commission on Dams, 2000.

---

sive base of knowledge about large dams—by far the largest ever assembled and a valuable product of the WCD in its own right. This knowledge base includes eight in-depth case studies of large dams (including, for instance, Tarbela in Pakistan, Grand Coulee in the United States, and Pak Mun in Thailand); the most comprehensive statistical survey of large dams to date; seventeen in-depth reviews of important dam-related issues; four separate reviews of options in the irrigation, water supply, flood control, and electricity supply sectors, as well as numerous voluntary submissions. The WCD also held four major regional consultations—one each for South Asia (held in Colombo, Sri Lanka), Latin America (in São Paulo, Brazil), Africa and the Middle East (in Cairo, Egypt), and East and Southeast Asia (in Hanoi, Vietnam). Some 1,400 people from fifty-nine different countries and all walks of life participated in these meetings.[24] The WCD offered travel stipends to all speakers at these events, ensuring that no stakeholder group went unheard because of insufficient travel funds, a decision that added significantly to the Commission's credibility. In addition, the Commission held twenty consultations in various countries and river basins around the world to discuss its case studies.[25] Coordinating all of these activities was a full-time secretariat based in Cape Town, South Africa.

This might seem like an overwhelmingly large undertaking. But in less time and for less money than it typically takes to build one large dam, the WCD reframed the debate over this intensely controversial issue and offered a set of principles for moving forward. Because of the WCD's widespread legitimacy and perceived moral authority, these principles carry substantial weight. They offer visible benchmarks against which to judge any process of decision-making by a government or other institution to build a large dam.

Not surprisingly, some governments have disavowed the WCD's findings and recommendations because they view them as an unwelcome intrusion into their dam-building affairs. This group includes, most notably, China, India, and Turkey—countries that account for a large share of the world's dams that are under construction or in the pipeline. In addition, several of the large international dam industry associations, including the International Commission on Large Dams, the International Hydropower Association, and the International Commission on Irrigation and Drainage, have repudiated the WCD's conclusions— although some individual chapters within these organizations have expressed some support.[26]

By contrast, a number of European countries—including the British, Dutch, German, and Swedish governments—have variously endorsed or shown support for the Commission's recommendations. Among the United Nations agencies, the World Health Organization and the UN Environment Programme have voiced the greatest support and praise. The latter agency has established a Dams and Development Project to help carry the WCD's work forward. In addition, there have been supportive reactions from some construction and engineering companies, including from a director of Chicago-based Harza Engineering who called the report "a sound approach."[27]

Despite being a cosponsor of the Commission, the World Bank has so far been unwilling to adopt the WCD's recommendations into its own policies and practices concerning dams. A draft of its new water resources sector strategy signals no intent to incorporate the WCD's core principles and guidelines.[28] The WCD's other co-convenor, the IUCN, has stated that it is firmly committed to fostering the implementation, adaptation, and testing of the WCD recommendations. To this end, according to IUCN, "it will use the full strength of its unique membership, which brings together 79 states, 113 government agencies, 754 NGOs (non-governmental organizations), and some 10,000 scientists and experts from 181 countries in a unique worldwide partnership."[29]

The final chapter of the World Commission on Dams will only be written some years from now, after its impact on the future of large dams and the people and ecosystems affected by them can be seen more clearly. The WCD had power only to make recommendations, not to implement them. It is up to the World Bank, the regional development banks, donor agencies, and governments themselves to take the WCD's core principles and recommendations to heart in their loan- and grant-making decisions. Organizations such as California-based International Rivers Network are working to hold these institutions' feet to the fire by spotlighting where dam-building decisions fall short of, or neglect altogether, the WCD's recommendations. It is up to existing institutions to put a solid structure on the foundation and frame that the WCD has built.

BOTTOM-UP GOVERNANCE GETS A TRY

Within a few years of its passage, South Africa's new water law became the buzz of international water talk. Nothing like its two-pronged water reserve had ever been designed at the national level. The idea was exciting; but was it workable? Its goals were laudable; but were they practical?

As every innovator learns, it is one thing to craft a new approach on paper and quite another to actually carry it out. South Africa's experiment with a water policy that incorporates the fundamental understanding that ecological health serves the common good presents a direct challenge to conventional modes of water governance. Only a broad and representative group of people with interests in a given river basin can determine what the optimum use of that river looks like. According to South Africa's new water policy, participatory decision-making is not just a nice thing to have; it is essential to carrying out the policy's core vision.[30]

In the South African context, the ecological water reserve has strong scientific underpinnings but is fundamentally a social construct. A major challenge facing implementers of the new law is correcting the misconception that the ecological reserve is water set aside for the environment for the environment's sake. Rather, the reserve is water purposely left in its natural channel in order to provide a valuable stream of goods and services that benefit people. Just like water extracted from its natural course, "reserve" water is aimed at social and economic growth and human well-being.

In this way, South Africa is actively attempting to align three stars for better river governance—the addition of ecosystem service values to the weighting of river benefits, the setting of environmental flow criteria to sustain those ecological values, and participatory decision-making to achieve more equitable and sustainable allocation of the full range of river benefits. It is up to the citizens living within a river basin to collectively define, through negotiation and dialogue, a shared vision for management and use of the river. This involves making explicit the trade-offs between extractive water uses (e.g., for irrigation) and the ecological services lost as a result of those extractions. Ideally, stakeholders accomplish this through consensus rather than compromise. Compromise involves splitting the difference between positions defined by individual self-interest and often results in an outcome that satisfies no one. By contrast, consensus results in a shared vision of a desirable future state, and derives from a coevolution of individual preferences within a spirit of community responsibility.[31] As people participating in the process gain more knowledge about a river's natural functions, as well as the needs and values of other participants, individual preferences coevolve, which, in turn, moves everyone closer to shared goals. This process takes more time, but is more likely to yield an outcome with legitimacy and staying power (see Table 5-1).

For nearly a decade, South African scientist Kevin Rogers has been helping to facilitate dialogues in the watersheds of the Sabie and other rivers that flow through Kruger National Park in the northeastern part of the country. Rogers and his colleagues have found that through such a cooperative process of "building their future" the watershed participants do indeed shift their preferences and desires as they listen to what others in the watershed want and need. Their interests also evolve from what is best for themselves to what is best for their community when viewed more holistically. This stakeholder dialogue is a critical part of what Rogers and others call strategic adaptive management, which aims, through an active partnership between science, management, and society, to arrive at a consensus on how to allocate and manage water for the good of all in the river basin. This approach is a homegrown variety of adap-

TABLE 5-1   Likely Outcomes of Top-Down Versus Bottom-Up
Approaches to River Governance

"Top Down" *Specialist-centered*	*"Bottom Up"* *Stakeholder-centered*
Compromise	Consensus
• Reached by confrontation	• Reached by cooperation
• Alienation—Disinvestment	• Ownership—Buy-in
• Relationships impaired	• Relationships improved
• Short-term efficiency high	• Short-term efficiency low
• Overall efficiency low	• Overall efficiency high

SOURCE: Sherwill and Rogers, 2002

tive management that integrates the South African notions of *Ubuntu* (I see you the individual), *Simunye* (we are one), and *Batho pele* (people first).[32]

Strategic adaptive management requires that stakeholders collectively set ecological goals by defining a preferred state or vision of the river ecosystem. For one river, the goal may be to maintain a very high degree of ecological health, whereas the desired ecological state for another river may allow for significant degradation to accommodate pressing human needs for water. This broad vision then gets translated into management objectives and operational goals—including a flow prescription—that then guide the work of land and water managers within that catchment.[33] The process may also involve categorizing different segments of a river according to their ecological health—natural, good, fair, or poor—and then comparing how the current status accords with that desired in the vision. In this way, river segments critical to achieving the stakeholders' desired future can be targeted for more intensive management and those in a near-pristine or natural state can be given strong protections. Rogers and others working with watershed groups have found that asking stakeholders to define their desired state for a river in ecological terms "elicits frustration and confusion," but because "everyone, regardless of background or training, can . . . discuss resource quality expressed in goods and services terminology" they use this to find common ground.[34]

Scientists play a critical role in helping categorize river segments by applying various indices of river health, such as for fish assemblages, aquatic insects, riparian vegetation, and overall habitat integrity. Besides providing a status report, these indices help the catchment management groups monitor progress. A major challenge to scientists and managers working in the Sabie catchment, where biodiversity protection is a key goal of the vision, has been to predict and monitor how biodiversity is affected by changes in the river's flow, sediment supply, and water quality—changes that originate at the catchment level[35] (see Chapter 4). Scientists working there have developed what they call "thresholds of probable concern"—a term that reflects the philosophy of adaptive management—in order to set limits of acceptable change in the ecosystem's structure, function, and composition. The science is driven by and responsive to the societal values reflected in the watershed's vision statement, which makes the scientists' work directly relevant to the achievement of social goals. The indicators and ecological thresholds that scientists derive therefore need to be practical enough to be applied broadly at the watershed scale. Ideally, a spirit of creativity and learning pervades the partnership among citizens, scientists, and managers as the process unfolds and all acquire new knowledge.

A good portion of the water professionals in South Africa are committed to making the nation's unique experiment in water policy and governance a success. But there are no guarantees, and many pitfalls. Like most national water bureaucracies around the world, South Africa's Department of Water Affairs and Forestry (DWAF) has a legacy of command-and-control management that officials are trying to revamp in order to accommodate new participatory approaches. The catchment management agencies being set up around the country to implement the act are largely drawing their expertise from the DWAF, which has much more experience with regulating water use and issuing water permits than with managing ecosystems. There is a danger, therefore, that the ecological reserves will not actively be managed, but rather be defined and protected only by a limit on the number of water use licenses issued—clearly not what was intended under the new law. In addition, adequate funding has not yet been committed to implement the flow prescriptions that scientists develop and to monitor changes to river ecosystems over time. As South African scientists Kevin Rogers, Dirk Roux, and Harry Biggs warn, "We must be sure that the institutions we set up to implement and administer this law are equally innovative and do it full justice. If not, the progressive legislation will flounder in the face of bureaucracy."[36]

South Africa's new experiment in river governance is just getting under way, but already it offers some useful lessons. Among the most important ones are the need to commit to a process of dialogue, inclusion, and consensus-building, and to create institutions that support working partnerships among citizens, river interests, scientists, and water managers. Although the verdict will remain out for some time, South Africa is on its way to replacing a dysfunctional and inequitable approach to river governance with one that is better.

RIVER BASIN COMMISSIONS WORK "OUTSIDE THE BOX"

Rivers occupy a very different place on maps of political geography than on maps of physical geography. Historically, rivers have often been used to delineate national or state boundaries, so on a political map they often appear to divide countries. Ecologically, however, rivers run through the middle of a watershed that spans those same countries; hence, on a physiographic map, rivers appear to unite countries. Managing such transboundary rivers in a sensible and holistic fashion requires that the different political entities see themselves as part of the same ecosystem, and work together to protect the river and to share its goods and services equitably.

Most rivers, unfortunately, are not managed this way. There are now 261 rivers that flow through two or more countries. Since the early 1800s, governments have signed some 145 treaties dealing with non-navigational uses of transboundary waters. An analysis of these treaties by Aaron Wolf of Oregon State University and his colleagues has found, however, that more than half of them have no monitoring provisions, two-thirds do not specify water allocations to the parties, and four-fifths have no enforcement mechanisms. Moreover, 86 percent of the treaties have only two signatories even though many of the rivers they address are shared by three or more countries.[37] Thus, in most cases, key parties have been missing from the negotiating table. One party absent in just about every case is the river system itself.

Institutions able to manage rivers at a watershed scale are essential to the administration of ecological flow allocations and the corresponding caps on water use and flow modifications that they entail. Increasingly they are also needed to reduce competition and conflict between upstream and downstream users of shared rivers, as well as between extractive and instream water uses. By bringing together representatives from each of the political entities that share a river, international or inter-state river basin commissions allow the full spectrum of river functions to be considered holistically—a prerequisite to equitably sharing a river's full range of benefits. Moreover, any effort to re-create a river's natural flow pattern must consider the river as a unified whole, regardless of political boundaries.

Recent experience also suggests that river basin commissions can promote more creative, out-of-the-box solutions than is often possible within the confines of state or national laws. International and inter-state compacts typically supercede national and state policies and they offer considerable flexibility in fashioning more integrated approaches to river protection and management. For example, Australia's policy innovation of the cap on water extractions came out of the Ministerial Council of the Murray-Darling Basin Commission, which is composed of the resource ministers from each basin state or territory and the Commonwealth. As described in Chapter 3, the Council had determined that a better balance had to be struck between conventional economic uses of the river and vital ecological functions of the river—hence the cap on diversions was born. It is hard to imagine that any one Australian state alone would have voluntarily limited its water extractions without a similar commitment from its neighbors.

In Europe, new international collaborations are breathing life back into the fabled Danube River. Rising in Germany's Black Forest, the Danube joins fourteen countries and some 80 million people within its watershed as it runs 2,840 kilometers eastward to the Black Sea (see Figure 5-1). Over the past two centuries, the river has been badly degraded by channelization, draining of wetlands, rampant pollution, and the construction of numerous dams—including more than fifty-eight of them along the river's first 1,000 kilometers. A good portion of the Danube's riparian forests are gone and former floodplains have dried out: in Bulgaria, for example, 90 percent of the river's floodplain wetlands have disappeared.[38] Moreover, the Danube Delta—Europe's largest wetland ecosystem and home to 320 species of birds—has been seriously degraded by the heavy pollution loads carried downstream and by the reduction of cleansing flood flows.

After the breakup of the Soviet bloc and the fall of the Iron Curtain, new opportunities for cooperation and collaboration arose for the nations of the Danube watershed. They did not waste much time. In September 1991, the environment ministers from a number of Danube countries met in Sofia, Bulgaria, to begin planning the river's restoration. In

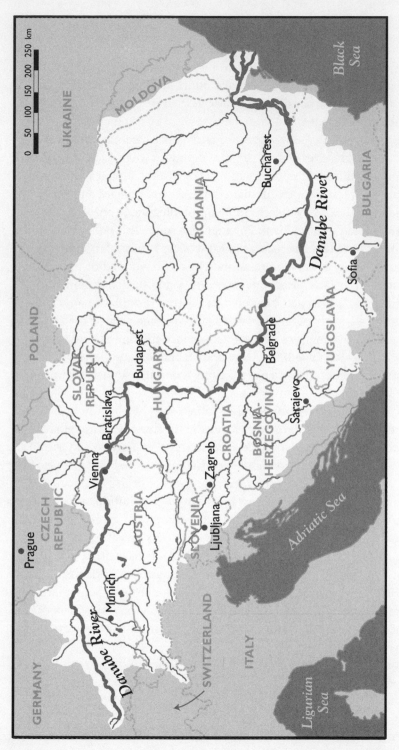

FIGURE 5-1. The Danube River Basin.

June 1994, a majority of Danube countries, plus the European Commission (the decision-making arm of the European Union [EU]), signed the Convention on Cooperation for the Protection and Sustainable Use of the Danube River, a legal instrument that directly calls for sustainable and equitable water management.[39] Later that year, in Bucharest, Romania, the environment ministers and the EU's environmental commissioner endorsed the Danube Strategic Action Plan, which states that "Conservation, restoration and management of riverine habitat and biodiversity is important for maintaining the natural capital of the basin . . . and to establish its natural purification and assimilative capacity."[40]

Remarkably, the Danube collaboration brings together former Communist countries with their western counterparts, and relatively rich nations such as Germany and Austria with poor ones such as Bulgaria and Romania. A key benefit of a cooperative river-basin framework is that it allows international agencies and groups to fund and help implement projects. For instance, the governments of Bulgaria, Romania, Moldova, and Ukraine have pledged to create a network of at least 600,000 hectares of floodplain habitat along the lower Danube, along the Prut River, and in the Danube Delta.[41] This joint effort is part of a project called Green Corridor for the Danube initiated in June 2000 by the World Wildlife Fund, a private conservation organization. With funding from United Nations agencies and others, the project aims initially to demonstrate how healthy floodplains can provide habitat, reduce pollution loads, and enhance fisheries. The hope is to extend the Green Corridor program to the entire length of the Danube.[42]

For Romania, which harbors more than 80 percent of the Danube Delta, restoration of the ecosystem must be accompanied by a reinvigoration of its weak economy. There, as in many poor countries, citizens are only likely to support restoration efforts if their livelihoods improve at the same time. Whether an upstream-downstream collaboration can meet this difficult test of sustainable development remains to be seen. One key to success likely will be acknowledging the value of revitalized ecosystem services. According to one estimate, a $275 million investment in wetland restoration in Romania alone would be recouped within six years from the ecosystem goods and services provided by the delta—including reduced pollution loads, flood control, and regenerated fisheries.[43] In an April 2001 speech, Romanian President Ion Iliescu set a supportive tone, noting that past development on the Danube had resulted in "unacceptable material and human costs," and he promised to cooperate with the other thirteen basin countries to restore the river and its delta.[44]

In the United States, three southeastern states have turned to a new inter-state water compact to help them resolve upstream-downstream conflicts and, at least so far, to prevent water-allocation decisions from being made by the courts. The controversy—which involves Georgia, Alabama, and Florida—is over how to share the waters of the Apalachicola-Chattahoochee-Flint (ACF) river system, which drains an area north of Atlanta south through the Florida panhandle to Apalachicola Bay (see Figure 5-2). Explosive population growth, particularly in the greater Atlanta region, along with irrigation expansion in southwestern Georgia, have greatly increased water demands in the basin. These human demands, in turn, are depleting and altering river flows needed by the rare mussels, fish, and other freshwater life in the watershed. The Apalachicola River is home to one of the highest concentrations of imperiled species in the United States. At the tail end of the watershed, Apalachicola Bay ranks among North America's most productive estuaries, yielding highly prized harvests of blue crabs, shrimps, and more than 90 percent of Florida's commercial oysters. Survival of these oysters depends on the Apalachicola River emptying enough fresh water into the bay to keep stone crabs and other saltwater predators from migrating in from the Gulf of Mexico and decimating the oyster reefs.

Sixteen dams control the flows of the Chattahoochee and Flint rivers, including five large multi-purpose federal dams operated by the U.S. Army Corps of Engineers. In 1989, the Corps agreed to a request from the state of Georgia to reallocate storage in a large reservoir upstream on the Chattahoochee from hydropower generation to water supply in order to meet the escalating water demands of Atlanta. Concerned about the possible downstream effects of this reallocation, Alabama filed a lawsuit against the Corps in 1990. Florida, wanting to protect flows of the Apalachicola River into the bay, joined Alabama's suit; Georgia sided with the Corps. Instead of pressing the matter through the courts, however, the states opted to talk, gather more information, and explore possible options for resolving their differences. These discussions led to the signing, in 1997, of the Apalachicola-Chattahoochee-Flint River Basin Compact, which provides a framework for the states "to develop a water allocation formula for equitably apportioning the surface waters of the ACF Basin among the states while protecting the water quality, ecology and biodiversity of the ACF."[45] It called for an ACF Commission made up of

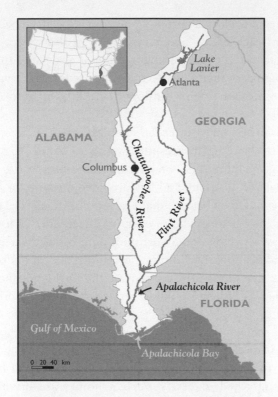

FIGURE 5-2. The Apalachicola River Basin.

the governors of the three states plus a representative of the federal government appointed by the president of the United States. Once the state commissioners agree on an allocation formula, the federal commissioner decides whether or not to concur after assessing the formula's compliance with federal laws.

The negotiations have proven lengthy and arduous, and as of June 2003 no final deal had been reached. Yet the compact has provided a vehicle for integrating ecological water needs into the process of allocating the ACF's flows. Florida's proposed allocation formula provides for ecological flows through two conditions. First, it would limit the amount of water that can be removed from Lake Lanier—the large federal reservoir behind Buford Dam on the Chattahoochee River and the principal water source for Atlanta. Nothing would prevent Georgia from importing water from outside the basin and storing it in Lake Lanier in order to augment supplies for Atlanta, but diversions of the Chattahoochee's water would effectively be capped. Second, Florida's proposal lays out a specific schedule of water releases from each of the major reservoirs in the system, one that is designed to mimic the natural flow regime. It also states that the Army Corps of Engineers shall operate the lower federal reservoirs so as to ensure a specified minimum outflow of fresh water into Apalachicola Bay.[46]

It remains to be seen whether the states can reach an acceptable agreement and avoid handing their dispute over to the courts. To date the commission has given more attention to ecological values than is typically the case in river-basin planning and has provided a venue for the different parties to try to strike a balance that is acceptable to all. The negotiations have been greatly hampered, however, by the absence of a scientifically based flow prescription and a corresponding cap on water extractions and flow modifications. In addition, none of the allocation formulas proposed by the states explicitly incorporate the flow guidelines developed jointly by the U.S. Fish and Wildlife Service and the Environmental Protection Agency to protect the ACF's freshwater biodiversity.[47] Moreover, any hope for achieving sustainability in the basin clearly hinges on much more aggressive water conservation—both in agriculture and in Atlanta and other urban areas. As in Massachusetts' Ipswich River basin, thirsty green lawns attached to new suburban homes are driving up water demands in the ACF basin.

Opportunities for river-basin commissions to promote more ecologically sound water management are particularly ripe in developing countries, where many rivers are not yet altered substantially but are slated for major dam construction. A hard lesson learned in developed countries is that it is difficult to restore healthy flows to rivers after those flows have been divvied up for various economic purposes. To the extent that the full range of river benefits can be assessed before dams and other infrastructure are built, a more efficient, fair, and sustainable water allocation regime will likely result.

The vast Mekong River of Southeast Asia originates on the Tibetan plateau of China and then borders or flows through five other countries—Myanmar (Burma), Laos, Thailand, Cambodia, and Vietnam (see Figure 5-3). This tropical basin has ample water in the wet season, but experiences shortages during the dry season, when less than 2 percent of the annual flow reaches the Mekong Delta. In recent decades, competition for water among the basin countries has increased greatly, as they each strive to expand their agricultural production and economies. With no

FIGURE 5-3. The Mekong River Basin.

clear allocation formulas setting out how much water each country should receive and ensuring that sufficient flows are provided for the delta and river itself, the familiar stage is set for water disputes and ecological decline.

Biologically, much is at stake. The Mekong basin supports at least five hundred species of fish (some estimates range as high as 1,200–2,000 species), placing it among the top three rivers in terms of fish diversity worldwide.[48] The natural flood regime also maintains an incredibly productive fishery in the downstream countries of Cambodia and Vietnam. During the wet season, the Mekong rises and flows into the Tonle Sap River, which in turn feeds into Southeast Asia's largest freshwater lake, the Tonle Sap in Cambodia. The lake expands to five times its dry-season size, allowing fish to move into the inundated swamp forests to feed and breed. Sustained largely by the flood pulse, Cambodia's fisheries yield at least 400,000 tons a year. A similar tonnage is provided by the Mekong Delta in Vietnam.[49] These fish provide much of the animal protein consumed by people in the region.

Cooperative management of the Mekong dates back to 1957, when Cambodia, Laos, Thailand, and Vietnam formed the Mekong Committee. War and political instability overshadowed the committee's work for several decades, with Cambodia variously participating or not at different times. In 1995, the four countries signed an "Agreement on the Cooperation for the Sustainable Development of the Mekong River Basin." Among other things, this compact created the Mekong River Commission (MRC) and charged it with drafting a strategy to guide water development in the lower Mekong basin. The MRC also has authority to help the parties negotiate agreements that determine minimum monthly flows at various points along the river.[50] As with the ACF compact, the Mekong agreement sets out general principles and procedures, but does not set specific water allocations for the signatories. As of late 2002, these specific allocations had not been resolved—testifying to the difficult trade-offs among various upstream-downstream and instream-offstream uses of the river.

So far, no dams have been built on the Mekong mainstem south of the Burma-Laos border, which includes about three-quarters of the watershed. The MRC has identified a dozen potential sites for hydropower development on the lower Mekong, but these dams seem unlikely to be built anytime soon. China, which is not a member of the MRC, has already constructed two large dams on the upper Mekong and has six more in the pipeline. According to biologist David Dudgeon of Hong Kong University, one prediction suggests that, by 2010, China's dams on the Mekong will substantially flatten the river's hydrograph—reducing flows during the wet season and increasing dry-season flows by as much as 50 percent.[51]

The incorporation of ecological flows into management decisions for the Mekong River is critical to protecting the region's unique biodiversity and equitably sharing the river's full range of benefits. The trade-offs among these potential benefits—which include hydropower generation, flood control, water supply, crop production, fisheries yield, and species conservation—are extremely complex. Coming up with a fair and ecologically sustainable water development strategy is not easy in this context. Moreover, all four nations in the MRC will be affected by China's decisions upstream—something they can do little about unless China is persuaded to join the MRC and to act cooperatively and responsibly.

At this juncture, it is impossible to discern how events in the basin will transpire, but there are at least some promising signs that ecological flows are under consideration. At a workshop in November 2001 attended by representatives of all four MRC countries, University of Cape Town ecologist Jackie King—one of South Africa's environmental flow pioneers—made a presentation to the commission on the importance of ecological flow requirements. As a World Bank–supported advisor to the MRC, she then traveled to each MRC member country in May 2002 in order to present the concept of environmental flows to a wider group of officials and stakeholders. The MRC is now planning a pilot study on ecological flows within the basin. Says King, "Environmental flow assessments provide decision makers with information that they have never had before on the predicted social and ecological impacts of proposed water-resource developments. They now have to consider these as well as the traditional engineering and economic information on costs of construction and the commercial value of water. It makes their decision more difficult, as they search for an acceptable trade-off, but hopefully more balanced."[52]

The Mekong is more than an important test case for integrating ecosystem-sustaining flows into management of a complex, transboundary river in the developing world. It is one of the world's most biologically rich river systems, and it is at risk of irreversible transformation. The existence of an institution capable of working out-of-the-box does not necessarily mean that it will do so. It remains to be seen whether the MRC, with outside assistance, will rise to the challenges of twenty-first century water management and chart a new path for sustainable management of a large international river.

SPARKS OF LEADERSHIP

It is no accident that South Africa has assumed a leadership role in water governance over the last decade. Former President Nelson Mandela emerged from his Robbins Island prison cell with a set of moral convictions that permeated the restructuring of the nation's post-apartheid political and social institutions. In establishing his first cabinet, he chose not a civil engineer but a human rights lawyer, Kader Asmal, to head the nation's water ministry. Mandela understood the need to go back to first principles of governance—ethics, justice, and equity—in setting his country on a new water course. He inspired new models of leadership not only within his cabinet, but among scientists, policymakers, and citizens in numbers out of proportion to the country's size. While the ultimate outcome of South Africa's efforts will not be known for many years—and the implementation hurdles are substantial—the exercise of leadership by Mandela and Asmal may well come to be seen by future water historians as a major turning point in world water affairs.

Societal change requires leadership. In the case of rivers, new knowledge about the value of freshwater ecosystem services and the vital role of natural flows in protecting river health is a necessary but not sufficient condition for a shift to new styles of river governance and management. That shift will require actions that spur change. Here and there, political institutions, private organizations, and dedicated individuals are beginning to exert that leadership, inspiring hope that their experiences will motivate larger actions.

By far the greatest near-term opportunities for shifting the balance of river management toward greater river protection reside within the agencies mandated to manage water. In functioning democracies, these agencies serve the public, but they have been slow to realign their activities to protect the public trust in water.

At the international level, the new water directive issued by the European Parliament and the Council of the European Union holds out the promise of a major turnaround for Europe's rivers. With this exercise of policy leadership, the fifteen countries of the European Union (and ten more are likely to be added within the next few years) are charged not only to prevent their rivers from deteriorating, but to ensure that all of them achieve at least good ecological health. Similarly, the eight U.S. states and two Canadian provinces that comprise the Great Lakes basin have taken a leadership step with the June 2001 adoption of an annex to The Great Lakes Charter. Noting that "the Great Lakes are a bi-national public treasure and are held in trust by the Great Lakes States and Provinces," the charter supplement requires that future modifications to the basin's rivers and streams be accompanied by flow restoration measures that result in a net ecological benefit for the basin's freshwater ecosystems.[53] With the stroke of two pens on different sides of the Atlantic, the rivers and streams of Europe and the Great Lakes basin now stand a good chance of being healthier two decades from now than they are today.

Also in North America, the Instream Flow Council (IFC), which is composed of state and provincial resource management agencies, is helping to fill the leadership vacuum on river flow protection. Founded in

1998, the IFC is working to improve the effectiveness of governmental instream flow programs in conserving aquatic ecosystems. The Council emphasizes the responsibility of public resource managers to protect the public trust, recommending that "harm to trust purposes be prevented or minimized whenever feasible."[54] In its guidance to public water managers, the Council says further that "even though many rivers have been highly modified, it should be an ultimate goal of all state and provincial natural resource management agencies to reestablish and sustain the natural flow-related processes."[55]

Leadership at the local level can be a force for wider change simply through the power of positive example. When Bob Biel of the U.S. Army Corps of Engineers collaborated with scientists at The Nature Conservancy in crafting new operating rules for dams on Kentucky's Green River, he cracked open a window of opportunity for broader reforms within his federal agency. One outgrowth of the Green River experience is the "Sustainable Rivers Project," a joint effort by the Corps and the Conservancy to evaluate how the operation of thirteen federal dams could be improved to better protect habitat and ecosystem functions while at the same time meeting human needs.[56]

Similarly, local efforts to reconnect rivers with their floodplains are giving the Corps some valuable test cases of alternative approaches to flood control and river restoration. By restoring natural meanders to the channelized Kissimmee River, the Corps and Florida water authorities will learn a great deal about how rivers heal, lessons they will hopefully apply elsewhere. In Napa County, the heart of California wine country, a dedicated citizens' group encouraged the Corps to develop a nonconventional flood-control plan that reconnects the Napa River with its floodplain and brings the river back into the community's life. After much hard work by these individuals to garner support for the new approach, county residents voted in 1998 to raise their local sales tax to help pay for it. They are now poised to reap myriad benefits from the restoration of the river's ecosystem services—including a revitalized downtown, reduced damage from flooding, lower rates for flood insurance, beautiful parks and trails for recreation and bird-watching, higher tourist revenues, and a river that inspires boating rather than dumping. Even though the plan will take several more years to complete, it has attracted delegations from around the world—including Argentina, Australia, and China—to learn from this experience.[57] Initially reluctant and skeptical, the Corps came to view the scheme very positively: "What we will be doing in Napa is radically different from anything we have ever done before," a Corps spokesman told reporters after the 1998 sales tax vote. "It's going to totally change the way we do business."[58]

In a similar fashion, villages in India have garnered a wealth of knowledge about the potential value of water harvesting and other watershed projects.[59] Researchers at the New Delhi-based Centre for Science and Environment see these methods as at least a partial alternative to ecologically damaging and increasingly controversial large dam projects. As evidence grows that in many cases water harvesting projects offer a practical, locally controlled, socially acceptable, and environmentally sustainable alternative to meeting village water supply needs, so does the likelihood that they will be incorporated more fully into India's national and state-level water policy, planning, and management.

The reshaping of river governance and management will take leadership of many kinds. It will take political champions willing to buck special interests in order to do what is right for river health and society at large. It will take water managers willing to think and work outside the box. It will take citizens willing to lead the charge for changes in river management in their particular watersheds, and others willing to toil hard behind the scenes. And it will take scientists willing to work for policy and management reforms, even if academia does not reward them for it. Legions of citizens, scientists, conservationists, and public servants care deeply about healthy rivers and the life they support. Given opportunities to put their passions to work, they collectively constitute a major force for constructive change.

Social and political reformer Eleanor Roosevelt said that "we should constantly be reminded of what we owe in return for what we have." It is a fitting call to leadership and hard work for those who possess the knowledge, skills, passion, or power to make a difference for the earth's rivers and all they give to our generation and those yet to come.

CHAPTER SIX

~

Epilogue: Can We Save Earth's Rivers?

Few findings beamed back from outer space generate more intrigue than evidence of the possibility of water on other cosmic spheres. Earth's moon may have ice at its poles. Mars, our colder neighbor, appears to have frozen water in ice caps and possibly beneath its land surface. Europa, one of Jupiter's moons, may have water in a liquid state, thanks to volcanic heat emanating from its core.

No planet or moon comes close, however, to having water like earth has, with its vast oceans, fluid ribbons of fresh water, and voluminous lakes and aquifers—all connected in a solar-powered cycle of renewal. The beauty and variety of earth's landscapes and life-forms are made possible by water. And nature is not making any more of it: the water that is here is all there will be.

No generation before ours would have asked the question posed in this closing chapter's title. It has an ominous ring: how can it possibly be up to us to save earth's rivers? But the degree of our dominion over rivers has put us in exactly this position. Most rivers are no longer controlled by nature, but by us.

Human impacts on the hydrologic environment have increased on the order of nine-fold since 1950.[1] This is an enormous change in a very short period of time. Only a portion of this impact stems directly from withdrawals of water for irrigation, industries, and cites, which have tripled over the last half century. Most of it stems from human manipulation of natural flow patterns through the construction and operation of dams, reservoirs, dikes, and levees. Species that evolved over the millennia within earth's aquatic ecosystems are now reeling from these human-induced impacts. We have cast them into a race for survival for which they are not evolutionarily prepared. By virtue of our domination, we have become their stewards.

Ecologists now are warning us that stewardship of nature is not an altruistic act, but rather a rational one of self-preservation. The goods and services that aquatic ecosystems provide are too central to human well-being for us to get along for any great length of time without them. They perform functions we depend upon and cannot replicate. Technology has not freed us from this dependence, but has blinded us to it. Whether we realize it or not, our staying power as a species depends upon our ability to coexist with other species.

The deep conundrum we face is how to exercise stewardship of other species when the needs and aspirations of our fellow Homo sapiens are so large, and still growing. Within a generation, some 3 billion people will be living in countries that hydrologists classify as water-stressed based simply on the amount of water available per person. Is there hope for rivers and freshwater species in those places? Between 1950 and today, about 3.5 billion people were added to the planet; 3 billion more will likely be added over the next half century. All people must have access to sufficient water, food, and energy for a healthy and secure life. At the same time, a large global middle class aspires to the high-consumption lifestyles now enjoyed by the richest 1 billion people—including meat-rich diets, luxurious caches of clothes and cars, recreational golfing, and sizeable homes with lush green lawns. Even as world population is growing, per capita global water demand is rising, intensifying total human impacts on freshwater ecosystems.

As if this predicament was not difficult enough, global climatic change from the buildup of greenhouse gases will greatly complicate our efforts to create a water-secure future. Glaciers and mountain snowpacks, the natural reservoirs that feed many of the world's rivers, are melting. As temperatures rise, and as more precipitation falls as rain rather than snow, they will melt faster. Glaciers are already retreating, from the Alps to Alaska. But they are retreating fastest in the high-altitude regions of Africa, Asia, and Latin America, where most of the world's poor people live and where most of the world's population growth will take place. For a period of time, accelerated glacial melting will produce an increase in river runoff; but then it will be gone. Officials in La Paz, Bolivia, for example, now openly worry about future water shortages because the glaciers that provide the city's water are retreating so quickly. As Robert Gallaire, a hydrologist with a French scientific institute studying the Bolivian glaciers told a reporter for the *New York Times*, "The problem is we are using reserves that are being reduced. So we have to ask, what will happen in fifty years? Fifty years, you know, is tomorrow."[2]

Against this backdrop of demographic, consumptive, and climatic pressures, rivers and the panoply of life they sustain would seem doomed. However, disastrous loss of freshwater biodiversity is not yet a foregone conclusion. Homo sapiens is among the life-forms that rivers sustain. At some point, the compulsion to save ourselves, as a species, will trigger an impulse to save the aquatic ecosystems that life depends upon.

The question is, what quality of life and earthly realm will be left when that instinctive impulse kicks us into action? Will the Colorado pikeminnow still ply its ancestral waters? Will the Yangtze River dolphin, which now numbers fewer than two hundred individuals, still grace China's largest river? Will salmon still carry out their legendary migrations within the great rivers of northern Europe, New England, and the Pacific Northwest, or will they move only from fish farms to our dinner tables? Will coastal estuaries receive enough fresh water and nutrients to remain productive enough to feed the growing populations that depend upon them? Will legions of filter-feeding mussels still cleanse the river water running by them? Will enough floodplain habitat remain for the feeding and breeding of fish populations that help sustain millions of subsistence dwellers in developing countries, not to mention tropical biodiversity?

Current trends strongly suggest that the answer to all of these questions will be no. We are moving rapidly toward a freshwater world of greater ecological degradation, species extinction, and loss of natural ecosystem services. This may not be the world we want for ourselves or our descendants, but it is the one that is coming if no course corrections are made.

We now have a narrow window of opportunity in which to redirect the ecological trajectory of the planet's rivers toward improvement rather than decline. With the scientific tools and innovative policies we have described in earlier chapters, the time is ripe for mobilizing a global river restoration movement. The good news coming from the restoration efforts now under way around the world is this: when given a chance, river systems often heal. Reconnect a river with its floodplain, and fish and riparian plant communities will rebound. Remove a dam, and species long gone will return upriver. Release a flood pulse from a reservoir, and key habitat improvements will materialize. The science supporting river restoration is now strong enough to warrant greater societal investment in rebalancing human and ecosystem water needs. Moreover, as several of our examples have shown, river health can often be improved with minimal social or economic disruption.

For this movement to gain steam, governments must act swiftly to enact policies that protect river health even as water continues to be appropriated for human needs. Following South Africa's lead, these policies must call for freshwater reserves that consist of the volume and timing of river flows needed to safeguard ecological health. For their part, water managers must embrace the new philosophy of adaptive management, or learning by doing. Delaying action because of uncertainty is no longer a valid excuse, because through experimentation, monitoring, and periodic resetting of goals, progress can be made even in the face of uncertainty. With species extinctions and other irreversible changes around the corner, it is simply essential to get started, and to learn while doing.

Ultimately, for these policy and management reforms to have a durable impact, society's relationship to freshwater ecosystems will need to change in several overarching ways. Water affects so many aspects of our lives that a move to live in better balance with it inevitably will involve some fundamental changes in societal priorities and individual choices.

First, human communities must learn to integrate better with nature's cycles. Homo sapiens, like every other species, is part of nature. But whereas all other life-forms live in synchrony with nature's variability, we actively negate or defy that variability in order to make water supplies reliable for us. Indeed, this is one of the principal aims of modern water engineering—bending natural conditions to create what we surmise to be the most beneficial conditions possible for our cities, towns, and farms. By doing this, however, we reduce the survival chances of many of our earthly companions whose life cycles are keyed to nature's cycles. They need floods to create good habitat. They need water in dry spells as desperately as we do. Once-perennial rivers that now routinely run dry because of heavy irrigation withdrawals will not long support the life that evolved within them. Unless human communities begin to adapt to natural cycles and coexist with aquatic communities, those natural communities will disappear and the ecological work they perform will be lost.

What this means from a practical standpoint is that instead of planning to make every year as good as it can be for us, we plan instead to share the hardship of water-deficit years and the surplus of water-abundant years with the natural communities around us. In periods of drought, we expect to adjust our water-use practices not just to stretch out the available supply for human uses, but because other species need water too. Rationing or other curbs on water use become not signals of failed water management but of the desire to coexist with the life around us. Of course, such a policy will result in short-term economic losses in some years; but the benefit will be healthier and more resilient ecosystems contributing valuable goods and services to the economy over the long term. For some people, the moral obligation to preserve all life will be reason enough to make this adjustment.

Second, we will need to reduce human pressures on the aquatic environment by slowing growth in population and consumption, and by boosting water productivity. Populations continue to grow rapidly in some of the most water-stressed regions of the world, including parts of western and south-central Asia, much of Africa, and the southwestern United States. Currently, about 77 million people are being added to the global population each year, the equivalent of adding another Germany.[3] Reduced population growth rates, both globally and regionally, are critical to meeting human and ecosystem needs for water. At the same time, reducing per capita use of both water and energy, particularly among the top 2 billion or so consumers, would reduce the number and size of dams and reservoirs required, and provide water managers greater flexibility in satisfying environmental flow requirements.

Raising water productivity—the output or benefit derived per liter of water extracted from the natural environment—is critical to remaining within any sustainability boundary established to protect river health. Higher water productivity in the global food system is particularly important. Nearly 70 percent of all the water withdrawn from freshwater ecosystems goes to irrigated agriculture, yet drip irrigation—which often doubles yield per liter of water compared with conventional irrigation methods—accounts for only 1 percent of world irrigated area.[4] From California to Central Asia, water-thirsty crops are grown in dry climates, often with inefficient irrigation methods. At the individual level, dietary choices make a large difference on per capita human impact on rivers and aquifers. A typical American diet requires about 1,970 cubic meters of water per year (in the form of evapotranspiration) to produce, while an equally nutritious vegetarian diet takes only 950 cubic meters.[5] A large-scale shift from animal to vegetable protein could save large quantities of water. Indeed, for the same volume of water consumption, two people could be fed instead of one.

Third, the globalized trend toward the commodification and privatization of water requires a strong reaffirmation that water is a public trust to be preserved for the common good of this generation and those to come. The relatively recent and quickly expanding search for profits from water ownership and management poses a large threat to ecosystem health and species preservation. Those aimed at profiting from water have little incentive to conserve it or to protect its ecological functions. With no "world ecosystem organization" to match the powers of the World Trade Organization, this protective action may need to come in the form of an international freshwater convention, comparable in scope to existing United Nations conventions on climate change and biodiversity. A principal aim of such a convention would be for signatories to agree to establish water allocations specifically to sustain ecosystem health—and to give these allocations priority over nonessential human uses of water.

Lastly, an ethic of stewardship toward fresh water and its dependent species requires that we err on the side of allocating too much water to ecosystems rather than too little. Each habitat and species in the natural world is a life-support component, performing tasks we may or may not be aware of or know the value of. For our own self-preservation, it makes sense to conserve all the components unless we can say with certainty that a particular piece can be eliminated without causing serious harm. With so many components already gone or at risk, there is a premium now on preserving those that remain.

Most deeply, an ethic of stewardship is about respecting the beauty and mystery of a natural world we did not create and cannot fully understand, but over which we have acquired dominance. It is about adding a healthy dose of humility as an antidote to our past hubris. And it is about applying the best of our science, policy, and technology not to further manipulate nature but to better adapt ourselves to its time-tested, life-sustaining cycles.

NOTES

CHAPTER ONE

1. Quoted in Stanley Roland Davison, *The Leadership of the Reclamation Movement, 1875–1902* (New York: Arno Press, 1979).

2. Goldwater makes these statements in "An American Nile," program two of the documentary series *Cadillac Desert: Water and the Transformation of Nature*, distributed by Public Broadcasting System and Columbia TriStar Television, first aired on July 1, 1997.

3. Sandra Postel, "Entering an Era of Water Scarcity: The Challenges Ahead," *Ecological Applications* 10 (August 2000): 941–948.

4. James A. Gore and F. Douglas Shields Jr., "Can Large Rivers Be Restored?" *BioScience* 45 (March 1995): 142–152.

5. Carmen Revenga et al., *Pilot Analysis of Global Ecosystems: Freshwater Systems* (Washington, D.C.: World Resources Institute, 2000).

6. Robert Costanza et al., "The Value of the World's Ecosystem Services and Natural Capital," *Nature* 387 (May 1997): 254–260.

7. N. LeRoy Poff et al., "The Natural Flow Regime: A Paradigm for River Conservation and Restoration," *BioScience* 47 (December 1997): 769–784; Brian Richter et al., "How Much Water Does a River Need?" *Freshwater Biology* 37 (1997): 231–249.

8. Sandra Postel, *Pillar of Sand: Can the Irrigation Miracle Last?* (New York: W. W. Norton, 1999).

9. See, for example, the collection of chapters in Gretchen C. Daily, ed., *Nature's Services: Societal Dependence on Natural Ecosystems* (Washington, D.C.: Island Press, 1997); also see Paul Hawken, Amory Lovins, and L. Hunter Lovins, *Natural Capitalism: Creating the Next Industrial Revolution* (Boston, Mass.: Back Bay Books, 1999).

10. Sandra Postel and Stephen Carpenter, "Freshwater Ecosystem Services," in Daily, ed., *Nature's Services* (note 9), pp. 195–214.

11. Costanza et al., "World's Ecosystem Services" (note 6).

12. Catherine M. Pringle, Mary C. Freeman, and Byron J. Freeman, "Regional

Effects of Hydrologic Alterations on Riverine Macrobiota in the New World: Tropical-Temperate Comparisons," *BioScience* 50 (September 2000): 807–823; Catherine M. Pringle, "River Conservation in Tropical Versus Temperate Latitudes," in P. J. Boon, B. R. Davies, and Geoffrey E. Petts, eds., *Global Perspectives on River Conservation: Science, Policy, and Practice* (New York: John Wiley & Sons, 2000), pp. 371–381.

13. Richard E. Sparks, "Need for Ecosystem Management of Large Rivers and Their Floodplains," *BioScience* 45 (March 1995): 168–182.

14. Postel, *Pillar of Sand* (note 8); quote from M. S. Drower, "Water-Supply, Irrigation, and Agriculture," in C. Singer, E. J. Holmyard, and A. R. Hall, eds., *A History of Technology* (New York: Oxford University Press, 1954).

15. Postel, *Pillar of Sand* (note 8).

16. Edward B. Barbier and Julian R. Thompson, "The Value of Water: Floodplain Versus Large-Scale Irrigation Benefits in Northern Nigeria," *Ambio* 27 (1998): 434–440.

17. Richard A. Haeuber and William K. Michener, "Natural Flood Control," *Issues in Science and Technology* (Fall 1998): 74–80.

18. E. Rykiel, "Ecosystem Science for the Twenty-First Century," *BioScience* 47 (October 1997): 705–708.

19. National Research Council, *Restoration of Aquatic Ecosystems: Science, Technology, and Public Policy* (Washington, D.C.: National Academy Press, 1992).

20. Michael S. Flannery, Part II Rule Revision: Evaluation of Potential Impacts to Streams and Estuaries, Memorandum, Respondent's Exhibit 442, February 28, 1989.

21. For a concise review of human alterations of the global hydrological environment, see David M. Rosenberg, Patrick McCully, and Catherine M. Pringle, "Global-Scale Environmental Effects of Hydrological Alterations: Introduction," *BioScience* 50 (September 2000): 746–751.

22. Charles Vörösmarty and Dork Sahagian, "Anthropogenic Disturbance of the Terrestrial Water Cycle," *BioScience* 50 (September 2000): 753–765.

23. Matts Dynesius and Christer Nilsson, "Fragmentation and Flow Regulation of River Systems in the Northern Third of the World," *Science* 266 (1994): 753–762.

24. B. F. Chao, "Anthropogenic Impact on Global Geodynamics Due to Reservoir Water Impoundment," *Geophysical Research Letters* 22 (1995): 3529–3532. For more on human impacts, see also Sandra Postel, Gretchen C. Daily, and Paul R. Ehrlich, "Human Appropriation of Renewable Fresh Water," *Science* 271: 785–788.

25. World Commission on Dams (WCD), *Dams and Development: A New Framework for Decision-Making* (London: Earthscan, 2000).

26. WCD, *Dams and Development*, pp. 8–10.

27. WCD, *Dams and Development*.

28. Pringle et al., "Hydrologic Alterations" (note 12).

29. C. J. Vörösmarty, P. Green, J. Salisbury, and R. B. Lammers, "Global Water Resources: Vulnerability from Climate Change and Population Growth," *Science* 289 (July 2000): 284–288.

30. Stuart E. Bunn and Angela H. Arthington, "Basic Principles and Ecological Consequences of Altered Flow Regimes for Aquatic Biodiversity," *Environmental Management* 30 (April 2002): 492–507.

31. This section draws from Steven W. Carothers and Bryan T. Brown, *The Colorado River Through Grand Canyon: Natural History and Human Change* (Tucson: University of Arizona Press, 1991).

32. David Dudgeon, "Large-Scale Hydrological Changes in Tropical Asia: Prospects for Riverine Biodiversity," *BioScience* 50 (September 2000): 793–806.

33. Michael Collier, Robert H. Webb, and John C. Schmidt, *Dams and Rivers: Primer on the Downstream Effects of Dams* (Denver, Colo.: U.S. Geological Survey, 1996).

34. William J. Mitsch et al., "Reducing Nitrogen Loading to the Gulf of Mexico from the Mississippi River Basin: Strategies to Counter a Persistent Ecological Problem," *BioScience* 51 (May 2001): 373–388.

35. Richard E. Sparks, John C. Nelson, and Yao Yin, "Naturalization of the Flood Regime in Regulated Rivers: The Case of the Upper Mississippi River," *BioScience* 48 (September 1998): 706–720.

36. Mitsch et al., "Reducing Nitrogen Loading" (note 34).

37. Pringle et al., "Hydrologic Alterations" (note 12).

38. Harald Frederiksen, Jeremy Berkoff, and William Barber, *Water Resources Management in Asia* (Washington, D.C.: The World Bank, 1993).

39. Dudgeon, "Hydrological Changes" (note 32).

40. Revenga et al., *Global Ecosystems* (note 5).

41. Revenga et al., *Global Ecosystems* (note 5).

42. Peter B. Moyle and Robert A. Leidy, "Loss of Biodiversity in Aquatic Ecosystems: Evidence from Fish Faunas," in P. L. Fiedler and S. K. Jain, eds., *Conservation Biology: The Theory and Practice of Nature Conservation, Preservation, and Management* (New York: Chapman and Hall, 1992).

43. Anthony Ricciardi and Joseph B. Rasmussen, "Extinction Rates of North American Freshwater Fauna, *Conservation Biology* 13 (1999): 1220–1222.

44. Bruce Stein, Lynn S. Kutner, and Jonathan S. Adams, eds., *Precious Heritage: The Status of Biodiversity in the United States* (New York: Oxford University Press, 2000).

45. Canary in the coal mine analogy from interview with Richard Neves, "The Man Behind the Mussel," *The Nature Conservancy*, January–February 2001.

46. Example taken from Stephen J. Chaplin et al., "The Geography of Imperilment: Targeting Conservation Toward Critical Biodiversity Areas," in Stein et al., eds., *Precious Heritage* (note 44), pp. 159–199.

47. Pringle et al., "Hydrologic Alterations" (note 12).

48. Stein et al., eds., *Precious Heritage* (note 44), p. 181.

49. Stein et al., eds., *Precious Heritage* (note 44), p. 157.

50. World Wildlife Fund, *The Status of Wild Atlantic Salmon: A River by River Assessment* (Washington, D.C.: 2001).

51. Pringle et al., "Hydrologic Alterations" (note 12).

52. Pringle et al., "Hydrologic Alterations" (note 12).

53. WCD, *Dams and Development* (note 25), pp. 380–381.

54. See Khalil H. Mancy, "The Environmental and Ecological Impacts of the Aswan High Dam," in Hillel Shuval, ed., *Developments in Arid Zone Ecology and Environmental Quality* (Philadelphia: Balaban ISS, 1981); also Gilbert White, "The Environmental Effects of the High Dam at Aswan," *Environment* (September 1988), pp. 5–11, 34–40.

55. Richard Beilfuss, Africa Program Director, International Crane Foundation, Baraboo, Wisc., private e-mail communication with authors, November 2002.

56. There is also a population of river dolphins in the Mekong River in Laos. These dolphins are believed to be genetically equivalent to the marine dolphins of the South China Sea, but are now completely isolated from the sea, according to Jackie King of the Freshwater Research Unit, Zoology Department, University of Cape Town, South Africa, in a private e-mail communication with authors.

57. David Dudgeon, "The Ecology of Tropical Asian Rivers and Streams in Relation to Biodiversity Conservation," *Annual Review of Ecological Systems* 31 (2000): 239–263.

58. Dudgeon, "Tropical Asian Rivers."

59. Dudgeon, "Hydrological Changes" (note 32); Dudgeon, "Tropical Asian Rivers" (note 57).

60. Dudgeon, "Hydrological Changes" (note 32).

61. Dudgeon, "Tropical Asian Rivers" (note 57).

62. Margaret A. Palmer et al., "Linkages Between Aquatic Sediment Biota and Life above Sediments as Potential Drivers of Biodiversity and Ecological Processes," *BioScience* 50 (December 2000): 1062–1075.

63. Palmer et al., "Linkages."

64. P. S. Lake et al., "Global Change and the Biodiversity of Freshwater Ecosystems: Impacts on Linkages Between Above-Sediment and Sediment Biota," *BioScience* 50 (December 2000): 1099–1107.

65. Both quotes contained in Sandra Postel, "Where Have All the Rivers Gone?" *World Watch*, May–June 1995.

66. Dam removals reported in American Rivers, Friends of the Earth, and Trout Unlimited, *Dam Removal Success Stories: Restoring Rivers Through Selective Removal of Dams That Don't Make Sense* (Washington, D.C.: 1999); for a good

overview of scientific aspects of dam removals, see N. LeRoy Poff and David D. Hart, "How Dams Vary and Why It Matters for the Emerging Science of Dam Removal," *BioScience* 52 (August 2002): 659–668.

67. Bruce Babbitt, "What Goes Up, May Come Down," *BioScience* 52 (August 2002): 656–658.

68. Susanne Wong, "Villagers Chart River Recovery Since Pak Mun Gates Opened," *World Rivers Review* 17 (August 2002): 10–11.

CHAPTER TWO

1. This river serpent god goes by various names across southern Africa. Nyaminyami is the namesake of a district in Zimbabwe, held sacred by villagers along the Zambezi River.

2. Patrick McCully, *Silenced Rivers: The Ecology and Politics of Large Dams* (London: Zed Books, 1996).

3. Michael Goulding, Nigel J. H. Smith, and Dennis J. Mahar, *Floods of Fortune: Ecology and Economy along the Amazon* (New York: Columbia University Press, 1996).

4. Donald L. Tennant, "Instream Flow Regimens for Fish, Wildlife, Recreation and Related Environmental Resources," *Fisheries* 1 (July/August 1975): 6–10.

5. Instream Flow Council, *Instream Flows for Riverine Resource Stewardship* (n.p.: Instream Flow Council, 2001).

6. Rebecca E. Tharme, "A Global Perspective on Environmental Flow Assessment: Emerging Trends in the Development and Application of Environmental Flow Methodologies for Rivers," *Rivers Research and Application* (in press).

7. Clair B. Stalnaker, "Low Flow as a Limiting Factor in Warmwater Streams," in L. A. Krumholz, ed., *The Warmwater Streams Symposium* (Bethesda, Md.: American Fisheries Society, 1981), pp. 192–199.

8. Tennant, "Instream Flow Regimens" (note 4).

9. Instream Flow Council, *Instream Flows* (note 5).

10. Kenneth D. Bovee, *A Guide to Stream Habitat Analysis Using the Instream Flow Incremental Methodology* (Denver, Colo.: U.S. Fish and Wildlife Service, 1982).

11. B. A. Richardson, "Evaluation of In-Stream Flow Methodologies for Freshwater Fish in New South Wales," in I. C. Campbell, ed., *Stream Protection: The Management of Rivers for Instream Uses* (Victoria, Australia: Water Studies Centre, Chisholm Institute of Technology, 1986), pp. 143–167.

12. D. Scott and C. S. Shirvell, "A Critique of the In-Stream Flow Incremental Methodology and Observations of Flow Determination in New Zealand," in J. F. Craig and J. B. Kemper, eds., *Regulated Streams: Advances in Ecology* (New York: Plenum Press, 1987), pp. 27–43; Angela H. Arthington and Brad J. Pusey, "In-Stream Flow Management in Australia: Methods, Deficiencies, and Future Direc-

tions," *Australian Biologist* 6 (1993): 52–60; Jackie M. King and Rebecca E. Tharme, *Assessment of the Instream Flow Incremental Methodology and Initial Development of Alternative Instream Flow Methodologies for South Africa* (Pretoria, South Africa: Water Research Commission, 1994).

13. Angela H. Arthington, Jackie M. King, Jay H. O'Keefe, Stuart E. Bunn, J. A. Day, Brad J. Pusey, David R. Bluhdorn, and Rebecca E. Tharme, "Development of an Holistic Approach for Assessing Environmental Flow Requirements of Riverine Ecosystems," in John J. Pigram and Bruce P. Hooper, eds., *Proceedings of an International Seminar and Workshop on Water Allocation for the Environment* (Armidale, Australia: The Centre for Water Policy Research, 1992), pp. 69–76; Merryl Alber, "A Conceptual Model of Estuarine Freshwater Inflow Management," *Estuaries* 25 (2002): 1246–1261; Instream Flow Council, *Instream Flows* (note 5); Jackie M. King and Delana Louw, "Instream Flow Assessments for Regulated Rivers in South Africa Using the Building Block Methodology," *Aquatic Ecosystem Health and Management* 1 (1998): 109–124.

14. Arthington et al., "Holistic Approach" (note 13).

15. Richard E. Sparks, "Risks of Altering the Hydrologic Regime of Large Rivers," in John Cairns, Barbara Niederlehner, and D. R. Orvos, eds., *Predicting Ecosystem Risk*, Vol. 20 (Princeton, N.J.: Princeton Scientific Publishing, 1992), pp. 119–152.

16. Keith F. Walker, Fran Sheldon, and James T. Puckridge, "A Perspective on Dryland River Ecosystems," *Regulated Rivers* 11 (1995): 85–104.

17. N. LeRoy Poff, J. David Allan, Mark B. Bain, James R. Karr, Karen L. Prestegaard, Brian D. Richter, Richard E. Sparks, and Julie C. Stromberg, "The Natural Flow Regime: A Paradigm for River Conservation and Restoration," *BioScience* 47 (December 1997): 769–784.

18. Poff et al., "The Natural Flow Regime."

19. Arthington et al., "Holistic Approach" (note 13).

20. Richardson, "In-Stream Flow Methodologies" (note 11); Scott and Shirvell, "Critique" (note 12); Rebecca E. Tharme, *Review of International Methodologies for the Quantification of the Instream Flow Requirements of Rivers* (Pretoria, South Africa: Department of Water Affairs and Forestry, 1996); Angela H. Arthington and M. Jacinta Zalucki, *Comparative Evaluation of Environmental Flow Assessment Techniques: Review of Methods* (Canberra, Australian Capitol Territory: Land and Water Resources Research and Development Corporation, 1998).

21. Angela H. Arthington, "Wounded Rivers, Thirsty Land: Getting Water Management Right," Inaugural Lecture, April 1997 (Nathan, Queensland, Australia: Centre for Catchment and In-Stream Research, Griffith University, 1997).

22. Arthington et al., "Holistic Approach" (note 13).

23. Tharme, *International Methodologies* (note 20).

24. Rebecca E. Tharme and Jackie M. King, *Development of the Building Block Methodology for Instream Flow Assessments and Supporting Research on the Effects*

of Different Magnitude Flows on Riverine Ecosystems (Cape Town, South Africa: Water Research Commission, 1998).

25. Tharme and King, *Development of the Building Block Methodology for Instream Flow Assessments.*

26. Jackie M. King, Rebecca E. Tharme, and M. S. DeVilliers, eds., *Environmental Flow Assessments for Rivers: Manual for the Building Block Methodology* (Pretoria, South Africa: Water Research Commission, 2000).

27. Tharme, "Global Perspective" (note 6).

28. Tharme, "Global Perspective" (note 6).

29. Angela H. Arthington and Rina Lloyd, *Logan River Trial of the Building Block Methodology for Assessing Environmental Flow Requirements* (Queensland, Australia: Griffith University, 1998).

30. Sandra O. Brizga, Angela H. Arthington, Brad J. Pusey, Mark J. Kennard, Stephen J. Mackay, Garry L. Werren, Neil M. Craigie, and Satish J. Choy, "Benchmarking, a 'Top-Down' Methodology for Assessing Environmental Flows in Australian Rivers," in *Proceedings of International Conference on Environmental Flows for Rivers* (Cape Town, South Africa: Southern Waters Consulting, 2002).

31. Sandra O. Brizga, *"Burnett Basin Water Allocation and Management Plan: Proposed Environmental Flow Performance Measures"* (Brisbane, Queensland, Australia: Department of Natural Resources, 2000).

32. Private communication with Jackie King, Freshwater Research Unit, Zoology Department, University of Cape Town, Cape Town, South Africa, October 2002.

33. Jackie M. King, Cate Brown, and Hossein Sabet, "A Scenario-Based Holistic Approach to Environmental Flow Assessments for Rivers," *Rivers Research and Applications* (in press).

34. Geoffrey E. Petts, "Water Allocation to Protect River Ecosystems," *Regulated Rivers* 12 (1996): 353–365.

35. Adaptive management is well described in a number of publications, including C. S. Holling, ed., *Adaptive Environmental Assessment and Management* (New York: John Wiley & Sons, 1978); Carl Walters, *Adaptive Management of Renewable Resources* (Caldwell, N.J.: Blackburn Press, 1986); C. S. Holling, "What Barriers? What Bridges?" Chap. 1 in Lance H. Gunderson, C. S. Holling, and Stephen S. Light, eds., *Barriers and Bridges to the Renewal of Ecosystems and Institutions* (New York: Columbia University Press, 1995); Kai N. Lee, *Compass and Gyroscope* (Washington, D.C.: Island Press, 1993).

36. Brian D. Richter, Ruth Mathews, David L. Harrison, and Robert Wigington, "Ecologically Sustainable Water Management: Managing River Flows for Ecological Integrity," *Ecological Applications* 13: 206–224.

37. Vicky J. Meretsky, David L. Wegner, and Larry E. Stevens, "Balancing Endangered Species and Ecosystems: A Case Study of Adaptive Management in the Grand Canyon," *Environmental Management* 25 (May 2000): 579–586; Carl Walters, Josh Korman, Larry E. Stevens, and Barry Gold, "Ecosystem Modeling

for Evaluation of Adaptive Management Policies in the Grand Canyon," *Conservation Ecology* 4(2): 1 [online] URL: http://www.consecol.org/vol4/iss2/art1.

38. Clair B. Stalnaker and Edmund J. Wick, "Planning for Flow Requirements to Sustain Stream Biota," Chap. 16 in Ellen E. Wohl, ed., *Inland Flood Hazards: Human, Riparian, and Aquatic Communities* (London: Cambridge University Press, 2000).

39. Lou A. Toth, "Principles and Guidelines for Restoration of River/Floodplain Ecosystems—Kissimmee River, Florida," in John Cairns, ed., *Rehabilitating Damaged Ecosystems* (Cherry Hill, N.J.: Lewis Publications, CRC Press, 1995), pp. 49–73.

40. Carl L. Walters, Lance Gunderson, and C. S. Holling, "Experimental Policies for Water Management in the Everglades," *Ecological Applications* 2 (May 1992): 189–202.

41. Richard E. Sparks, John C. Nelson, and Yao Yin, "Naturalization of the Flood Regime in Regulated Rivers: The Case of the Upper Mississippi River," *BioScience* 48 (September 1998): 706–720.

42. A. I. Robertson, P. Bacon, and G. Heagney, "The Responses of Floodplain Primary Production to Flood Frequency and Timing," *Journal of Applied Ecology* 38 (February 2001): 126–136.

43. Kevin H. Rogers and Regina Bestbier, *Development of a Protocol for the Definition of the Desired State of Riverine Systems in South Africa* (Pretoria, South Africa: Department of Environmental Affairs and Tourism, 1997); Elise R. Irwin and Mary C. Freeman, "Proposal for Adaptive Management to Conserve Biotic Integrity in a Regulated Segment of the Tallapoosa River, Alabama, U.S.A.," *Conservation Biology* 16 (October 2002): 1212–1222.

44. Private e-mail communication with James T. Peterson, University of Georgia, Athens, Ga., July 2002.

45. Robert Glennon, *Water Follies: Groundwater Pumping and the Fate of America's Fresh Waters* (Washington, D.C.: Island Press, 2002).

46. Glennon, *Water Follies*.

47. Carmen Revenga, Jake Brunner, Norbert Henninger, Ken Kassem, and Richard Payne, *Pilot Analysis of Global Ecosystems: Freshwater Systems* (Washington, D.C.: World Resources Institute, 2000).

48. Glennon, *Water Follies* (note 45); Wayne B. Solley, Robert R. Pierce, and Howard A. Perlman, *Estimated Use of Water in the United States in 1995*, Circular 1200 (Denver, Colo.: U.S. Geological Survey, 1998).

49. Mario Sophocleous, "From Safe Yield to Sustainable Development of Water Resources—the Kansas Experience," *Journal of Hydrology* 235 (August 2000): 27–43.

50. Glennon, *Water Follies* (note 45).

51. Poster presented at "Environmental Flows for River Systems" conference in Cape Town, South Africa, March 3–8, 2002.

52. See "Flow Restoration Database" at www.freshwaters.org.

53. Private e-mail communication with Jon Hornsby, Division of Wildlife and Freshwater Fisheries, Alabama, July 2002.

54. Stalnaker and Wick, "Flow Requirements" (note 38).

55. Solley et al., *Estimated Use of Water* (note 48).

56. Peter R. Wilcox, G. Mathias Kondolf, W. V. Matthews, and A. F. Barta, "Specification of Sediment Maintenance Flows for a Large Gravel-Bed River," *Water Resources Research* 32 (1996): 2911–2921.

57. McBain and Trush, *Trinity River Restoration Program: A Summary of the United States Secretary of the Interior Record of Decision, December 19, 2000* (Arcata, Calif.: 2001).

58. Stalnaker and Wick, "Flow Requirements" (note 38).

59. See "Flow Restoration Database" at www.freshwaters.org.

60. M. C. Acreman, F. A. K. Farquharson, M. P. McCartney, C. Sullivan, K. Campbell, N. Hodgson, J. Morton, D. Smith, M. Birley, D. Knott, J. Lazenby, and E. B. Barbier, *Managed Flood Releases from Reservoirs: Issues and Guidance*, Report to DFID and the World Commission on Dams (Wallingford, U.K.: Centre for Ecology and Hydrology, 2000).

61. See "Flow Restoration Database" at www.freshwaters.org.

62. See "Flow Restoration Database" at www.freshwaters.org.

63. Robert T. Muth, Larry W. Crist, Kirk E. LaGory, John W. Hayse, Kevin R. Bestgen, Thomas P. Ryan, Joseph K. Lyons, and Richard A. Valdez, *Flow and Temperature Recommendations for Endangered Fishes in the Green River Downstream of Flaming Gorge Dam* (Lakewood, Colo.: Upper Colorado River Recovery Program, 2000).

64. David B. Irving and Timothy Modde, "Home-Range Fidelity and Use of Historical Habitat by Adult Colorado Squawfish (*Ptychocheilus lucius*) in the White River, Colorado and Utah," *Western North American Naturalist* 60 (2000): 16–25.

65. Robert J. Behnke and D. E. Benson, *Endangered and Threatened Fishes of the Upper Colorado River Basin* (Fort Collins, Colo.: Colorado State University Cooperative Extension Service, 1983).

66. U.S. Fish and Wildlife Service, *Colorado Squawfish* (Ptychocheilus lucius) *Recovery Goals: Amendment and Supplement to the Colorado Squawfish Recovery Plan* (Denver, Colo.: U.S. Fish and Wildlife Service Region 6, 2002); Muth et al., *Temperature Recommendations* (note 63).

67. Muth et al., *Temperature Recommendations* (note 63).

68. U.S. Fish and Wildlife Service, *Final Biological Opinion on Operation of Flaming Gorge Dam* (Denver, Colo.: U.S. Fish and Wildlife Service, 1992).

69. Kevin R. Bestgen, *Interacting Effects of Physical and Biological Processes on Recruitment of Colorado Squawfish* (Ph.D. diss., Colorado State University, 1997).

CHAPTER THREE

1. Jefferson quote from National Research Council, *The Missouri River Ecosystem: Exploring the Prospects for Recovery* (Washington, D.C.: National Academy Press, 2002), p. 109.

2. Amy Vickers, *Handbook of Water Use and Conservation* (Amherst, Mass.: WaterPlow Press, 2001); Sandra Postel, *Last Oasis: Facing Water Scarcity* (New York: W. W. Norton, 1992, rev. ed. 1997).

3. World Commission on Dams (WCD), *Dams and Development: A New Framework for Decision-Making* (London: Earthscan, 2000).

4. International Conference on Freshwater, *Water—A Key to Sustainable Development: Recommendations for Action*, Bonn, Germany, December 3–7, 2001.

5. European Parliament and Council of the European Union, Directive 2000/60/EC establishing a framework for Community action in the field of water policy, *Official Journal of the European Communities* (December 22, 2000) L 327: 1–72.

6. See articles and links at the World Wildlife Fund—Europe Web site at www.panda.org/about_wwf/what_we_do/freshwater/news/news.cfm?uNewsID=2753.

7. Institutes of Justinian 2.1.1. as cited in Supreme Court of California, *National Audubon Society et al., Petitioners v. The Superior Court of Alpine County, Respondent; Department of Water and Power of the City of Los Angeles et al., Real Parties in Interest*. 33 Cal.3d 419, 1983.

8. Will Durant, *Caesar and Christ* (New York: Simon and Schuster, 1944).

9. South African Department of Water Affairs and Forestry, White Paper on Water Policy, Pretoria, South Africa, 1997.

10. Jackie M. King, Rebecca E. Tharme, and M. S. DeVilliers, eds., *Environmental Flow Assessments for Rivers: Manual for the Building Block Methodology* (Pretoria, South Africa: Water Research Commission, 2000); Jackie King, private e-mail communication, September 2002.

11. South African National Water Act No. 36 of 1998, *Government Gazette* Vol. 398, No. 19182, Cape Town, August 26, 1998.

12. South African National Water Act No. 36 of 1998 (note 11), Part 3: "The Reserve," and Appendix 1: "Fundamental Principles and Objectives for a New Water Law in South Africa."

13. Jay H. O'Keefe, "Environmental Flow Assessments Within the South African Integrated Planning Process for Water Resources," in King et al., *Flow Assessments* (note 10), pp. 41–64.

14. IUCN (The World Conservation Union), *Vision for Water and Nature: A World Strategy for Conservation and Sustainable Management of Water Resources in the Twenty-First Century* (Gland, Switzerland, and Cambridge, U.K.: 2000), p. 15.

15. Industry Commission, "A Full-Repairing Lease: Inquiry into Ecologically Sustainable Land Management," Draft Report, 1997.

16. Number of dams from WCD, *Dams and Development* (note 3); population from Population Reference Bureau, *World Population Data Sheet* (Washington, D.C.: 2000).

17. This concern is reflected in Department of Resources and Energy, *Water 2000: A Perspective on Australia's Water Resources to the Year 2000* (Canberra: Australian Government Publishing Service, 1983).

18. Background information obtained from agency Web site at www.affa.gov.au/water-reform/facts2.html.

19. Agriculture and Resource Management Council of Australia and New Zealand, and the Australian and New Zealand Environment and Conservation Council, "National Principles for the Provision of Water for Ecosystems," Revised Draft, November 2001.

20. Jon Nevill, *Freshwater Biodiversity: Protecting Freshwater Ecosystems in the Face of Infrastructure Development* (Canberra, Australia: Water Research Foundation of Australia, 2001).

21. "The Delicate Balance of Sharing Water," *World Water and Environmental Engineering*, July–August 2001.

22. Angela Arthington, "The Water Act (Qld) 2000: Environmental Flow Objectives," Paper delivered to the Queensland Environmental Law Association Seminar, *Water Bill 2000*, University of Queensland, St. Lucia, 2000.

23. Arthington, "The Water Act (Qld) 2000."

24. Angela Arthington, private communication with author, Brisbane, Queensland, Australia, August 28, 2001.

25. Don J. Blackmore, "The Murray-Darling Basin Cap on Diversions—Policy and Practice for the New Millennium," *National Water* (June 1999): 1–12.

26. Murray-Darling Basin Commission (MDBC), "The Cap" (Canberra, Australia: 1999).

27. MDBC, "Cap."

28. MDBC, *Striking the Balance: Murray-Darling Basin Cap on Diversions—Water Year 1997/98* (Canberra, Australia: 1998).

29. MDBC, "Cap" (note 26).

30. Blackmore, "Murray-Darling Basin Cap" (note 25).

31. Nevill, *Freshwater Biodiversity* (note 20).

32. J. Whittington et al., "Ecological Sustainability of Rivers of the Murray-Darling," in *Review of the Operation of the Cap* (Canberra, Australian Capital Territory: Murray-Darling Basin Ministerial Council, 2000); author communication with scientists at *Riversymposium 2001*, Brisbane, Australia, August 27–31, 2001.

33. Chris Gippel, Trevor Jacobs, and Tony McLeod, "Environmental Flows and Water Quality Objectives for the River Murray," presented at *Riversymposium 2001*, Brisbane, Australia, August 27–31, 2001.

34. Arthur C. Benke, "A Perspective on America's Vanishing Streams," *Journal of the North American Benthological Society* 9 (March 1990): 77–88.

35. U.S. Environmental Protection Agency (USEPA), New England Office, "Ensuring Adequate Instream Flows in New England" (Boston: 2000).

36. U.S. Geological Survey, *Concepts for National Assessment of Water Availability and Use* (Reston, Va.: 2002).

37. David H. Getches, "The Metamorphosis of Western Water Policy: Have Federal Laws and Local Decisions Eclipsed the States' Role?" *Stanford Environmental Law Journal* 20 (1): 3–72.

38. David M. Gillilan and Thomas C. Brown, *Instream Flow Protection: Seeking a Balance in Western Water Use* (Washington, D.C.: Island Press, 1997), p. 178.

39. Gillilan and Brown, *Instream Flow Protection*.

40. Lois G. Witte, "Still No Water for the Woods," Paper prepared for the ALI-ABA Federal Lands Law Conference, Salt Lake City, Utah, October 19, 2001. The U.S. Forest Service temporarily won an implied reserved instream flow right in Idaho, but the decision was overturned upon a rehearing of the case by the Idaho Supreme Court after the Justice who wrote the original opinion had been voted off the bench.

41. Quote from Organic Administration Act, 16 U.S.C. 473 et seq., June 4, 1897, as cited in Witte, "Still No Water for the Woods"; figure on Forest Service lands important to aquatic biodiversity also from Witte, "Still No Water for the Woods."

42. National Park Service Organic Act of 1916, as quoted in Gillilan and Brown, *Instream Flow Protection* (note 38), p. 182.

43. Field presentation in Rocky Mountain National Park for "Managing River Flows for Biodiversity Conservation: A Conference on Science, Policy, and Conservation Action," Fort Collins, Colo., July 30–August 2, 2001.

44. Gillilan and Brown, *Instream Flow Protection* (note 38). In the end, however, the Tellico Dam was built. A federal appropriations bill signed into law in 1979 exempted the project from the ESA. The Tennessee Valley Authority relocated the remaining snail darters to other streams in the region and then finished constructing the dam.

45. "Conservation Groups Support Endangered Species Deal to Restore Flows in the Walla Walla River," press release, June 28, 2001, accessed from the Web site of American Rivers at www.amrivers.org/pressrelease/instreamflow6.28.01.htm.

46. American Rivers and Trout Unlimited, "International Report Reveals Flaws in United States Regulation of Dams," press release, November 20, 2000, Washington, D.C.

47. Brent Israelsen, "Grand Canyon Flood, Part 2," *The Salt Lake Tribune*, September 24, 2002.

48. Michael Collier, Robert H. Webb, and John C. Schmidt, *Dams and Rivers: Primer on the Downstream Effects of Dams*, Circular 1126 (Denver, Colo.: U.S.

Geological Survey, 1996); Upper Colorado River Case Study Panel Presentation at the conference, "River Flows" (note 43).

49. Sandra Postel, *Pillar of Sand: Can the Irrigation Miracle Last?* (New York: W. W. Norton, 1999).

50. Gillilan and Brown, *Instream Flow Protection* (note 38).

51. Margaret B. Bowman, "Legal Perspectives on Dam Removal," *BioScience* 52 (August 2002): 739–747.

52. U.S. Department of the Interior, "Interior Secretary Signs Landmark Conservation Agreement to Remove Edwards Dam," press release, Washington, D.C., May 26, 1998.

53. Michael S. Flannery, Ernst B. Peebles, Ralph T. Montgomery, "A Percent-of-Flow Approach for Managing Reductions of Freshwater Inflows from Unimpounded Rivers to Southwest Florida Estuaries," *Estuaries* 25 (December 2002): 1318–1331.

54. USEPA, New England Office, "Adequate Instream Flows" (note 35).

55. Gillilan and Brown, *Instream Flow Protection* (note 38).

56. Nicole Silk, Jack McDonald, and Robert Wigington, "Turning Instream Flow Water Rights Upside Down," *Rivers* 7 (April 2000): 298–313.

57. Gillilan and Brown, *Instream Flow Protection* (note 38).

58. Supreme Court of the United States, Majority opinion in *PUD No. 1 of Jefferson County v. Washington Department of Ecology*, Washington, D.C.: 1994; for more on the context and implications of this important case, and how it could be used to protect and restore flows, see Katherine Ransel, "The Sleeping Giant Awakens: *PUD No. 1 of Jefferson County v. Washington Department of Ecology*," *Environmental Law* 25 (Spring 1995): 255–283.

59. USEPA, New England Office, "Adequate Instream Flows" (note 35).

60. American Rivers Web site at www.amrivers.org/instreamflow/regulatorystrategies.htm.

61. Katherine Ransel, Senior Counsel, American Rivers, private e-mail communication, September 2002; for the court decision, see www.courts.wa.gov/opinions/.

62. Melissa Scanlan, "Access to Wisconsin Water: The Public Trust Doctrine—Past, Present, and Future," presented at *Waters of Wisconsin Forum*, Madison, Wisc., October 22, 2002.

63. Barry Usagawa, "Landmark Hawaii Supreme Court Decision Creates Water Use Prioritization and Re-Use May Become the Key Solution," in *Proceedings of the Water Sources Conference* (American Water Works Association and others), Las Vegas, Nev., January 27–30, 2002. Text of the court decision is available at www.hawaii.gov/jud.

64. Dan A. Tarlock, Presentation for Water Resource Management for Line Officers, U.S. Forest Service, Prescott, Ariz., 2000.

65. State of Connecticut Superior Court, *City of Waterbury, Town of Wolcott,*

Town of Middlebury and Town of Watertown v. Town of Washington, Town of Roxbury, Steep Rock Association, Inc., Roxbury Land Trust, and Shepaug River Association, Inc., No. X01-UWY-CV97-140886 Waterbury, Conn., February 16, 2000.

66. Rivers Alliance of Connecticut, "CT Supreme Court Reverses Shepaug River Decision," Web site at www.riversalliance.org/legal_watch.htm. The state Supreme Court decision is available at the Court's Web site at www.jud.state.ct.us/supapp/external/Cases/AROcr/260cr80.pdf.

67. For an excellent review of the evolution of and controversy over the doctrine, see Helen Ingram and Cy R. Oggins, "The Public Trust Doctrine and Community Values in Water," *Natural Resources Journal* 32 (1992): 515–537.

68. Supreme Court of California, *National Audubon Society et al., Petitioners v. The Superior Court of Alpine County, Respondent; Department of Water and Power of the City of Los Angeles et al., Real Parties in Interest,* 33 Cal.3d 419, 1983.

69. Getches, "Metamorphosis" (note 37).

70. Dan A. Tarlock, "Water Policy Adrift," *Forum for Applied Research and Public Policy* (Spring 2001): 63–70.

71. Richard W. Wahl, "United States," in Ariel Dinar and Ashok Subramanian, eds., *Water Pricing Experiences: An International Perspective* (Washington, D.C.: The World Bank, 1997).

72. Mateen Thobani, "Formal Water Markets: Why, When, and How to Introduce Tradable Water Rights," *The World Bank Research Observer* 12 (February 1997): 161–179.

73. Thobani, "Formal Water Markets."

74. Thobani, "Formal Water Markets."

75. Blackmore, "Murray-Darling Basin Cap" (note 25).

76. Stephen Wyatt, "Trading in Water Licenses Attracts Big Money," *Financial Times,* February 17, 1999.

77. Gillilan and Brown, *Instream Flow Protection* (note 38).

78. Clay Landry, "Market Transfers of Water for Environmental Protection in the Western United States," *Water Policy* 1 (1998): 457–469.

79. "Washington Department of Ecology Buys Private Water Rights for Fish," *U.S. Water News,* January 2001.

80. Landry, "Market Transfers" (note 78).

81. Josh Newcom, "Is the California Water Market Open for Business?" *Western Water* (March–April 2001).

82. Aldo Leopold, *A Sand County Almanac* (New York: Oxford University Press, 1949), p. 203.

83. Edward O. Wilson, *Consilience: The Unity of Knowledge* (New York: Vintage Books, 1998), p. 262.

84. International Joint Commission, *Protection of the Waters of the Great Lakes: Interim Report to the Governments of Canada and the United States* (Washington, D.C., and Ottawa, Ontario: 1999), p. 28.

CHAPTER FOUR

1. The Nature Conservancy, Freshwater Initiative, "Flow Restoration Database," at www.freshwaters.org.

2. Thomas Schmidt and Jeremy Schmidt, *The Saga of Lewis and Clark* (New York: DK Publishing, 1999).

3. National Research Council (NRC), *The Missouri River Ecosystem: Exploring the Prospects for Recovery* (Washington, D.C.: National Academy Press, 2002).

4. David L. Galat and Robin Lipkin, "Restoring Ecological Integrity of Great Rivers: Historical Hydrographs Aid in Defining Reference Conditions for the Missouri River," *Hydrobiologia* 422/423 (2000): 29–48.

5. Galat and Lipkin, "Great Rivers."

6. NRC, *Missouri River Ecosystem* (note 3).

7. NRC, *Missouri River Ecosystem* (note 3).

8. Summaries of the most endangered rivers, accessed from the American Rivers Web site at www.americanrivers.org.

9. NRC, *Missouri River Ecosystem* (note 3).

10. David L. Galat, U.S. Geological Survey, Biological Resources Division, Missouri Cooperative Fish and Wildlife Research Unit, University of Missouri, Columbia, Mo., private e-mail communication, September 2002.

11. NRC, *Missouri River Ecosystem* (note 3), p. 3.

12. NRC, *Missouri River Ecosystem* (note 3).

13. U.S. Army Corps of Engineers, *Missouri River Master Water Control Manual—Review and Update*, Revised Draft Environmental Impact Statement, August 2001; American Rivers Web site at www.americanrivers.org.

14. David L. Galat et al., "Flooding to Restore Connectivity of Regulated, Large-River Wetlands," *BioScience* 48 (September 1998): 721–733.

15. NRC, *Missouri River Ecosystem* (note 3).

16. NRC, *Missouri River Ecosystem* (note 3).

17. City Council of Brisbane (Queensland, Australia), "The Jagara Are the People of the Brisbane River Watershed," at www.brisbane-stories.powerup.com.au/maggil/02mag_pages/mag_aborigines21.htm.

18. Cooperative Research Centre for Catchment Hydrology (CRC), background information at www.catchment.crc.org.au, accessed April 2002; all dollar figures are U.S. dollars.

19. CRC, www.catchment.crc.org.au.

20. Sandra O. Brizga, "Hydrology," in Angela H. Arthington et al., *Environmental Flow Requirements of the Brisbane River Downstream from Wivenhoe Dam* (Brisbane, Queensland: South East Queensland Water Corporation, and Centre for Catchment and In-Stream Research, Griffith University, 2000), pp. 65–85.

21. Angela H. Arthington et al., *Environmental Flow Requirements of the Brisbane River Downstream from Wivenhoe Dam* (Brisbane, Queensland: South East

Queensland Water Corporation, and Centre for Catchment and In-Stream Research, Griffith University, 2000).

22. Angela H. Arthington, "Brisbane River Trial of a Flow Restoration Methodology (FLOWRESM)," in A. H. Arthington and J. M. Zalucki, eds., *Water for the Environment: Recent Approaches to Assessing and Providing Environmental Flows* (Brisbane: AWWA, 1998), pp. 35–50; Arthington et al., *Flow Requirements* (note 21).

23. Angela Arthington, Centre for Catchment and In-Stream Research, Griffith University, Queensland, Australia, private e-mail communication with author, March 27, 2002.

24. Quote appears in Commission for Environmental Cooperation (CEC), *Ribbon of Life: An Agenda for Preserving Transboundary Migratory Bird Habitat on the Upper San Pedro River* (Montreal: 1999).

25. San Pedro Expert Study Team, *Sustaining and Enhancing Riparian Migratory Bird Habitat on the Upper San Pedro River* (Montreal: CEC, 1999).

26. San Pedro Expert Study Team, *Bird Habitat*.

27. Patricia Orr and Bonnie Colby, "Nature-Oriented Visitors and Their Expenditures: Upper San Pedro River Basin," University of Arizona, Tucson, 2002.

28. Tomas Charles Goode and Thomas Maddock III, *Simulation of Groundwater Conditions in the Upper San Pedro Basin for the Evaluation of Alternative Futures* (Tucson, Ariz.: University of Arizona, 2000).

29. San Pedro Expert Study Team, *Bird Habitat* (note 25).

30. San Pedro Expert Study Team, *Bird Habitat* (note 25).

31. San Pedro Expert Study Team, *Bird Habitat* (note 25).

32. Upper San Pedro Partnership (USPP), *Upper San Pedro Conservation Plan 2002 Progress Report* (Sierra Vista, Ariz.: 2002a).

33. USPP, *Upper San Pedro Conservation Plan*.

34. USPP, *Upper San Pedro Partnership Planning Activity: 2002 Progress Report* (Sierra Vista, Ariz.: 2002b).

35. USPP, *Upper San Pedro Conservation Plan* (note 32).

36. "Upper San Pedro Partnership Water Conservation Strategies," *Sierra Vista Herald*, November 11, 2001.

37. USPP, *Upper San Pedro Conservation Plan* (note 32).

38. Catherine M. Pringle and Frederick N. Scatena, "Freshwater Resource Development: Case Studies from Puerto Rico and Costa Rica," in L. U. Hatch and M. E. Swisher, eds., *Managed Ecosystems: The Mesoamerican Experience* (New York: Oxford University Press, 1999).

39. Jonathan P. Benstead, James G. March, Catherine M. Pringle, and Frederick N. Scatena, "Effects of a Low-Head Dam and Water Abstractions on Migratory Tropical Stream Biota," *Ecological Applications* 9 (February 1999): 656–668.

40. Frederick N. Scatena and Sherri L. Johnson, *Instream-Flow Analysis for the*

Luquillo Experimental Forest, Puerto Rico: Methods and Analysis (Rio Piedras, Puerto Rico: U.S. Forest Service and International Institute of Tropical Forestry, 2001).

41. Catherine M. Pringle, "Exploring How Disturbance Is Transmitted Upstream: Going Against the Flow," *Journal of the North American Benthological Society* 16 (February 1997): 425–438.

42. Benstead et al., "Effects of a Low-Head Dam" (note 39).

43. James G. March, Jonathan P. Benstead, Catherine M. Pringle, and Frederick N. Scatena, "Migratory Drift of Larval Freshwater Shrimps in Two Tropical Streams, Puerto Rico," *Freshwater Biology* 40 (1998): 261–273.

44. Benstead et al., "Effects of a Low-Head Dam" (note 39).

45. Pringle and Scatena, "Freshwater Resource Development" (note 38).

46. March et al., "Larval Freshwater Shrimps" (note 43).

47. Benstead et al., "Effects of a Low-Head Dam" (note 39).

48. Benstead et al., "Effects of a Low-Head Dam" (note 39).

49. James G. March, Jonathan P. Benstead, Frederick N. Scatena, and Catherine M. Pringle, "Damming Tropical Island Streams: Problems, Solutions, and Alternatives," *BioScience* (in review).

50. Pringle, "Disturbance" (note 41).

51. U.S. National Park Service, Web site for Mammoth Cave National Park at www.nps.gov/maca/home.htm.

52. U.S. Army Corps of Engineers, *Environmental Assessment—Green River Lock and Dam Nos. 3, 4, 5, 6 and Barren River No. 1* (Louisville, Ky.: Louisville District, June 2001).

53. D. C. Weeks, Jay H. O'Keeffe, A. Fourie, and Brian R. Davies, *A Pre-Impoundment Study of the Sabie-Sand River System, Mpumalanga with Special Reference to Predicted Impacts on the Kruger National Park*, Vol. 1 (Pretoria, South Africa: Water Research Commission, 1996).

54. G. L. Heritage, A. W. van Niekerk, B. P. Moon, L. J. Broadhurst, K. H. Rogers, and C. S. James, *The Geomorphological Response to Changing Flow Regimes of the Sabie and Letaba River Systems* (Pretoria, South Africa: Water Research Commission, 1997).

55. Rebecca E. Tharme, *Sabie-Sand River System: Instream Flow Requirements* (Pretoria, South Africa: Department of Water Affairs and Forestry, 1997).

56. Kevin H. Rogers, Dirk Roux, and Harry Biggs, "Challenges for Catchment Management Agencies: Lessons from Bureaucracies, Business, and Resource Management," *Water SA* 26 (October 2000): 505–511.

57. Kevin H. Rogers and Regina Bestbier, *Development of a Protocol for the Definition of the Desired State of Riverine Systems in South Africa* (Pretoria, South Africa: Department of Environmental Affairs and Tourism, 1997).

58. Rogers and Bestbier, *Protocol*.

59. Heritage et al., *Geomorphological Response* (note 54).

60. Heritage et al., *Geomorphological Response* (note 54).

61. Jay H. O'Keeffe, D. C. Weeks, A. Fourie, and Brian R. Davies, *A Pre-Impoundment Study of the Sabie-Sand River System, Mpumalanga with Special Reference to Predicted Impacts on the Kruger National Park*, Vol. 3 (Pretoria, South Africa: Water Research Commission, 1996).

62. O'Keeffe et al., *Sabie-Sand River System* (note 61).

CHAPTER FIVE

1. Blaine Harden, "Dams, and Politics, Channel Flow of the Mighty Missouri," *The New York Times*, May 5, 2002.

2. Khayyám quoted in Patrick McCully, *Silenced Rivers: The Ecology and Politics of Large Dams* (London: Zed Books, 1996), p. 238.

3. Donald Worster, *Rivers of Empire: Water, Aridity, and the Growth of the American West* (New York: Oxford University Press, 1985), p. 329.

4. Fikret Berkes, Mina Kislalioglu, Carl Folke, and Madhav Gadgil, "Exploring the Basic Ecological Unit: Ecosystem-Like Concepts in Traditional Societies," *Ecosystems* 1 (1998): 409–415.

5. A similar idea is fleshed out in Geoffrey Heal et al., "Protecting Natural Capital Through Ecosystem Service Districts," *Stanford Environmental Law Journal* 20 (2001): 333–364.

6. Michael M. Horowitz, "The Management of an African River Basin: Alternative Scenarios for Environmentally Sustainable Economic Development and Poverty Alleviation," in Proceedings of the International UNESCO Symposium, *Water Resources Planning in a Changing World* (Karlsruhe, Germany: Bundesanstalt für Gewässerkundef, 1994).

7. World Commission on Dams (WCD), *Dams and Development: A New Framework for Decision-Making* (London: Earthscan, 2000).

8. Peter Bosshard, "An Act of Economic and Environmental Nonsense," 1999, accessed via the Web site of International Rivers Network at www.irn.org/programs/safrica/index.asp?id=bosshard.study.html.

9. As quoted in Bosshard, "An Act of Economic and Environmental Nonsense."

10. W. M. Adams, *Wasting the Rain: Rivers, People, and Planning in Africa* (London: Earthscan Publications, 1992).

11. The World Bank, *Water Resources Sector Strategy: Strategic Directions for World Bank Engagement*, draft (Washington, D.C.: March 2002).

12. Susanne Wong, "Villagers Chart River Recovery since Pak Mun Gates Opened," *World Rivers Review* 17 (August 2002).

13. IUCN (The World Conservation Union), *Vision for Water and Nature: A World Strategy for Conservation and Sustainable Management of Water Resources in the Twenty-First Century* (Gland, Switzerland, and Cambridge, U.K.: IUCN, 2000).

14. European Union Life-Environment Project, "Wise Use of Floodplains," Web site at www.floodplains.org (accessed November 21, 2002).

15. For a good overview of these methods, see Lawrence H. Goulder and Donald Kennedy, "Valuing Ecosystem Services: Philosophical Bases and Empirical Methods," in Gretchen C. Daily, ed., *Nature's Services* (Washington, D.C.: Island Press, 1997).

16. Quote is contained in Geoffrey Heal, *Nature and the Marketplace: Capturing the Value of Ecosystem Services* (Washington, D.C.: Island Press, 2000), pp. 50–51.

17. Martha Echavarria, "FONAG: The Water-Based Finance Mechanism of the Condor Bioreserve in Ecuador," working draft (Quito, Ecuador: The Nature Conservancy, November 2001).

18. Brian W. van Wilgen, Richard M. Cowling, and Chris J. Burgers, "Valuation of Ecosystem Services: A Case Study from South African Fynbos Ecosystems," *BioScience* 46 (March 1996): 184–189.

19. U.S. Geological Survey, *Concepts for National Assessment of Water Availability and Use* (Reston, Va.: 2002).

20. Brian D. Richter and Kent H. Redford, "The Art (and Science) of Brokering Deals Between Conservation and Use," *Conservation Biology* 13 (June 1999): 1235–1237.

21. This section draws heavily upon Navroz K. Dubash, Mairi Dupar, Smitu Kothari, and Tundu Lissu, *A Watershed in Global Governance? An Independent Assessment of the World Commission on Dams* (India: World Resources Institute, Lokayan, and Lawyers' Environmental Action Team, 2001).

22. Dubash et al., *Watershed in Global Governance?*

23. Kader Asmal, "Globalisation from Below," Preface to WCD, *Dams and Development* (note 7).

24. World Commission on Dams, CD-ROM, World Commission on Dams Secretariat, Cape Town, South Africa, 2000.

25. Dubash et al., *Watershed in Global Governance?* (note 21).

26. Patrick McCully, "One Year after the World Commission on Dams: Reflections on the Diverse Reactions to Groundbreaking Report," *World Rivers Review* 16: June 2001.

27. McCully, "One Year After" (including quote).

28. The World Bank, *Water Resources Sector Strategy* (note 11).

29. IUCN (The World Conservation Union), "Statement on the World Commission on Dams," Gland, Switzerland, 2001.

30. Tamsyn Sherwill and Kevin Rogers, "Public Participation in Setting the Goals for Integrated Water Resource Management: A Means to Equity and Sustainability?" Appendix 6 in Brian E. van Wilgen et al., "Principles and Processes for Supporting Stakeholder Participation in Integrated River Management: Lessons from the Sabie-Sand Catchment," Final Report Project K5/1062, Water Research Commission, Pretoria, South Africa, 2002.

31. For more on the idea of coevolution of preferences, see Robert Costanza and Carl Folke, "Valuing Ecosystem Services with Efficiency, Fairness, and Sustainability as Goals," in Daily, ed., *Nature's Services* (note 15), pp. 49–68.

32. Kevin Rogers, Dirk Roux, and Harry Biggs, "Challenges for Catchment Management Agencies: Lessons from Bureaucracies, Business, and Resource Management," *Water SA* 26 (April 2000): 505–511. The authors articulate SAM (strategic adaptive management) as a local derivative of adaptive resource management, as originally developed by C. S. Holling (see C. S. Holling, ed., *Adaptive Environmental Assessment and Management* [London: John Wiley & Sons, 1978]).

33. Kevin Rogers and Harry Biggs, "Integrating Indicators, Endpoints, and Value Systems in Strategic Management of the Rivers of the Kruger National Park," *Freshwater Biology* 41 (1999): 439–451.

34. Ernita van Wyk et al., "Big Vision, Complex Reality: Building Common Understanding of Policy Intention for River Management in South Africa," Appendix 8 in van Wilgen et al., "Stakeholder Participation" (note 30).

35. Rogers and Biggs, "Integrating Indicators" (note 33).

36. Rogers et al., "Challenges" (note 32).

37. Aaron T. Wolf, "Transboundary Waters: Sharing Benefits, Lessons Learned," Thematic Background Paper prepared for the Secretariat of the International Conference on Freshwater, Bonn, Germany, 2001. See also Sandra L. Postel and Aaron T. Wolf, "Dehydrating Conflict," *Foreign Policy* (September–October 2001): 60–67.

38. World Wildlife Fund (WWF), Living Waters Program—Europe, "A Green Corridor for the Danube," Web site at http://www.panda.org/about_wwf/where_we_work/europe/where/danube_carpathian/danube_river_basin/lower_danube_green_corridor.cfm, accessed June 17, 2003.

39. Rhoda Margesson, "Reducing Conflict over the Danube Waters: Equitable Utilization and Sustainable Development," *Natural Resources Forum* 21 (January 1997): 23–38.

40. Quote appears on the Web site of WWF, Living Waters Program—Europe (note 38).

41. Karen F. Schmidt, "A True-Blue Vision for the Danube," *Science* 294 (2001): 1444–1447.

42. WWF, Living Waters Program—Europe (note 38).

43. Schmidt, "Vision for the Danube" (note 41).

44. Schmidt, "Vision for the Danube" (note 41).

45. Quote is contained in Brian Richter, Ruth Mathews, David L. Harrison, and Robert Wigington, "Ecologically Sustainable Water Management: Managing River Flows for Ecological Integrity," *Ecological Applications* 13: 206–224.

46. State of Florida, "ACF Allocation Formula Agreement—Apalachicola-Chattahoochee-Flint River Basin," Draft proposal, January 14, 2002.

47. Richter et al., "Ecologically Sustainable Water Management" (note 45).

48. The 500 figure is from David Dudgeon, "Large-Scale Hydrological Changes in Tropical Asia: Prospects for Riverine Biodiversity," *BioScience* 50 (September 2000): 793–806.

49. Claudia Ringler, *Optimal Water Allocation in the Mekong River Basin*, Discussion Papers on Development Policy (No. 38) (Bonn, Germany: Center for Development Research, 2001).

50. Ringler, *Mekong River Basin*.

51. Dudgeon, "Hydrological Changes" (note 48).

52. Jackie King, Freshwater Research Unit, Zoology Department, University of Cape Town, Rondebosch, South Africa, private e-mail communication with authors, September 2002.

53. *The Great Lakes Charter Annex: A Supplementary Agreement to The Great Lakes Charter*, signed June 18, 2001.

54. Instream Flow Council (IFC), *Instream Flows for Riverine Resource Stewardship* (n.p.: IFC, 2002), p. 17.

55. IFC, *Instream Flows*, pp. 91–92.

56. For more information, see The Nature Conservancy's Freshwater Initiative Web site at www.freshwaters.org.

57. Gretchen C. Daily and Katherine Ellison, *The New Economy of Nature: The Quest to Make Conservation Profitable* (Washington, D.C.: Island Press, 2002).

58. Quote contained in Timothy Egan, "For a Flood-Weary Napa Valley, a Vote to Let the River Run Wild," *The New York Times*, April 25, 1998.

59. Anil Agarwal and Sunita Narain, eds., *Dying Wisdom* (New Delhi: Centre for Science and Environment, 1997).

CHAPTER SIX

1. We use the increase in the number of large dams as a proxy for the increase in total human impact.

2. Juan Forero, "As Andean Glaciers Shrink, Water Worries Grow," *The New York Times*, November 24, 2002.

3. Danielle Nierenberg, "Population Growing Steadily," in Linda Starke, ed., *Vital Signs* (New York: W. W. Norton, 2002).

4. Sandra Postel, *Pillar of Sand* (New York: W. W. Norton, 1999).

5. Frank Rijsberman and David Molden, "Balancing Water Uses: Water for Food and Water for Nature," Background Paper prepared for the International Conference on Freshwater, Bonn, Germany, 2001.

BIBLIOGRAPHY

Acreman, M. C., F. A. K. Farquharson, M. P. McCartney, C. Sullivan, K. Campbell, N. Hodgson, J. Morton, D. Smith, M. Birley, D. Knott, J. Lazenby, and E. B. Barbier. *Managed Flood Releases from Reservoirs: Issues and Guidance.* Report to DFID and the World Commission on Dams. Wallingford, U.K.: Centre for Ecology and Hydrology, 2000.

Adams, W. M. *Wasting the Rain: Rivers, People, and Planning in Africa.* London: Earthscan Publications, 1992.

Agarwal, Anil, and Sunita Narain, eds. *Dying Wisdom.* New Delhi: Centre for Science and Environment, 1997.

Agriculture and Resource Management Council of Australia and New Zealand, and the Australian and New Zealand Environment and Conservation Council. "National Principles for the Provision of Water for Ecosystems." Revised Draft, November 2001.

Alber, Merryl. "A Conceptual Model of Estuarine Freshwater Inflow Management." *Estuaries* 25 (2002): 1246–1261.

American Rivers. Web site at www.amrivers.org/instreamflow/regulatorystrategies.htm.

———. "Conservation Groups Support Endangered Species Deal to Restore Flows in the Walla Walla River." Press release, June 28, 2001, accessed from the Web site www.amrivers.org/pressrelease/instreamflow6.28.01.htm.

———. Summaries of the most endangered rivers. Accessed from the Web site www.americanrivers.org.

American Rivers, Friends of the Earth, and Trout Unlimited. *Dam Removal Success Stories: Restoring Rivers Through Selective Removal of Dams That Don't Make Sense.* Washington, D.C.: 1999.

American Rivers and Trout Unlimited. "International Report Reveals Flaws in United States Regulation of Dams." Washington, D.C. Press release, November 20, 2000.

Arthington, Angela. "The Water Act (Qld) 2000: Environmental Flow Objectives." Paper delivered to the Queensland Environmental Law Association Seminar, *Water Bill 2000.* University of Queensland, St. Lucia, 2000.

Arthington, Angela H. "Wounded Rivers, Thirsty Land: Getting Water Management Right." Inaugural Lecture, Centre for Catchment and In-Stream Research, Griffith University, Nathan, Queensland, Australia. April 1997.

———. "Brisbane River Trial of a Flow Restoration Methodology (FLOWRESM)." Pp. 35–50 in A. H. Arthington and J. M. Zalucki, eds., *Water for the Environment:*

Recent Approaches to Assessing and Providing Environmental Flows. Brisbane: AWWA, 1998.

Arthington, Angela H., Jackie M. King, Jay H. O'Keefe, Stuart E. Bunn, J. A. Day, Brad J. Pusey, David R. Bluhdorn, and Rebecca E. Tharme. "Development of an Holistic Approach for Assessing Environmental Flow Requirements of Riverine Ecosystems." Pp. 69–76 in John J. Pigram and Bruce P. Hooper, eds., *Proceedings of an International Seminar and Workshop on Water Allocation for the Environment.* Armidale, Australia: The Centre for Water Policy Research, 1992.

Arthington, Angela H., and Rina Lloyd. *Logan River Trial of the Building Block Methodology for Assessing Environmental Flow Requirements.* Queensland, Australia: Griffith University, 1998.

Arthington, Angela H., and Brad J. Pusey. "In-Stream Flow Management in Australia: Methods, Deficiencies, and Future Directions." *Australian Biologist* 6 (1993): 52–60.

Arthington, Angela H., and M. Jacinta Zalucki. *Comparative Evaluation of Environmental Flow Assessment Techniques: Review of Methods.* Canberra, Australian Capitol Territory: Land and Water Resources Research and Development Corporation, 1998.

Arthington, Angela H., et al. *Environmental Flow Requirements of the Brisbane River Downstream from Wivenhoe Dam.* Brisbane, Queensland: South East Queensland Water Corporation, and Centre for Catchment and In-Stream Research of Griffith University, 2000.

Asmal, Kader. "Globalisation from Below." Preface to World Commission on Dams. *Dams and Development: A New Framework for Decision-Making.* London: Earthscan, 2000.

Babbitt, Bruce. "What Goes Up, May Come Down." *BioScience* 52 (August 2002): 656–658.

Barbier, Edward B., and Julian R. Thompson. "The Value of Water: Floodplain Versus Large-Scale Irrigation Benefits in Northern Nigeria." *Ambio* 27 (1998): 434–440.

Behnke, Robert J., and D. E. Benson. *Endangered and Threatened Fishes of the Upper Colorado River Basin.* Fort Collins, Colo.: Colorado State University Cooperative Extension Service, 1983.

Beilfuss, Richard. Africa Program Director, International Crane Foundation, Baraboo, Wisconsin, e-mail communication with authors, November 2002.

Benke, Arthur C. "A Perspective on America's Vanishing Streams." *Journal of the North American Benthological Society* 9 (March 1990): 77–88.

Benstead, Jonathan P., James G. March, Catherine M. Pringle, and Frederick N. Scatena. "Effects of a Low-Head Dam and Water Abstractions on Migratory Tropical Stream Biota." *Ecological Applications* 9 (February 1999): 656–668.

Berkes, Fikret, Mina Kislalioglu, Carl Folke, and Madhav Gadgil. "Exploring the Basic Ecological Unit: Ecosystem-Like Concepts in Traditional Societies." *Ecosystems* 1 (1998): 409–415.

Bestgen, Kevin R. *Interacting Effects of Physical and Biological Processes on Recruitment of Colorado Squawfish.* Ph.D. diss., Colorado State University, 1997.

Blackmore, Don J. "The Murray-Darling Basin Cap on Diversions—Policy and Practice for the New Millennium." *National Water* (June 1999): 1–12.

Bosshard, Peter. "An Act of Economic and Environmental Nonsense." (1999). Accessed via the Web site of International Rivers Network at www.irn.org/programs/safrica/index.asp?id=bosshard.study.html.

Bovee, Kenneth D. *A Guide to Stream Habitat Analysis Using the Instream Flow Incremental Methodology*. Denver, Colo.: U.S. Fish and Wildlife Service, 1982.

Bowman, Margaret B. "Legal Perspectives on Dam Removal." *BioScience* 52 (August 2002): 739–747.

Brizga, Sandra O. "Hydrology." Pp. 65–85 in Arthington et al., *Environmental Flow Requirements of the Brisbane River Downstream from Wivenhoe Dam*. Brisbane, Queensland: South East Queensland Water Corporation, and Centre for Catchment and In-Stream Research, Griffith University, 2000.

———. *Burnett Basin Water Allocation and Management Plan: Proposed Environmental Flow Performance Measures*. Brisbane, Queensland, Australia: Department of Natural Resources, 2000.

Brizga, Sandra O., Angela H. Arthington, Brad J. Pusey, Mark J. Kennard, Stephen J. Mackay, Garry L. Werren, Neil M. Craigie, and Satish J. Choy. "Benchmarking, a 'Top-Down' Methodology for Assessing Environmental Flows in Australian Rivers." In *Proceedings of International Conference on Environmental Flows for Rivers*. Cape Town, South Africa: Southern Waters Consulting, 2002.

Bunn, Stuart E., and Angela H. Arthington. "Basic Principles and Ecological Consequences of Altered Flow Regimes for Aquatic Biodiversity." *Environmental Management* 30 (April 2002): 492–507.

Carothers, Steven W., and Bryan T. Brown. *The Colorado River Through Grand Canyon: Natural History and Human Change*. Tucson: University of Arizona Press, 1991.

Chao, B. F. "Anthropogenic Impact on Global Geodynamics Due to Reservoir Water Impoundment." *Geophysical Research Letters* 22 (1995): 3529–3532.

Chaplin, Stephen J., et al. "The Geography of Imperilment: Targeting Conservation Toward Critical Biodiversity Areas." In Stein et al., eds., *Precious Heritage*.

City Council of Brisbane (Queensland, Australia). "The Jagara Are the People of the Brisbane River Watershed," at www.brisbane-stories.powerup.com.au/maggil/02mag_pages/mag_aborigines21.htm.

Collier, Michael, Robert H. Webb, and John C. Schmidt. *Dams and Rivers: Primer on the Downstream Effects of Dams*. Circular 1126. Denver, Colo.: U.S. Geological Survey, 1996.

Commission for Environmental Cooperation (CEC). *Ribbon of Life: An Agenda for Preserving Transboundary Migratory Bird Habitat on the Upper San Pedro River*. Montreal: 1999.

Cooperative Research Centre for Catchment Hydrology (CRC). Background information at www.catchment.crc.org.au.

Costanza, Robert, and Carl Folke. "Valuing Ecosystem Services with Efficiency, Fairness, and Sustainability as Goals." Pp. 49–68 in Gretchen C. Daily, ed., *Nature's Services: Societal Dependence on Natural Ecosystems*. Washington, D.C.: Island Press, 1997.

Costanza, Robert, et al. "The Value of the World's Ecosystem Services and Natural Capital." *Nature* 387 (May 1997): 254–260.

Daily, Gretchen C., ed. *Nature's Services: Societal Dependence on Natural Ecosystems*. Washington, D.C.: Island Press, 1997.

Daily, Gretchen C., and Katherine Ellison. *The New Economy of Nature: The Quest to Make Conservation Profitable*. Washington, D.C.: Island Press, 2002.

Davison, Stanley Roland. *The Leadership of the Reclamation Movement, 1875–1902*. New York: Arno Press, 1979.

Department of Resources and Energy. *Water 2000: A Perspective on Australia's Water Resources to the Year 2000*. Canberra: Australian Government Publishing Service, 1983.

Drower, M. S. "Water-Supply, Irrigation, and Agriculture." In C. Singer, E. J. Holmyard, and A. R. Hall, eds., *A History of Technology*. New York: Oxford University Press, 1954.

Dubash, Navroz K., Mairi Dupar, Smitu Kothari, and Tundu Lissu. *A Watershed in Global Governance? An Independent Assessment of the World Commission on Dams*. India: World Resources Institute, Lokayan, and Lawyers' Environmental Action Team, 2001.

Dudgeon, David. "Large-Scale Hydrological Changes in Tropical Asia: Prospects for Riverine Biodiversity." *BioScience* 50 (September 2000): 793–806.

——. "The Ecology of Tropical Asian Rivers and Streams in Relation to Biodiversity Conservation." *Annual Review of Ecological Systems* 31 (2000): 239–263.

Durant, Will. *Caesar and Christ*. New York: Simon and Schuster, 1944.

Dynesius, Matts, and Christer Nilsson. "Fragmentation and Flow Regulation of River Systems in the Northern Third of the World." *Science* 266 (1994): 753–762.

Echavarria, Martha. "FONAG: The Water-Based Finance Mechanism of the Condor Bioreserve in Ecuador." Working Draft. Quito, Ecuador: The Nature Conservancy, November 2001.

Egan, Timothy. "For a Flood-Weary Napa Valley, a Vote to Let the River Run Wild." *The New York Times*, April 25, 1998.

European Parliament and Council of the European Union. Directive 2000/60/EC establishing a framework for Community action in the field of water policy. *Official Journal of the European Communities* (December 22, 2000). L 327: 1–72.

European Union Life-Environment Project. "Wise Use of Floodplains." Web site at www.floodplains.org (accessed November 21, 2002).

Flannery, Michael S. Part II Rule Revision: Evaluation of Potential Impacts to Streams and Estuaries. Memorandum. Respondent's Exhibit 442, February 28, 1989.

Flannery, Michael S., Ernst B. Peebles, and Ralph T. Montgomery. "A Percent-of-Flow Approach for Managing Reductions of Freshwater Inflows from Unimpounded Rivers to Southwest Florida Estuaries." *Estuaries* 25 (December 2002): 1318–1331.

Forero, Juan. "As Andean Glaciers Shrink, Water Worries Grow." *The New York Times*, November 24, 2002.

Frederiksen, Harald, Jeremy Berkoff, and William Barber. *Water Resources Management in Asia*. Washington, D.C.: The World Bank, 1993.

Galat, David L., et al. "Flooding to Restore Connectivity of Regulated, Large-River Wetlands." *BioScience* 48 (September 1998): 721–733.

Galat, David L., and Robin Lipkin. "Restoring Ecological Integrity of Great Rivers: Historical Hydrographs Aid in Defining Reference Conditions for the Missouri River." *Hydrobiologia* 422/423 (2000): 29–48.

Getches, David H. "The Metamorphosis of Western Water Policy: Have Federal Laws and Local Decisions Eclipsed the States' Role?" *Stanford Environmental Law Journal* 20 (1): 3–72.

Gillilan, David M., and Thomas C. Brown. *Instream Flow Protection: Seeking a Balance in Western Water Use*. Washington, D.C.: Island Press, 1997.

Gippel, Chris, Trevor Jacobs, and Tony McLeod. "Environmental Flows and Water Quality Objectives for the River Murray." Presented at *Riversymposium 2001*. Brisbane, Australia, August 27–31, 2001.

Glennon, Robert. *Water Follies: Groundwater Pumping and the Fate of America's Fresh Waters*. Washington, D.C.: Island Press, 2002.

Goode, Tomas Charles, and Thomas Maddock III. *Simulation of Groundwater Conditions in the Upper San Pedro Basin for the Evaluation of Alternative Futures*. Tucson, Ariz.: University of Arizona, 2000.

Gore, James A., and F. Douglas Shields Jr. "Can Large Rivers Be Restored?" *BioScience* 45 (March 1995): 142–152.

Goulder, Lawrence H., and Donald Kennedy. "Valuing Ecosystem Services: Philosophical Bases and Empirical Methods." In Gretchen C. Daily, ed., *Nature's Services: Societal Dependence on Natural Ecosystems*. Washington, D.C.: Island Press, 1997.

Goulding, Michael, Nigel J. H. Smith, and Dennis J. Mahar. *Floods of Fortune: Ecology and Economy along the Amazon*. New York: Columbia University Press, 1996.

Haeuber, Richard A., and William K. Michener. "Natural Flood Control." *Issues in Science and Technology* (Fall 1998): 74–80.

Harden, Blaine. "Dams, and Politics, Channel Flow of the Mighty Missouri." *The New York Times*, May 5, 2002.

Hawken, Paul, Amory Lovins, and L. Hunter Lovins. *Natural Capitalism: Creating the Next Industrial Revolution*. Boston, Mass.: Back Bay Books, 1999.

Heal, Geoffrey. *Nature and the Marketplace: Capturing the Value of Ecosystem Services*. Washington, D.C.: Island Press, 2000.

Heal, Geoffrey, et al. "Protecting Natural Capital Through Ecosystem Service Districts." *Stanford Environmental Law Journal* 20 (2001): 333–364.

Heritage, G. L., A. W. van Niekerk, B. P. Moon, L. J. Broadhurst, K. H. Rogers, and C. S. James. *The Geomorphological Response to Changing Flow Regimes of the Sabie and Letaba River Systems*. Pretoria, South Africa: Water Research Commission, 1997.

Holling, C. S. "What Barriers? What Bridges?" In Lance H. Gunderson, C. S. Holling, and Stephen S. Light, eds., *Barriers and Bridges to the Renewal of Ecosystems and Institutions*. New York: Columbia University Press, 1995.

——, ed. *Adaptive Environmental Assessment and Management*. New York: John Wiley & Sons, 1978.

Horowitz, Michael M. "The Management of an African River Basin: Alternative Scenarios for Environmentally Sustainable Economic Development and Poverty Alleviation." In

Proceedings of the International UNESCO Symposium, *Water Resources Planning in a Changing World*. Karlsruhe, Germany: Bundesanstalt für Gewärkundef, 1994.

Industry Commission. "A Full-Repairing Lease: Inquiry into Ecologically Sustainable Land Management," Draft Report, 1997.

Ingram, Helen, and Cy R. Oggins. "The Public Trust Doctrine and Community Values in Water." *Natural Resources Journal* 32 (1992): 515–537.

Instream Flow Council. *Instream Flows for Riverine Resource Stewardship*. N.p.: Instream Flow Council, 2001.

International Conference on Freshwater. *Water—A Key to Sustainable Development: Recommendations for Action*. Bonn, Germany, December 3–7, 2001.

International Joint Commission. *Protection of the Waters of the Great Lakes: Interim Report to the Governments of Canada and the United States*. Washington, D.C., and Ottawa, Ontario: 1999.

Irving, David B., and Timothy Modde. "Home-Range Fidelity and Use of Historical Habitat by Adult Colorado Squawfish (*Ptychocheilus lucius*) in the White River, Colorado, and Utah." *Western North American Naturalist* 60 (2000): 16–25.

Irwin, Elise R., and Mary C. Freeman. "Proposal for Adaptive Management to Conserve Biotic Integrity in a Regulated Segment of the Tallapoosa River, Alabama, U.S.A." *Conservation Biology* 16 (October 2002): 1212–1222.

Israelsen, Brent. "Grand Canyon Flood, Part 2." *The Salt Lake Tribune*, September 24, 2002.

IUCN (The World Conservation Union). "Statement on the World Commission on Dams." Gland, Switzerland, 2001.

——. *Vision for Water and Nature: A World Strategy for Conservation and Sustainable Management of Water Resources in the Twenty-First Century*. Gland, Switzerland, and Cambridge, U.K.: IUCN, 2000.

King, Jackie M., Cate Brown, and Hossein Sabet. "A Scenario-Based Holistic Approach to Environmental Flow Assessments for Rivers." *Rivers Research and Applications*, in press.

King, Jackie M., and Delana Louw. "Instream Flow Assessments for Regulated Rivers in South Africa Using the Building Block Methodology." *Aquatic Ecosystem Health and Management* 1 (1998): 109–124.

King, Jackie M., and Rebecca E. Tharme. *Assessment of the Instream Flow Incremental Methodology and Initial Development of Alternative Instream Flow Methodologies for South Africa*. Pretoria, South Africa: Water Research Commission, 1994.

King, Jackie M., Rebecca E. Tharme, and M. S. DeVilliers, eds., *Environmental Flow Assessments for Rivers: Manual for the Building Block Methodology*. Pretoria, South Africa: Water Research Commission, 2000.

Lake, P. S., et al. "Global Change and the Biodiversity of Freshwater Ecosystems: Impacts on Linkages Between Above-Sediment and Sediment Biota." *BioScience* 50 (December 2000): 1099–1107.

Landry, Clay. "Market Transfers of Water for Environmental Protection in the Western United States." *Water Policy* 1 (1998): 457–469.

Lee, Kai N. *Compass and Gyroscope*. Washington, D.C.: Island Press, 1993.

Leopold, Aldo. *A Sand County Almanac*. New York: Oxford University Press, 1949.

Mancy, Khalil H. "The Environmental and Ecological Impacts of the Aswan High Dam." In Hillel Shuval, ed., *Developments in Arid Zone Ecology and Environmental Quality*. Philadelphia: Balaban ISS, 1981.

March, James G., Jonathan P. Benstead, Catherine M. Pringle, and Frederick N. Scatena. "Migratory Drift of Larval Freshwater Shrimps in Two Tropical Streams, Puerto Rico." *Freshwater Biology* 40 (1998): 261–273.

March, James G., Jonathan P. Benstead, Frederick N. Scatena, and Catherine M. Pringle. "Damming Tropical Island Streams: Problems, Solutions, and Alternatives." *BioScience* (in review).

Margesson, Rhoda. "Reducing Conflict over the Danube Waters: Equitable Utilization and Sustainable Development." *Natural Resources Forum* 21 (January 1997): 23–38.

McBain and Trush. *Trinity River Restoration Program: A Summary of the United States Secretary of the Interior Record of Decision, December 19, 2000*. Arcata, Calif.: 2001.

McCully, Patrick. "One Year after the World Commission on Dams: Reflections on the Diverse Reactions to Groundbreaking Report." *World Rivers Review* 16: June 2001.

———. *Silenced Rivers: The Ecology and Politics of Large Dams*. London: Zed Books, 1996.

Meretsky, Vicky J., David L. Wegner, and Larry E. Stevens. "Balancing Endangered Species and Ecosystems: A Case Study of Adaptive Management in the Grand Canyon." *Environmental Management* 25 (May 2000): 579–586.

Mitsch, William J., et al. "Reducing Nitrogen Loading to the Gulf of Mexico from the Mississippi River Basin: Strategies to Counter a Persistent Ecological Problem." *BioScience* 51 (May 2001): 373–388.

Moyle, Peter B., and Robert A. Leidy. "Loss of Biodiversity in Aquatic Ecosystems: Evidence from Fish Faunas." In P. L. Fiedler and S. K. Jain, eds., *Conservation Biology: The Theory and Practice of Nature Conservation, Preservation, and Management*. New York: Chapman and Hall, 1992.

Murray-Darling Basin Commission (MDBC). "The Cap." Canberra, Australia: 1999.

———. *Striking the Balance: Murray-Darling Basin Cap on Diversions—Water Year 1997/98*. Canberra, Australia: 1998.

Muth, Robert T., Larry W. Crist, Kirk E. LaGory, John W. Hayse, Kevin R. Bestgen, Thomas P. Ryan, Joseph K. Lyons, and Richard A. Valdez. *Flow and Temperature Recommendations for Endangered Fishes in the Green River Downstream of Flaming Gorge Dam*. Lakewood, Colo.: Upper Colorado River Recovery Program, 2000.

National Research Council (NRC). *Restoration of Aquatic Ecosystems: Science, Technology, and Public Policy*. Washington, D.C.: National Academy Press, 1992.

———. *The Missouri River Ecosystem: Exploring the Prospects for Recovery*. Washington, D.C.: National Academy Press, 2002.

Neves, Richard. "The Man Behind the Mussel." *The Nature Conservancy*. January–February 2001.

Nevill, Jon. *Freshwater Biodiversity: Protecting Freshwater Ecosystems in the Face of Infra-*

structure Development. Canberra, Australia: Water Research Foundation of Australia, 2001.

Newcom, Josh. "Is the California Water Market Open for Business?" *Western Water* (March–April 2001).

Nierenberg, Danielle. "Population Growing Steadily." In Linda Starke, ed., *Vital Signs.* New York: W. W. Norton, 2002.

O'Keeffe, Jay H. "Environmental Flow Assessments Within the South African Integrated Planning Process for Water Resources." Pp. 41–64 in King et al., eds., *Environmental Flow Assessments for Rivers: Manual for the Building Block Methodology.* Pretoria, South Africa: Water Research Commission, 2000.

O'Keeffe, Jay H., D. C. Weeks, A. Fourie, and Brian R. Davies. *A Pre-Impoundment Study of the Sabie-Sand River System, Mpumalanga with Special Reference to Predicted Impacts on the Kruger National Park.* Vol. 3. Pretoria, South Africa: Water Research Commission, 1996.

Orr, Patricia, and Bonnie Colby. "Nature-Oriented Visitors and Their Expenditures: Upper San Pedro River Basin." University of Arizona, Tucson, 2002.

Palmer, Margaret A., et al. "Linkages Between Aquatic Sediment Biota and Life above Sediments as Potential Drivers of Biodiversity and Ecological Processes." *BioScience* 50 (December 2000): 1062–1075.

Petts, Geoffrey E. "Water Allocation to Protect River Ecosystems." *Regulated Rivers* 12 (1996): 353–365.

Poff, N. LeRoy, J. David Allan, Mark B. Bain, James R. Karr, Karen L. Prestegaard, Brian D. Richter, Richard E. Sparks, and Julie C. Stromberg. "The Natural Flow Regime: A Paradigm for River Conservation and Restoration," *BioScience* 47 (December 1997): 769–784.

Poff, N. LeRoy, and David D. Hart. "How Dams Vary and Why It Matters for the Emerging Science of Dam Removal." *BioScience* 52 (August 2002): 659–668.

Population Reference Bureau. *World Population Data Sheet.* Washington, D.C.: 2000.

Postel, Sandra. "Entering an Era of Water Scarcity: The Challenges Ahead." *Ecological Applications* 10 (August 2000): 941–948.

——. *Last Oasis: Facing Water Scarcity.* New York: W. W. Norton, 1992, rev. ed., 1997.

——. *Pillar of Sand: Can the Irrigation Miracle Last?* New York: W. W. Norton, 1999.

——. "Where Have All the Rivers Gone?" *World Watch,* May–June 1995.

Postel, Sandra, and Stephen Carpenter. "Freshwater Ecosystem Services." Pp. 195–214 in Gretchen C. Daily, ed., *Nature's Services: Societal Dependence on Natural Ecosystems.* Washington, D.C.: Island Press, 1997.

Postel, Sandra, Gretchen C. Daily, and Paul R. Ehrlich. "Human Appropriation of Renewable Fresh Water." *Science* 271 (1996): 785–788.

Postel, Sandra L., and Aaron T. Wolf. "Dehydrating Conflict." *Foreign Policy* (September–October 2001): 60–67.

Pringle, Catherine M. "Exploring How Disturbance Is Transmitted Upstream: Going Against the Flow." *Journal of the North American Benthological Society* 16 (February 1997): 425–438.

——. "River Conservation in Tropical Versus Temperate Latitudes." Pp. 371–381 in P. J. Boon, B. R. Davies, and Geoffrey E. Petts, eds., *Global Perspectives on River Conservation: Science, Policy and Practice*. New York: John Wiley & Sons, 2000.

Pringle, Catherine M., Mary C. Freeman, and Byron J. Freeman. "Regional Effects of Hydrologic Alterations on Riverine Macrobiota in the New World: Tropical-Temperate Comparisons." *BioScience* 50 (September 2000): 807–823.

Pringle, Catherine M., and Frederick N. Scatena. "Freshwater Resource Development: Case Studies from Puerto Rico and Costa Rica." In L. U. Hatch and M. E. Swisher, eds., *Managed Ecosystems: The Mesoamerican Experience*. New York: Oxford University Press, 1999.

Ransel, Katherine. "The Sleeping Giant Awakens: PUD No. 1 of Jefferson County v. Washington Department of Ecology." *Environmental Law* 25 (Spring 1995): 255–283.

Revenga, Carmen, Jake Brunner, Norbert Henninger, Ken Kassem, and Richard Payne. *Pilot Analysis of Global Ecosystems: Freshwater Systems*. Washington, D.C.: World Resources Institute, 2000.

Ricciardi, Anthony, and Joseph B. Rasmussen. "Extinction Rates of North American Freshwater Fauna. *Conservation Biology* 13 (1999): 1220–1222.

Richardson, B. A. "Evaluation of In-Stream Flow Methodologies for Freshwater Fish in New South Wales." Pp. 143–167 in I. C. Campbell, ed., *Stream Protection: The Management of Rivers for Instream Uses*. Victoria, Australia: Water Studies Centre, Chisholm Institute of Technology, 1986.

Richter, Brian D., Ruth Mathews, David L. Harrison, and Robert Wigington. "Ecologically Sustainable Water Management: Managing River Flows for Ecological Integrity." *Ecological Applications* 13: 206–224.

Richter, Brian D., and Kent H. Redford. "The Art (and Science) of Brokering Deals Between Conservation and Use." *Conservation Biology* 13 (June 1999): 1235–1237.

Richter, Brian, et al. "How Much Water Does a River Need?" *Freshwater Biology* 37 (1997): 231–249.

Rijsberman, Frank, and David Molden. "Balancing Water Uses: Water for Food and Water for Nature." Background paper prepared for the International Conference on Freshwater, Bonn, Germany, 2001.

Ringler, Claudia. *Optimal Water Allocation in the Mekong River Basin*. Discussion Papers on Development Policy (No. 38). Bonn, Germany: Center for Development Research, 2001.

Rivers Alliance of Connecticut. "CT Supreme Court Reverses Shepaug River Decision." Web site at www.riversalliance.org/legal_watch.htm.

Robertson, A. I., P. Bacon, and G. Heagney. "The Responses of Floodplain Primary Production to Flood Frequency and Timing." *Journal of Applied Ecology* 38 (February 2001): 126–136.

Rogers, Kevin, and Harry Biggs. "Integrating Indicators, Endpoints, and Value Systems in Strategic Management of the Rivers of the Kruger National Park." *Freshwater Biology* 41 (1999): 439–451.

Rogers, Kevin H., and Regina Bestbier. *Development of a Protocol for the Definition of the*

Desired State of Riverine Systems in South Africa. Pretoria, South Africa: Department of Environmental Affairs and Tourism, 1997.

Rogers, Kevin H., Dirk Roux, and Harry Biggs. "Challenges for Catchment Management Agencies: Lessons from Bureaucracies, Business, and Resource Management." *Water SA* 26 (October 2000): 505–511.

Rosenberg, David M., Patrick McCully, and Catherine M. Pringle. "Global-Scale Environmental Effects of Hydrological Alterations: Introduction." *BioScience* 50 (September 2000): 746–751.

Rykiel, E. "Ecosystem Science for the Twenty-First Century." *BioScience* 47 (October 1997): 705–708.

San Pedro Expert Study Team. *Sustaining and Enhancing Riparian Migratory Bird Habitat on the Upper San Pedro River.* Montreal: CEC, 1999.

Scanlan, Melissa. "Access to Wisconsin Water: The Public Trust Doctrine—Past, Present, and Future." Paper presented at *Waters of Wisconsin Forum*. Madison, Wisc., October 22, 2002.

Scatena, Frederick N., and Sherri L. Johnson. *Instream-Flow Analysis for the Luquillo Experimental Forest, Puerto Rico: Methods and Analysis.* Rio Piedras, Puerto Rico: U.S. Forest Service and International Institute of Tropical Forestry, 2001.

Schmidt, Karen F. "A True-Blue Vision for the Danube." *Science* 294 (2001): 1444–1447.

Schmidt, Thomas, and Jeremy Schmidt. *The Saga of Lewis and Clark.* New York: DK Publishing, 1999.

Scott, D., and C. S. Shirvell. "A Critique of the In-Stream Flow Incremental Methodology and Observations of Flow Determination in New Zealand." Pp. 27–43 in J. F. Craig and J. B. Kemper, eds., *Regulated Streams: Advances in Ecology.* New York: Plenum Press, 1987.

Sherwill, Tamsyn, and Kevin Rogers. "Public Participation in Setting the Goals for Integrated Water Resource Management: A Means to Equity and Sustainability?" Appendix 6 in Brian E. van Wilgen et al., "Principles and Processes for Supporting Stakeholder Participation in Integrated River Management: Lessons from the Sabie-Sand Catchment." Final Report Project K5/1062, Water Research Commission, Pretoria, South Africa, 2002.

Shiklomanov, Igor A. "Assessment of Water Resources and Water Availability in the World." St. Petersburg, Russia: State Hydrological Institute, 1996.

Silk, Nicole, Jack McDonald, and Robert Wigington. "Turning Instream Flow Water Rights Upside Down." *Rivers* 7 (April 2000): 298–313.

Solley, Wayne B., Robert R. Pierce, and Howard A. Perlman. *Estimated Use of Water in the United States in 1995.* Circular 1200. Denver, Colo.: U.S. Geological Survey, 1998.

Sophocleous, Mario. "From Safe Yield to Sustainable Development of Water Resources—the Kansas Experience." *Journal of Hydrology* 235 (August 2000): 27–43.

South African Department of Water Affairs and Forestry. White Paper on Water Policy. Pretoria, South Africa, 1997.

South African National Water Act No. 36 of 1998. *Government Gazette* Vol. 398, No. 19182. Cape Town, August 26, 1998.

Sparks, Richard E. "Need for Ecosystem Management of Large Rivers and Their Flood-plains." *BioScience* 45 (March 1995): 168–182.

——. "Risks of Altering the Hydrologic Regime of Large Rivers." Pp. 119–152 in John Cairns, Barbara Niederlehner, and D. R. Orvos, eds., *Predicting Ecosystem Risk.* Vol. 20. Princeton, N.J.: Princeton Scientific Publishing, 1992.

Sparks, Richard E., John C. Nelson, and Yao Yin. "Naturalization of the Flood Regime in Regulated Rivers: The Case of the Upper Mississippi River." *BioScience* 48 (September 1998): 706–720.

Stalnaker, Clair B. "Low Flow as a Limiting Factor in Warmwater Streams." Pp. 192–199 in L. A. Krumholz, ed., *The Warmwater Streams Symposium.* Bethesda, Md.: American Fisheries Society, 1981.

Stalnaker, Clair B., and Edmund J. Wick. "Planning for Flow Requirements to Sustain Stream Biota." Chap. 16 in Ellen E. Wohl, ed., *Inland Flood Hazards: Human, Riparian, and Aquatic Communities.* London: Cambridge University Press, 2000.

State of Connecticut Superior Court. City of Waterbury, Town of Wolcott, Town of Middlebury and Town of Watertown v. Town of Washington, Town of Roxbury, Steep Rock Association, Inc., Roxbury Land Trust, and Shepaug River Association, Inc. No. X01-UWY-CV97-140886 Waterbury, Conn., February 16, 2000.

State of Florida. "ACF Allocation Formula Agreement—Apalachicola-Chattahoochee-Flint River Basin." Draft proposal, January 14, 2002.

Stein, Bruce, Lynn S. Kutner, and Jonathan S. Adams, eds., *Precious Heritage: The Status of Biodiversity in the United States.* New York: Oxford University Press, 2000.

Stiassny, Melanie L. J. "An Overview of Freshwater Biodiversity." *Fisheries* 21 (September 1996): 7–13.

Supreme Court of California. *National Audubon Society et al., Petitioners v. The Superior Court of Alpine County, Respondent; Department of Water and Power of the City of Los Angeles et al., Real Parties in Interest.* 33 Cal.3d 419, 1983.

Supreme Court of the United States. Majority opinion in *PUD No. 1 of Jefferson County v. Washington Department of Ecology.* Washington, D.C.: 1994.

Tarlock, Dan A. Presentation for Water Resource Management for Line Officers. U.S. Forest Service, Prescott, Ariz., 2000.

——. "Water Policy Adrift." *Forum for Applied Research and Public Policy* (Spring 2001): 63–70.

Tennant, Donald L. "Instream Flow Regimens for Fish, Wildlife, Recreation and Related Environmental Resources." *Fisheries* 1 (July/August 1975): 6–10.

Tharme, Rebecca E. *Sabie-Sand River System: Instream Flow Requirements.* Pretoria, South Africa: Department of Water Affairs and Forestry, 1997.

——. "A Global Perspective on Environmental Flow Assessment: Emerging Trends in the Development and Application of Environmental Flow Methodologies for Rivers." *Rivers Research and Application,* in press.

——. *Review of International Methodologies for the Quantification of the Instream Flow Requirements of Rivers.* Pretoria, South Africa: Department of Water Affairs and Forestry, 1996.

Tharme, Rebecca E., and Jackie M. King. *Development of the Building Block Methodology for Instream Flow Assessments and Supporting Research on the Effects of Different Magnitude Flows on Riverine Ecosystems.* Cape Town, South Africa: Water Research Commission, 1998.

"The Delicate Balance of Sharing Water." *World Water and Environmental Engineering* (July–August 2001).

The Great Lakes Charter Annex: A Supplementary Agreement to The Great Lakes Charter. Signed June 18, 2001.

The Nature Conservancy. Freshwater Initiative. "Flow Restoration Database." www.freshwaters.org.

The World Bank. *Water Resources Sector Strategy: Strategic Directions for World Bank Engagement.* Draft. Washington, D.C.: March 2002.

Thobani, Mateen. "Formal Water Markets: Why, When, and How to Introduce Tradable Water Rights." *The World Bank Research Observer* 12 (February 1997): 161–179.

Toth, Lou A. "Principles and Guidelines for Restoration of River/Floodplain Ecosystems—Kissimmee River, Florida." Pp. 49–73 in John Cairns, ed., *Rehabilitating Damaged Ecosystems.* Cherry Hill, N.J.: Lewis Publications, CRC Press, 1995.

Upper San Pedro Partnership (USPP). *Upper San Pedro Conservation Plan 2002 Progress Report.* Sierra Vista, Ariz.: 2002a.

———. *Upper San Pedro Partnership Planning Activity: 2002 Progress Report.* Sierra Vista, Ariz.: 2002b.

"Upper San Pedro Partnership Water Conservation Strategies." *Sierra Vista Herald*, November 11, 2001.

Usagawa, Barry. "Landmark Hawaii Supreme Court Decision Creates Water Use Prioritization and Re-Use May Become the Key Solution." In *Proceedings of the Water Sources Conference.* American Water Works Association and others, Las Vegas, Nev., January 27–30, 2002.

U.S. Army Corps of Engineers. *Missouri River Master Water Control Manual—Review and Update.* Revised Draft Environmental Impact Statement, August 2001.

———. *Environmental Assessment—Green River Lock and Dam Nos. 3, 4, 5, 6 and Barren River No. 1.* Louisville, Ky.: Louisville District, June 2001.

U.S. Department of the Interior. "Interior Secretary Signs Landmark Conservation Agreement to Remove Edwards Dam." Press release, Washington, D.C., May 26, 1998.

U.S. Environmental Protection Agency (USEPA). New England Office. "Ensuring Adequate Instream Flows in New England." Boston, 2000.

U.S. Fish and Wildlife Service. *Colorado Pikeminnow* (Ptychocheilus lucius) *Recovery Goals: Amendment and Supplement to the Colorado Squawfish Recovery Plan.* Denver, Colo.: U.S. Fish and Wildlife Service Region 6, 2002.

———. *Final Biological Opinion on Operation of Flaming Gorge Dam.* Denver, Colo.: U.S. Fish and Wildlife, 1992.

U.S. Geological Survey. *Concepts for National Assessment of Water Availability and Use.* Reston, Va.: 2002.

U.S. National Park Service. Web site for Mammoth Cave National Park at www.nps.gov/maca/home.htm.

van Wilgen, Brian W., Richard M. Cowling, and Chris J. Burgers. "Valuation of Ecosystem Services: A Case Study from South African Fynbos Ecosystems." *BioScience* 46 (March 1996): 184–189.

van Wyk, Ernita, et al. "Big Vision, Complex Reality: Building Common Understanding of Policy Intention for River Management in South Africa." Appendix 8 in van Wilgen et al. "Principles and Processes for Supporting Stakeholder Participation in Integrated River Management: Lessons from the Sabie-Sand Catchment," Final Report Project K5/1062, Water Research Commission, Pretoria, South Africa, 2002.

Vickers, Amy. *Handbook of Water Use and Conservation*. Amherst, Mass.: WaterPlow Press, 2001.

Vörösmarty, C. J., P. Green, J. Salisbury, and R. B. Lammers. "Global Water Resources: Vulnerability from Climate Change and Population Growth." *Science* 289 (July 2000): 284–288.

Vörösmarty, Charles, and Dork Sahagian. "Anthropogenic Disturbance of the Terrestrial Water Cycle." *BioScience* 50 (September 2000): 753–765.

Wahl, Richard W. "United States." In Ariel Diners and Ashok Subramanian, eds., *Water Pricing Experiences: An International Perspective*. Washington, D.C.: The World Bank, 1997.

Walker, Keith F., Fran Sheldon, and James T. Puckridge. "A Perspective on Dryland River Ecosystems." *Regulated Rivers* 11 (1995): 85–104.

Walters, Carl. *Adaptive Management of Renewable Resources*. Caldwell, New Jersey: Blackburn Press, 1986.

Walters, Carl L., Lance Gunderson, and C. S. Holling. "Experimental Policies for Water Management in the Everglades." *Ecological Applications* 2 (May 1992): 189–202.

Walters, Carl, Josh Korman, Larry E. Stevens, and Barry Gold. "Ecosystem Modeling for Evaluation of Adaptive Management Policies in the Grand Canyon." *Conservation Ecology* 4 (2000).

"Washington Department of Ecology Buys Private Water Rights for Fish." *U.S. Water News* (January 2001).

Weeks, D. C., Jay H. O'Keeffe, A. Fourie, and Brian R. Davies. *A Pre-Impoundment Study of the Sabie-Sand River System, Mpumalanga with Special Reference to Predicted Impacts on the Kruger National Park*. Vol. 1. Pretoria, South Africa: Water Research Commission, 1996.

White, Gilbert. "The Environmental Effects of the High Dam at Aswan." *Environment* (September 1988).

Whittington, J., et al. "Ecological Sustainability of Rivers of the Murray-Darling." In *Review of the Operation of the Cap*. Canberra, Australian Capital Territory: Murray-Darling Basin Ministerial Council, 2000.

Wilcox, Peter R., G. Mathias Kondolf, W. V. Matthews, and A. F. Barta. "Specification of Sediment Maintenance Flows for a Large Gravel-Bed River." *Water Resources Research* 32 (1996): 2911–2921.

Wilson, Edward O. *Consilience: The Unity of Knowledge*. New York: Vintage Books, 1998.

Witte, Lois G. "Still No Water for the Woods." Paper prepared for the ALI-ABA Federal Lands Law Conference, Salt Lake City, Utah, October 19, 2001.

Wolf, Aaron T. "Transboundary Waters: Sharing Benefits, Lessons Learned." Thematic background paper prepared for the Secretariat of the International Conference on Freshwater. Bonn, Germany, 2001.

Wong, Susanne. "Villagers Chart River Recovery since Pak Mun Gates Opened." *World Rivers Review* 17 (August 2002): 10–11.

World Commission on Dams (WCD). CD-ROM, World Commission on Dams Secretariat, Cape Town, South Africa, 2000.

——. *Dams and Development: A New Framework for Decision-Making.* London: Earthscan, 2000.

World Wildlife Fund. Living Waters Program—Europe. "A Green Corridor for the Danube," Web site: http://archive.panda.org/europe/freshwater/initiatives/danube.html, accessed June 8, 2002.

——. *The Status of Wild Atlantic Salmon: A River by River Assessment.* Washington, D.C.: 2001.

Worster, Donald. *Rivers of Empire: Water, Aridity, and the Growth of the American West.* New York: Oxford University Press, 1985.

Wyatt, Stephen. "Trading in Water Licenses Attracts Big Money." *Financial Times*, February 17, 1999.

ABOUT THE AUTHORS

SANDRA POSTEL is director of the Global Water Policy Project in Amherst, Massachusetts. She is author of *Pillar of Sand* and of *Last Oasis*, which was the basis for a 1997 PBS television documentary, and of "Troubled Waters," which appears in the 2001 edition of *Best American Science and Nature Writing*. In November 2002, she was named one of the "Scientific American 50," by *Scientific American* magazine, a new award recognizing contributions to science and technology.

BRIAN RICHTER is director of the Freshwater Initiative of The Nature Conservancy and is based in Charlottesville, Virginia. In his sixteen years with the Conservancy he has provided technical support and strategic advice to more than eighty river conservation projects around the world. His experiences have engendered many scientific journal articles and the development of numerous practical methods and tools for river management.

INDEX